Christ, Ethics and Tragedy

Donald MacKinnon, Emeritus Professor of Divinity at Cambridge, has been the most influential philosopher of religion in Britain this century. His work has ranged widely, covering such topics as the metaphysics of Aristotle, the ethical significance of tragedy, Kant's epistemology, Christology, the relations between Marxism and Christianity, and trinitarian reflection.

The essays in this volume constitute the proceedings of a conference on MacKinnon's work, held in Cambridge in 1986. They take as their starting-point the writings of Professor Mac-Kinnon, and are presented to him on his seventy-fifth birthday. This multi-contributor volume covers such topics as the relation between Barth's theology and MacKinnon's thought, the controversy between realism and idealism, Trinity and ontology, incarnation and kenosis, the problem of evil, and MacKinnon and ethical reflection.

Christ, Ethics and Tragedy

ESSAYS IN HONOUR OF DONALD MacKINNON

edited by KENNETH SURIN

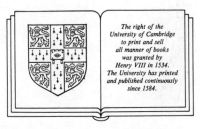

The right of the
University of Cambridge
to print and sell
all manner of books
was granted by
Henry VIII in 1534.
The University has printed
and published continuously
since 1584.

CAMBRIDGE UNIVERSITY PRESS

Cambridge

New York   New Rochelle

Melbourne   Sydney

Published by the Press Syndicate of the University of Cambridge
The Pitt Building, Trumpington Street, Cambridge CB2 1RP
32 East 57th Street, New York, NY 10022, USA
10 Stamford Road, Oakleigh, Melbourne 3166, Australia

First published 1989

Printed in Great Britain at
the University Press, Cambridge

British Library cataloguing in publication data
Christ, ethics and tragedy
1. Christian theology – Philosophical perspectives.
I. Surin, Kenneth, 1948–   II. Mackinnon, D. M.
(Donald Mackenzie), 1913–   .
230′.01

Library of Congress cataloguing in publication data
Christ, ethics, and tragedy: essays in honour of Donald MacKinnon /
edited by Kenneth Surin.
    p.   cm.
Papers presented at a conference held at St. John's College,
Cambridge on July 22–5, 1986.
ISBN 0 521 34137 X
1. MacKinnon, Donald MacKenzie, 1913–   . – Congresses.
2. Philosophical theology – Congresses.   I. MacKinnon, Donald
MacKenzie, 1913–   . II. Surin, Kenneth, 1948–
BX4827.M244C48 1989
230–dc19   88-18939   CIP

ISBN 0 521 34137 X

Contents

Preface

The papers in this volume represent the proceedings of a conference on the work of Donald MacKinnon, Norris-Hulse Professor Emeritus of Divinity in the University of Cambridge. Through the good offices of the conference chairman, Professor Stephen Sykes, it was possible to hold the conference at St John's College, Cambridge, on 22–5 July 1986. The editor is grateful to Professor Sykes for his work in chairing the conference and for facilitating the publication process.

The conference would not have been held but for a very generous subvention provided by St John's College. A subvention and conference reception were also provided by Corpus Christi College, Cambridge. A grant from the College of St Paul and St Mary, Cheltenham, subsidized the cost of organizing the conference, and the travelling expenses of the conference speakers were met by grants from the British Academy and the Cadbury Trust. Illness prevented Dr Paskins from presenting his own paper, and the editor is very grateful to Professor Rowan Williams for reading Dr Paskins's paper at short notice, and to the Revd Dr Peter Sedgwick for auditing the subsequent discussion. Professor MacKinnon was present throughout the proceedings, and the speakers are grateful to him for his generous and penetrating responses to their presentations. These essays, by colleagues, students and friends, are presented to Professor MacKinnon on the occasion of his seventy-fifth birthday.

object of the conference which provided the contents for this volume.

The authors do not aim to undertake 'MacKinnon exegesis', but to press his thought further, to clarify and evaluate his philosophical and theological assumptions, and to relate his ideas to current debates on certain key issues (the nuclear weapons debate, the problem of ethical 'foundations', 'realism' *versus* 'idealism', etc.). It is never easy for an editor of a volume like this to decide on the particular order in which its contents are to be presented. I have decided to follow, very roughly, the chronological sequence in which MacKinnon himself has dealt with the topics discussed by the contributors, and having established this principle, to cluster the relevant essays round a topic already selected in this way.

The 'early MacKinnon' was deeply influenced by Karl Barth, and the first essay in this volume, by Richard Roberts, discusses the nature and scope of this influence. From the beginning MacKinnon displayed a pervasive concern with the theological implications of the age-old debate between respective exponents of the several versions of 'realism' and 'idealism'. MacKinnon's treatment of this subject is considered by Fergus Kerr in the second essay. Central to any explicitly theological understanding of this debate is the question of the 'representation' of the divine, and both Patrick Sherry and Roger White deal with this issue in their contributions. MacKinnon, like Barth, adheres uncompromisingly to the principle that the discourse of Christian faith and practice is an irreducibly trinitarian discourse. MacKinnon's charting of some of the primary claims of such discourse, and the related discourses of 'incarnation' and 'kenosis', is the subject of the essays by Rowan Williams and Kenneth Surin. In the mid 1960s MacKinnon produced a series of articles on the themes of tragedy and atonement. These papers are the point of departure for the essays by David Ford and Brian Hebblethwaite. In his reflections on the tragic vision MacKinnon returned to some of the issues he had broached in a number of articles on the ethics of nuclear warfare published immediately after the Second World War. These reflections provide the basis for Barrie Paskins's essay. The tenth essay, by John Milbank, furnishes a historico-philosophical narrative which situates several strands of Mackinnon's thinking. Stanley Hauerwas, whose own *sittlich* ethics is contrasted with what Milbank regards as MacKinnon's 'retreat into deontology', concludes this volume by questioning the tenability of Milbank's historical narrative.

It should be emphasized that these essays, with the exception of the one by Surin, originated as spoken presentations in the Cambridge conference on MacKinnon's work. It has not been possible to eliminate every trace of spoken delivery from some of the essays.

and his work, as an inside 'outsider', presents very considerable difficulties. In addition, for those of us who have undergone some degree of 'formation' under his direct influence, the task is even more taxing because of the process of psychological embodiment which means that criticism has at the same time to be self-criticism. Moreover, the often highly oblique and sometimes seemingly perversely allusive aspects of MacKinnon's style invite the possibility of disastrous imitation. Such a self-cancelling and nugatory step has at all costs to be avoided.[2]

Thus far I have concentrated in my remarks upon a cluster of difficulties (and there are more than I have alluded to) which attend serious engagement with the thought of Donald MacKinnon. How, more positively, might we apply ourselves to it? Reading and re-reading of MacKinnon's œuvre convinces me that his most obvious achievements lie in the ruthless exposure of intellectual flabbiness in theological writers who venture incautious judgements. The deflation of pretension is, of course, a necessary but scarcely a sufficient condition of a positive contribution to theological self-understanding. MacKinnon's participation in the latter is contained mainly in four works: the wartime expanded pamphlets ('tracts' would be a happier term), *God the Living and the True* and *The Church of God* of 1940, and the substantial post-war texts, *A Study in Ethical Theory* (1957) and *The Problem of Metaphysics* (1974). It is relatively easy to couple the first and second and the third and fourth and see in each pair internal consistency and coherence. What are we to make, however, of the relation between the two groups of texts? It is not good enough, I believe, to disclaim the former or consign them to the category of fevered juvenilia. If we tackle MacKinnon's work on lines applied to other significant constructive theological and philosophical writers then it would be reasonable to assume a pattern of initial dialectical exploration of issues which then, in maturity, undergo attempted resolution. If, then, we may assume the possibility in principle of such a pattern of question and attempted answer, what may it be that relates the 'early' to the 'mature' MacKinnon? Is there continuity or discontinuity? How, beyond such an internal investigation, do MacKinnon's most fundamental concerns relate to the wider history of British theological reflection? In this essay I attempt to begin a substantial answer to the former question, but must, through pressure of space, merely allude to the latter, contextualizing question. I shall focus primarily upon one text, the first, *God the Living and the True*, and on this basis generate a series of supplementary questions that will show the continuing historical relevance (yet also the highly problematic character) of the 'early' MacKinnon to the present day.

II Dialectical initiation: theological rhetoric and the crisis of 1940

I have chosen to use the provocative term 'theological rhetoric'[3] to characterize MacKinnon's early work because it best encapsulates the difficulties in interpreting the curious extremity and stridency of tone in both *God the Living and the True* (*GLT*) and *The Church of God*. I, and I suspect most of my readers, are not in a position to speculate upon the personal genesis of these texts. It is largely as self-subsistent entities that we must take them and in these terms we must try to understand why they failed, certainly so far as I can judge, to have any significant *Wirkungsgeschichte* upon contemporary or subsequent discussion. Why should this be? It is my interpretative contention that these texts have a 'surface grammar', a brutal style, which, as we shall see, functions as a near-totalitarian rhetorical diatribe, imposing in impossibilist terms demands upon Christians and the Church (and here by 'Church' we must certainly mean the Church of England as by law established in the first instance) that were not eventually met. This sophisticated fundamentalism, the 'surface grammar', conceals to a large degree the 'depth grammar' of a growing, pervasive concern with the transcendental capacity of the human, what I have called the 'moral passion'. This is a term which I intend to convey the fullest range of meanings, for at this deeper level we certainly have to do with a Christ- and a Cross-centred, as well as a moral, 'passion'. It is the latter which, I believe, compels the allegiance, even the devotion, of many of those who have come under MacKinnon's influence. Here Karl Barth's truest words, that there can be no real theology without distress, yet none without courage in distress, have been realized in the individual: there is the authenticity that attracts despite the rhetoric that repels.[4]

It is extremely difficult to summarize the early and certainly problematic texts of 1940. Running very close to the rocks of sheer perversity, MacKinnon could, while evincing a concern 'primarily with the character of God, Creator and Redeemer, as he is presented in the Christian Gospel' (*GLT*, 9), see this in the light of Fr Victor White's gloss upon *Quem Deus vult salvare, prius dementat*, that is, 'Whom God wills to save he first drives mad' (*GLT*, 14).[5] Thus, in terms surely inseparable from Hoskyn's brilliant mediation of Barth's second *Römerbrief*, grace appears under the form of contradiction, even to the point of 'dementia'. This form of linguistic shock treatment is surely both rhetorical, a tactical ploy intended to obtrude upon a cultural consciousness weary of religious commonplace, and yet, in a sense, frighteningly, even if tangentially, true. Whilst MacKinnon wrote, that process of the inner estrangement of religion from social normality gathered pace, and it has now, possibly, extended over the whole of a sick social system and its enfeebled culture.

In *God the Living and the True* the ambiguous dalliance with divinely-induced dementia is not pursued at length: we note, however, on the one hand the emergence of a persisting theme – the equal inevitability of the historical form of the Gospel narrative and of the wider implications of its language, which is 'of necessity metaphysical in character' (*GLT*, 15). On the other hand, the description of this narrative scheme through the use of such conceptions as a 'meta-history' that 'invades the historical series' (*GLT*, 16), and of time broken in upon and 'invalidated' (*GLT*, 15) by God's eternity, besides the use of the adjective 'terrible' to describe the 'tale of Christ's coming and rejection' (*GLT*, 16), once more owes much to MacKinnon's 'Barth', despite the disclaimer that he had not 'surrendered himself to the contemporary mood of anti-rationalism' (*GLT*, 16). His further defence against the charge of 'Barthianism' consists of an appeal, again later consistently pursued, to the combination of rationalism in method with a recognition of the incapacity of reason exemplified in the scholastic theologies of Gardeil and Penido. MacKinnon's recognition, with Barth, that 'There can be no way from man to God unless there has been first set in the wilderness a way from God to man' (*GLT*, 21), is complemented by the equally mutual (although differently executed) later appeal to analogy. The rhetorical use of a conceptual vocabulary drawn from dialectical theology (in the first instance, as regards its extremity, Barthian, but later, with the increasing stress upon rationality, Brunnerian) coexists with scholastic conceptions flowing from the neo-Thomist revival. Overshadowing all is a massive commitment and adherence to the paradoxes of Crucifixion and Resurrection into which the dialectic of nature and grace is assumed (*GLT*, 20). In a passage specifically prefiguring the stauro-logical revival in recent German Lutheran theology MacKinnon focused upon the Crucifixion in the Biblical narrative:[6]

Any exposition of the Christian doctrine of God must first posit the Cross. For Christians, theology is, and must be, a *theologia crucis*, a theology of the Cross. (*GLT*, 22)

There are other features (including the polemic conducted against 'idealism') which strengthen the analogy of the 'early MacKinnon' with the 'early Barth'. Barth, above all, shares a rhetorical stridency, a tendency towards excess which is, it is to be feared, a function of weakness rather than strength. Is it not possible, moreover plausi-ble, that the very extremity of the presentation of the disruption of the created order by the onset, as MacKinnon puts it later, of God's 'attack' upon man in the Incarnation, should be understood as varying *inversely* with the *actual* categorical purchase of the 'mighty acts of God' upon reality? The context of this poignant dilemma is recognizably social: we can deny revelation because 'around us, furnishing the centre of our national life, is an elaborate social structure that is the fruit of human apostasy' and 'we are its prisoners more intimately than we know' (*GLT*, 25). Here MacKinnon displays a refracted response to the concerns of the Christendom group to which he owed a critical allegiance, even to the extent of acknowledging the social fact that in 'liberal culture, which we all inherit to a greater or lesser degree, religion is an adventure of the privileged few' (*GLT*, 26).

I have already presented sufficient material to indicate that there is, in however problematic a form, a systematic theology *in nuce* in *God the Living and the True*. This theology was never expanded and developed: it remains a strident and rhetorical combination of insights drawn from the dialectical and neo-scholastic tradition, set over against the pervasive corruption of liberal theology. It has, to use an offensive image, the potential and the pathos of a stillborn foetus. Why was it that MacKinnon turned from this area of intellectual operation into the 'borderland' that is the dominant feature of his mature work? The answer to this question may lie at least in part in the rhetorical character of the early work, which carried MacKinnon into a form of untenable theological and moral absolutism, the presuppositions and conditions of which remained both problematic and obscure. What were the transcendental conditions of the juxtaposed categories of philosophy and theology? Unlike many more famous but perhaps less courageous thinkers, but again like Barth, MacKinnon did not pursue a programme of simple question and subsequent answer, but had to reformulate and redirect the questions themselves. Thus, whilst on an immediate level MacKinnon presumed to exploit the theological analogue of philosophical positivism:

It is not for philosophy, whatever philosophy may be, to tell us whether or not God has intervened in the way in which he must have intervened for that intervention to merit the name of a revelation. That he has or has not is a matter of fact. We can only look and see.   (GLT, 33)

Both at a deeper level of transcendental presupposition *and* in terms of global plausibility, tensions mounted which would lead to a philosophical redirection of effort accompanied by what must have surely been a pain-bound personal advocacy of the *disciplina arcani* and ascesis with regard to the sphere of theology itself. It is not then surprising that the divine self-communication is understood as tragedy informed by kenosis:

The tragedy of our situation is that God can speak no other language to us, and that is the language we find it hardest to understand. For that sets over against human achievement divine failure. It is not a transvaluation, but an inversion of human failure.   (GLT, 40)

The Nietzschian overtones indicate how close to the wind MacKinnon attempted to sail in the exploration of paradox. It is not, I believe, implausible to conceive of MacKinnon's professional commitment to the philosophical mode of discourse as a means of expressing what must ultimately be judged as a profound and yet risk-fraught engagement with the contemporary theological expression of the Christian tradition, which has as its leitmotiv that acceptance of self-denigration, even self-destruction, which has constantly haunted his grasp of the Christian Gospel and twentieth-century reality. To this we shall return.

I am trying to indicate in this substantial passage devoted to Mac-Kinnon's first book that a variety of currents of thought coalesce, but that their strident, forced synthesis is, once seen with historical hindsight, a staying operation. In contemporary terms it was otherwise, because whilst the demand for transcendental justification existed in the 'surface grammar' and its potent, violent rhetoric, it then found expression in an extension of that rhetoric into a form of transcendental ecclesiology in *The Church of God*,[7] the first signs of which we find in the latter chapters of *God the Living and the True*. It was upon the rock of the Church that MacKinnon's desperate and paradoxical optimism was to founder; this ecclesiological betrayal still confronts us, as it was to confront MacKinnon in the aftermath of war. What are we to do with a Church that has effectively entered into a state of contradiction with its original nature?

Despite MacKinnon's recognition within Christianity of an analogue to the classical Greek virtue of *sophrosune*[8] in the 'continual tragedy of frustrated achievement' (*GLT*, 46) and his juxtaposition of the ultimacy of the Cross with the penultimacy of all human achievement, he nevertheless invests very heavily, too heavily, in the Church. In a passage that combines intense ecclesiological optimism with the Barthian dialectic of 'dissolution' MacKinnon tries to generate a conception of the Church that fuses social critique, theological objectivity and the renewal of the human:

To some extent the Christian baptised into the death of Christ must always, if he is loyal to his Master, be a disruptive force in society. For in and through his baptism he accepts the verdict of rejection pronounced from the Cross upon man's cultural achievement and is thereby irrevocably committed to the task of pointing the whole social frame to its origin beyond itself. The Church in its members is both involved in, and independent of, the historical cultural moment. It is involved in it, for it is [a] compact of individual historical men and women who are here to-day and gone to-morrow, but it is independent of it, for it is at the same time the Body of him who is the dissolver of all cultural forms that destroy and impede the attainment by the creature of his true status. The instrument, whereby the sub-human processes that ever threaten to absorb the individual persons are themselves revealed as demonic, is the revelation of the Cross of Christ.

(*GLT*, 47)

It is perhaps understandable that in the heat and dust of 1940 the pacifist MacKinnon should lay considerable reliance upon the invasive metaphor (as indeed the Swiss neutral Barth had done in the context of the First World War), but to this is added what we may describe analogously as *Gleichschaltung*. Thus whilst the Church originates in

an event in time that is the fruit of the interaction of time by eternity. It is the mission of the Church, the mystical body of Christ, to be his instrument for the extension of that irruptive and disruptive activity that was his coming. In a memorable phrase, Kierkegaard described the Incarnation as God's attack upon man.   (*GLT*, 53–4)

Are we wholly unfair if we see in this conception of the Church something of a triumphalist *Gleichschaltung* in the practical enactment, the ecclesial praxis, that is to follow *immediately* upon the incarnational 'fact'? This is a twentieth-century repristination of the Christian *Mythus* with, on the face of it, distinct totalitarian implications.

Our scheme has been to lay bare the whole character of the impact of the saving work of Christ upon our particular cultural situation. The Church exists for no other purpose than that through her ministry and her life she may continually refer human conflicts to the point in history at which they find their resolution. Apologetics properly conceived is the allotting to successive human aspirations and human tragedies of their place within the whole context of the Christ-drama.   (*GLT*, 55)

Again the Germanic undertones are further emphasized by MacKinnon's assertion of Brunner's conception of 'verbicompetence' in the setting of Maritain and Demant's neo-Thomism; for in 'the sphere of decisions rather than that of intelligence is to be found that potentiality which Christ in his coming actualises' (*GLT*, 58). That supremacy of *Tat* (act) over *Wort* (word), traceable to Goethe's self-conscious revision of German cultural expectations and values in the opening passage of *Faust*,[9] has its darker side, not least apparent when a theologian struggles with the perverse and extreme internalization and privatization of Christian practice in contemporary industrialized culture and society. The question is still with us: how do we renew Christian obedience without, putting it as directly (and crudely) as possible, relapsing into forms of authoritarian 'Christian fascism', or, as is all too apparent in the sociological literature, the analogous heteronomous and infantilized patterns of behaviour in the new religious movements? In this further sense MacKinnon's early work remains topical.

From under this potentially questionable 'surface grammar', MacKinnon's positive engagement with the inter-connection of intelligence and will that precludes any encounter with revelation emerges. This is beautifully expressed in a passage which itself prefigures his later concerns with the foundations of moral discourse as the presupposition of divine knowledge:

We can and must so scrutinise the human intelligence as to understand how it is that man can even in a measure comprehend the possibility of an intersection of the historical by the meta-historical. It is impossible to maintain the primacy of the practical reason in the face of the necessity that man should, at least in a measure comprehend the character of that which has shattered his conceit . . . the character of that act of decision is itself open to a distinctively intellectual scrutiny. His character as decision is discerned by an act of definitely intellectual recognition.   (*GLT*, 60)

This intricate and sophisticated discourse, the 'depth grammar' of *God the Living and the True*, cohabits uneasily with the totalitarian demand encapsulated in the rhetoric of staurological obedience:[10]

Christian theology is a *theologia crucis* simply in so far as it is the operation whereby the human intelligence adjusts its own appreciation of the human situation in the light of the impact upon it of the divine Word. (*GLT*, 63)

If we were to scrutinize these levels of assertion in terms of the 'post-modern' debate how would we categorize MacKinnon's assertions? There are, I believe, all the three elements, pre-critical, modern and post-modern, at work. Indeed, part of MacKinnon's great strength has been a refusal to accept any premature resolution of this restless tri-polarity, not least because of his constant interest in, and appreciation of, the particularities of pastoral life in which the struggle in and for faith is so informed. In the rhetoric of 'catastrophe', contradiction and saving act jostle upon the surface of MacKinnon's discourse, and this occasionally reaches a point near to *reductio ad absurdum*: the incarnational narrative of the Fourth Gospel is seen as 'the description of a divine attack upon man in mercy and a corresponding counter attack of man upon God in hate' (*GLT*, 72). At the same time the nascent 'depth grammar' intones themes that are to be pursued with both passion and agnostic caution in the mature work:

We have seen how tenuously man retains hold upon that sense of the transcendent character of the ground of his existence. We have seen again and again in human history how that intuition of finitude which is the most profound natural human intuition is debased, and how the infinite by reference to whom alone man discerns his individual finitide is located within and not without the initial process. None the less, the possibility of that intuition remains itself a guarantee of the at least partial validity of human ratiocination and of the possibility of man's being not unable to represent to himself the content of that which in Christ is revealed to him.

(GLT, 66)

I am acutely conscious that in trying to juxtapose the 'surface grammar' of extravagant and violent theological rhetoric with the 'depth grammar' and the birth of a subtle and agnostic moral passion I have not done justice to the emergent intellectual personality which finds fuller expression in the mature works, *A Study in Ethical Theory* and *The Problem of Metaphysics*. This deliberate exploitation of the unresolved ambiguities of the 'early' MacKinnon has, however, a further motive. Recent doctrinal controversy in the Church of England indicates, in my judgement, that an analogous irresolution persists in the wider context which allows public discussion to proceed with no real meeting of minds. Thus it would be possible for a conservative of High or Low Church persuasion to appeal to MacKinnon's consistent insistence upon the historical particularity of the Crucifixion and Resurrection narratives, or, alternatively, for a liberal to draw upon MacKinnon's cautious, even agnostic, epistemology and ontology such as we find it in the mature work.

MacKinnon concludes *God the Living and the True* with an emphatic flourish: 'It is through man's cruelty that the glory of God is revealed' (*GLT*, 88). This little book culminates in a brutal attack upon the domestication of the doctrine of the Incarnation in English Anglican theology, and if intellectual convulsion therapy could bring back critical life to a tradition then this perhaps ought to; but signally it did not. But are we not now in a position to see, with hindsight, that the malaise in Western European Christianity is certainly more complex, if not more profound, than MacKinnon then understood it? MacKinnon then stated the Christian vocation in perennial terms:

We can only come to ourselves through the death of ourselves, and the place of our burial we share with him whom we crucified. To know our worth we must admit we are worthless. Rather . . . to say that we are, we must first say that we are not. (*GLT*, 88)

This indicates more precisely that pattern of 'intellectual apostleship' to which we have already alluded. Whilst he was professionally to be a philosopher, MacKinnon's vocation was undertaken, may one suggest, as an incognito, a deliberate or perhaps not fully conscious assumption of a contrary nature behind which there still burns a theological furnace ignited under the original influence of Hoskyns. Purged of sentimentality and flaccid incarnationalism MacKinnon glimpses the Cross through the mysterious mutual involution of knowledge of God and of self-knowledge, and in that instant we know that of ourselves, we, the perpetrators of cruelty, *hate* what we see there displayed. Now we know why, in Hoskyns's words, the Incarnation is 'a dagger thrust in the heart of the world':

As he is . . . we need to see him as he is. When we see him, we are at first shocked that his face is marred above the sons of men. But as he confronts us, we are enabled to see of what stuff we ourselves are. Then no longer does it surprise us that there is no beauty that *we* should *desire in him*.[11]

Here, at what is inevitably the attainment of the first summit of a long mountain-range to be traversed in the years that were to come, MacKinnon's uncompromising renewed refraction of theological language owes much to Barth, certainly, but beyond that acknowledged influence there lies something even deeper and more tremendous. I suspect that it is perhaps Calvin, and his sense of the awful nature of God rejected by a perverse and depraved humanity, mediated through the Scottish Reformed tradition, that has likewise so impressed itself upon both MacKinnon and his great Scots compatriot Thomas Forsyth Torrance. Whatever else this consciousness may be, it succeeds in making unconditional grace in respect of both human particularity and structural sin the incontrovertible departure point of the Christian life and its conception of human growth. The contradiction between this conviction and the lived doctrine and behavioural pattern of the Church (not least the Church of England) and, in particular, its senior ecclesiastics, has, I believe, led a considerable number of MacKinnon's disciples either consciously or unconsciously to follow his example and resist the temptation of ordination.

III   Conclusion: moral passion and the failure of the Church

In *The Church of God*, MacKinnon further outlines, again in language at times of considerable brutality, the role of the Church, using the 'Messianic' motifs then current in Anglican theology (one has only to recall A. M. Ramsey's *The Gospel and the Catholic Church* for confirmation of this). Where the former misperceived the nature of the Church was in the presentation of a *contrasting* rather than a *similar* parallel between Israel and the Church. Whilst in the liturgy the Church 'stands most assuredly as witness to a tortured world that, where its self-contradiction was most hideously manifest, in the apostasy of the very chosen people of God, there was Christ attested as victor in his resurrection from the dead' (*CG*, 30) this contrast can no longer be sustained: it is the Church of God as a 'chosen people' that stands apostate, completing a deep irony in that the Church has *become* what it was called into existence to *deny*. The emblematic measure of this apostasy, seen by MacKinnon in his repeated later allusions to Bishop G. K. A. Bell and to the actions of senior ecclesiastics, is a recurrent theme that stems from an ecclesiological impossibilism grounded at least in part in an appropriation of dialectical theology, a 'MacKinnon's "Barth" ' that stalks the pages of *God the Living and the True* and *The Church of God*. There is a legitimate sense in which it could be asserted that the history of twentieth-century Western theology ought to be written around the attempted responses to Barth's impossibilism, his dialectical reduction. In *A Study in Ethical Theory* and *The Problem of Metaphysics* MacKinnon promoted a highly Anglo-Saxon version of a 'back to Kant' move, effectively abandoning the explicit use of the dialectical mode.

If, as I believe is the case, dialectical theology continues to be the key to understanding the fate of Christian theology in this century, and if, as I also believe, it contains the only *theological* tools capable of cutting through the entangled misconceptions that obscure the enactment of the tradition in contemporary reality, then MacKinnon's early work as the supreme British assimilation of that theology as mediated by Hoskyns deserves a partial and qualified rehabilitation. Such a rehabilitation has to be an *interpretation*, a hermeneutical mediation that recognizes the different, even incommensurable levels of argument and conflicting centres of intellectual consciousness which have, as I indicated at the outset, to be understood *both* in relation to MacKinnon's development *and* in the historical social and cultural context of that development.[12] Last but not least, a serious appropriation of the 'early' MacKinnon might help that lame, often lazy and usually undernourished English tradition to crystallize the Church of England's historical sense of time and place and wean it from the vaporous confusion of recent, often ineffectual theological controversy into serious theological engagement in the late twentieth century.

Notes

1 An obvious *lacuna* in this respect is a comprehensive account of the influence of E. C. Hoskyns's mediation of Barth.

2 MacKinnon himself has consistently run the risk of misunderstanding alluded to by Marx in his robust and arrogant treatment of Proudhon:

> M. Proudhon has the misfortune of being peculiarly misunderstood. In France he has the right to be a bad economist, because he is reputed to be a good German philosopher. In Germany he has the right to be a bad philosopher, because he is reputed to be one of the oldest of French economists. Being both a German and an economist at the same time, we desire to protest against this double error.
>
>   (*Collected Works*, 6:109)

MacKinnon in his 'borderland' has escaped Proudhon's error where other of his contemporaries have perhaps not.

3 I mean 'rhetoric' here primarily in the sense of an 'art of using language so as to persuade or influence others', but also in the potentially deprecatory sense of 'language characterised by artificial or ostentatious expression' (*COD*, p. 2535). Macaulay's judgement upon Milton that he had 'the sublime wisdom of the Areopagitica and the nervous rhetoric of the Iconoclast', *Essays* on Milton, 1825, indicates something of the sense of rhetoric as the language of emergency that I seek to convey here.

4 The analysis of rhetoric in theology offers important possibilities which I propose to explore more fully elsewhere.

5 This is a deliberate reformulation of '*Quem Deus vult perdere, prius dementat*', a Latin phrase originating in a scholastic's quotation of an unknown poet in commentary on Sophocles's *Antigone*. I am indebted to Dr E. D. Hunt of the Department of Classics, University of Durham, for tracing this reference.

6 The 'prophetic' prefiguring of the fully developed theologies of Moltmann and Jüngel is unmistakable.

7 For example, MacKinnon asserted that changed (and more sympathetic) attitudes towards Rome in England indicated that 'the Church of God suddenly again stands for something. And that something we may describe as the final and absolute revelation of Almighty God, given in the Word made flesh' (CG, 13). The difficulty of reconciling 'absoluteness' with the 'scandal of particularity' on the Cross remains with us.

8 A word defined as 'soundness of mind, providence, discretion, moderation in desire'. See H. G. Liddle and R. Scott, *A Greek–English Lexicon*, revised edn (Oxford, 1958), p. 1751.

9 Notoriously, 'Am Anfang war die Tat'.

10 The affinity between the view expressed in the following citation and that developed at length in T. F. Torrance's *Theological Science* (London, 1969) scarcely needs to be stressed.

11 Further to this,

It is the recognition that his being is contingent upon the necessary Being that is ever against him which constitutes the deepest intellectual appreciation of which he is capable. And the corollary of this discernment is the recognition that we do not know what God is; we know only what he is not and what relation everything else has with him. We cannot deny that this particular metaphysical assertion is vested with the ethical character of genuine humility (here the obliqueness of double negation almost subverts the statement of this, or one of MacKinnon's most fundamental and continuing postulates – R. H. R.). In the individual the appreciation of his own contingency is a psychological event which is fraught with a consciousness of his own insignificance. It is surely plain that such a recognition is distinguishable both in content and quality from the suggestion that man's significance is discernible in his own spiritual and material achievement.   (GLT, 73)

12 I explore this context at length in 'The Reception of the Theology of Karl Barth in the Anglo-Saxon World: History, Typology and Prospect', in S. W. Sykes, ed., *Karl Barth: Centenary Essays* (Cambridge, forthcoming).

2 Idealism and realism: an old controversy dissolved

FERGUS KERR

This essay is concerned with the dispute between realists and idealists, particularly in the form given to it in the immensely influential work of Michael Dummett, because Donald MacKinnon has insisted on its importance for theologians. That they should pay much more attention to their philosophical presuppositions is something that he has urged, not without some success, over many years. The reopening of the controversy may, however, prompt an attempt, not to resolve it so much as to make it superfluous. It will be suggested, at any rate, that the work of Charles Taylor, although at present much less influential, offers a perspective which it would be more fruitful for theologians to explore.

I

That Donald MacKinnon has conducted an anti-idealist campaign throughout his career need not be documented at great length. As an undergraduate at Oxford in 1934 he found himself being liberated from the theologically seductive doctrines of the British idealists by having to study the writings of the Cambridge realists, G. E. Moore and Bertrand Russell.[1] In 1935, as another autobiographical note discloses, he was taken by Isaiah Berlin to hear John Wisdom deliver a paper on Moore and Wittgenstein. If he appreciated how Wisdom had made his own Wittgenstein's 'emancipating insight' that we are philosophically misled by the habit of supposing the meaning of a word to be an object, he also responded positively to Wisdom's communication of 'the ruthlessly honest meticulous realism of Moore'.[2]

15

For all his realist insistence that religious belief has to do with what is the case, MacKinnon treated Richard Braithwaite's famous Eddington Memorial Lecture with surprising benevolence.[3] A decade later his attitude to tendencies that he detected in modern theology had greatly hardened. A paper on Aristotle concludes by suggesting that proper consideration of the doctrine of substance would 'issue in raising in a new way the perennially recurrent philosophical disputes between realism and subjectivism'.[4] In the exchange with Geoffrey Lampe on the doctrine of the Resurrection the same concern reappears. Here he speaks of 'continually renewed controversies', in the history of philosophy, 'between those who, where the theory of knowledge is concerned, are commonly called realists, and those who are sometimes called idealists, but also constructivists, between those for whom truth resides in the end in correspondence between propositions and fact, and those for whom it is something brought into being by more or less autonomous understanding'. And he goes as far as to force us to a choice: 'I suspect that, very much as Coleridge said that all men were at bottom either Platonists or Aristotelians, so we are, most of us, if we are informed enough philosophically to be self-conscious about these things, idealists or realists.'[5]

For years, then, sometimes with a certain ferocity, MacKinnon has sought to expose an idealist bias in much modern theology. Theologians whom he suspects of idealism are castigated for sup- posedly ecclesiocentric theology: 'Professor Macquarrie reveals himself in this book as a person who finds himself obviously very happy in church.'[6] Or again: Professor John Knox finds himself censured as one 'for whom theology has rotted away into the mere articulation of the presuppositions of a narrowly ecclesiastical piety'.[7]

MacKinnon voices his oppposition in such terms as the following:

If the Christian faith is true (and unless its truth-claims can be sustained we had better have done with it for ever), its truth is constituted by the correspondence of its credenda with harsh, human reality, and with the divine reality that met that human reality and was broken by it, only in that breaking to achieve its healing. At the foundation of the faith there lies a deed done, an incarnating of the eternal in the stuff of human history. It is not the delicate subtlety of our imaginative interpretations that is constitu- tive of this penetration of our human lot; what these interpretations seek to represent is the *act* that sets our every essay in conceptualization in restless vibration.[8]

The contrast between the 'deed done' and 'our imaginative interpretations' expresses the choice between realism and idealism – but is it necessarily to exhibit idealist tendencies if one questions the validity of this choice?

In 1976, MacKinnon writes of 'the radical subjectivism that may be judged the central blemish of the theological interpretation of the New Testament by Rudolf Bultmann' – but cites, as a worse case, 'the sort of radical subjectivism, which surely reaches its *reductio ad absurdum*, in the excursions into general theology by the much admired New York *Neutestamentler*, John Knox'. Contrasting Bultmann with Oscar Cullmann, MacKinnon notes 'the vibration within theology proper of the unresolved metaphysical controversy between idealism or constructivism and realism'. He now refers, parenthetically, to Michael Dummett's revival of the dispute between realism and idealism.[9] In his Presidential Address to the Aristotelian Society in the same year he placed great emphasis on the new debate between realism and anti-realism.[10]

Finally, writing of the report of the Doctrinal Commission of the Church of England which appeared in 1976, MacKinnon reached this judgement:

Its bias is undoubtedly subjectivist in the sense that it obstinately treats Christian believing ... as if it could be scrutinized in virtually complete aversion from what it is that is believed ... in the end, it is impossible to acquit the statement on *Christian Believing* of treating the certainly complex universe of Christian faith as if it were a universe of human activity that could be scrutinized as something self-contained, even as a kind of awareness that in a measure created its own objects.[11]

Such criticism of the 'pervasive bias', so he goes on at once to note, has been made by others with regard to modern theology in general, and he cites an article by Michael Dummett on tendencies in Roman Catholic theology which came 'like a breath of fresh air, for all the author's ignorance of recent study of the relevant New Testament material':

This because suddenly into an argument that much rehearsal had made tired, we had an intrusion by an absolutely first-class philosophical and formal logician, to whom vague generalization concerning the 'sudden or gradual birth of the conviction that Jesus was alive' is no substitute for precise and rigorous conceptual analysis. It is as if a detachment of the Welsh Guards had engaged with 'Dad's Army'.[12]

One might be pardoned for wondering if all the 'rigorous conceptual analysis' in the world would make up for 'ignorance of recent study of the relevant New Testament material' when anxieties on the latter score are aired. Dummett's essay,[13] which begins with trenchant denunciation of the 'dishonesty' that 'infects *most* modern Catholic biblical exegesis' (my italics), takes severely to task, as its first target, those who appeal to the literary convention of pseudonymous writing to justify rejecting Petrine authorship of the Second Epistle of St Peter. The protagonist in the revived dispute between realism and idealism, although widely regarded as himself anti-realist in his sympathies by professional colleagues, soon emerges as a realist in theological matters at least.

II

Donald MacKinnon once noted the hostility of R. G. Collingwood, sustained throughout his work, to what he called 'realism': the work of John Cook Wilson and H. A. Prichard, his colleagues at Oxford, as well as that of Moore and Russell at Cambridge. For Collingwood, as MacKinnon illuminatingly says, the trouble with the realists was that they were running away from the problem of our historical existence: 'they sought some point at which men could give an unconditioned validity to their commerce with the real'.[14] They were of course reacting against the doctrine of their idealist predecessors, who, with the slogan that 'all cognition is judgement', insisted so much on the role of interpretation in perception that they tended to the extreme conclusion that things as we know them cannot but be the creation of our minds. If we can never get the constructive function of our minds out of our knowledge of things, it appears that we never have knowledge of things as they are in themselves.

The realist urges, against all this, that the objects of our knowledge are independent of our knowing them. They hold to the doctrine, according to Collingwood, that 'knowing makes no difference to what is known'.[15] But his point is that, if the presence or absence of a certain condition, e.g., our being or not being on the scene, makes no difference to a thing, then one has to conclude that knowing what the thing is like *with* the condition and knowing what it is like *without* the condition may be *compared* – which would mean that the thing can be known *unconditionally*. Realism thus apparently trades on one's having access to some position outside one's own mundane perspective.

The anti-realism propounded by Collingwood in Oxford in the 1930s has much in common with the searching interrogation of realism conducted by Michael Dummett in Oxford since the late 1950s, although there is no direct indebtedness. Realism he redefines as the doctrine that a sentence can be true even though unverifiable. There is something in the world which confers truth value on it – even if we have no access to it. What Dummett sets out to do, starting in 1959 with his paper on 'Truth', is to probe the coherence of such a realist theory of knowledge.[16] Like many original philosophers he has some very simple examples.

Take, then, the case of Jones,[17] a man now dead who was never exposed to danger in his life: does it make sense to say 'Jones was brave'? I may say that, knowing that he had allied virtues, we may be sure that, if he had ever actually encountered danger, Jones would have acted bravely. But does 'If Jones had encountered danger he would have acted bravely' allow me to say 'Jones was brave'? It might be that, however many facts we knew of this kind which would be regarded as grounds for asserting our counterfactual conditional, we should still lack the decisive piece of information. In the end, since Jones never actually had to face danger, we just lack the crucial evidence that would enable us to decide whether he was brave. It appears that the sentence 'Jones was brave', in this story, can be neither verified nor falsified. We had better not say such things. Since we have no means of verifying that sentence we might as well admit that it is senseless.

It certainly seems that we cannot go on maintaining that a sentence must be true or false when there is no evidence that we should count as deciding the issue. Or rather – and this is Dummett's point – if we feel inclined to go on saying that 'Jones was brave' *must* be true or false, and it is not difficult to find oneself with this inclination, then we are trading on the belief that there is some fact somewhere in the world of the sort to which we appeal when settling counterfactual conditionals, if only we had access to it – 'or else . . . there is some fact of an extraordinary kind, perhaps known only to God'.

Whether Jones was brave thus becomes a truth that God alone can settle. But in that case, so Dummett goes on to suggest, we are imagining a kind of spiritual or psychic mechanism, Jones's character, which supposedly determines how he acts: 'his acting in such-and-such a way reveals to us the state of this spiritual mechanism, which was however already in place before its observable effects were displayed in his behaviour'. If we could have seen inside him when he was alive, we could say now, after his death, that Jones, who never had to face danger, was brave or otherwise. After all, the case is not so strange: we never have access to anyone's inner character; it always has to be revealed. Courage, or lack of it, must be *there*, 'inside', independently of whether circumstances require its being manifested. In no time at all, under Dummett's pressure, the inclination to say that there must be some fact about Jones, radically inaccessible to us, not just because he is dead but because facts of the relevant kind always are so, which would settle the truth or otherwise of 'Jones was brave', entangles us in a Cartesian philosophy of mind and even a certain disguised theism.

Dummett's example opens the way to his doubting the intelligibility (in the current jargon) of verification-transcendent truth. If the conditions for the truth or otherwise of a sentence lie completely beyond our powers to recognize, then that sentence has no meaning. The difference between realism and idealism is thus neatly redefined. Those who would say that 'Jones was brave' (in the story) does not mean anything unless we have the means of determining its truth belong to the anti-realist camp: the meaning of a sentence is inextricable from the means of verifying it. The strong undertow towards realism suggests, on the other hand, that, even if *we* have no way of verifying the statement, *some* way of doing so must exist: its truth or otherwise can be established, if not by us, then by 'some being whose intellectual capacities and powers of observation exceed our own'.

The theological implications of Dummett's interrogation of realism have never been concealed. In an unpublished paper in which he apparently undertakes what is in effect a reconstruction of Berkeley's proof of the existence of God, Dummett has suggested that 'anti-realism is ultimately incoherent but that realism is tenable only on a theistic basis'.[18] The anti-realist project is thus (partly) to lay bare the theistic assumptions with which realists, no doubt for the most part unwittingly, support their position. They are challenged to explain how a sentence can be true or false when the evidence for its being one or the other is radically inaccessible – at least to such beings as we humans are. For realism to work, that is to say, it has to allow for a supratemporal perspective on the world.

Dummett has formulated the difference in the following way:

> What the realist would like to do is to stand in thought outside the whole temporal process and describe the world from a point which has no temporal position at all, but surveys all temporal positions in a single glance ... The anti-realist takes more seriously the fact that we are immersed in time: being so immersed, we cannot frame any description of the world as it would appear to one who was not in time, but we can only describe it as it is, i.e. as it is now.[19]

Thus, as Collingwood had said, the anti-realist turns out to be the one who is peculiarly sensitive to the historical conditions of our existence. In terms perhaps more familiar to theologians, Dummett's anti-realist pays due attention to our *Geschichtlichkeit*. On the other hand, as Dummett confesses, he himself is strongly inclined to believe with the realist that there must be some description of reality which transcends any particular point of view: 'of anything which is real, there must be a complete – that is, observer-independent – description'.[20]

A deep difference, then. But the realist *versus* anti-realist dispute now begins to seem so profound that one cannot help remembering what Renford Bambrough has called Ramsey's maxim: when a dispute between two parties is chronic there must be some false assumption that is common to the two parties, the denial of which will lead to the resolution of the dispute.[21]

III

Consider these remarks from an important text which Wittgenstein completed in 1930:

> What I wanted to say is that it is remarkable that those who ascribe reality only to things and not to our ideas move about so unquestioningly in the world as idea and never look outside it.

That is: how unquestioned the given still is. It would be the very devil if it were a tiny picture taken from an oblique, distorting angle. The unquestioned – *life* – is supposed to be something accidental, marginal; while something over which I never normally puzzle at all is regarded as the real thing![22]

Philosophers have been tempted into the habit of ascribing reality either to 'things', *die Dinge*, or to 'our conceptions', *unsere Vorstellungen* – but this choice leaves 'the given' – 'life', *das Leben* – unquestioned. Even those who insist most strongly on the priority of *things*, rather than that of our *ideas*, and who may thus be regarded as anti-idealist, move about unquestioningly within 'the world as idea', *die Vorstellungswelt*. The realist, for all his insistence on our having knowledge of things outside our minds, never looks outside the world as that which is *representable*. The realist, just as much as the idealist, marginalizes 'life', 'the real thing', 'the given'.

The simple but essential point that Wittgenstein is making comes out in the immediately preceding passage:

That it doesn't strike us at all when we look around us, move about in space, feel our own bodies, etc., etc., shows how natural these things are to us. We do not notice that we see space perspectively or that our visual field is in some sense blurred towards the edges. It doesn't strike us and never can strike us because it is *the* way we perceive. We never give it a thought and it's impossible we should, since there is nothing that contrasts with the form of our world.

We cannot compare our relationship to the world with some alternative. Thus Wittgenstein rejects the temptation to posit some extra-mundane perspective from which observer-independent knowledge of things as they really are would become available. The suggestion is that the realist's concern for objective knowledge of things in themselves is entangled with the idealist's insistence that knowledge of things has to be knowledge of them as they are conceived by us. Either way, so Wittgenstein is suggesting, 'the real thing', *das Eigentliche*, is marginalized: *'life'* is overlooked in this dispute over 'things' and 'ideas'.

Clearly, Wittgenstein's remarks here remain programmatic. The thought goes somewhat as follows. I notice something by seeing its difference from something else, but I am in no position to set the world off against anything. The world does not strike us, if we look around, move, feel our bodies, and so on, because there is nothing with which to contrast the form of our world. But, as the passage concludes:

Time and again the attempt is made to use language to limit the world and set it in relief – but it can't be done. The self-evidence of the world expresses itself in the very fact that language can and does only refer to it.

For since language only derives the way in which it means from its meaning, from the world, no language is conceivable which does not represent the world.

The world is so obvious as to escape notice. By forgetting our immersion in the world we can be tempted to split language from life and find ourselves with a problem about how language can 'represent' the world. A little later, Wittgenstein makes the following remark:

From the very outset 'Realism', 'Idealism', etc., are names which belong to metaphysics. That is, they indicate that their adherents believe they can say something specific about the essence of the world.[23]

Several other themes are woven into this text, in characteristically Wittgensteinian fashion. But realism and idealism are here categorized as metaphysical beliefs about the essence of the world, while the upshot of the remarks which we have just discussed seems to be that, by setting language over against reality, a problem is generated about 'representation'.

In effect, then, Wittgenstein, by reminding us of our already 'being in the world' (to coin a phrase), aspires to bypass the problem of realism *versus* idealism. He wants to dissipate the illusion that language is a peculiar kind of picture of the world – that there is something extraordinary about *sentences*.

Consider the following discussion:

Why do we say a proposition is something remarkable? On the one hand, because of the enormous importance attaching to it. (And that is correct.) On the other hand this, together with a misunderstanding of the logic of language, seduces us into thinking that something extraordinary, something unique, must be achieved by propositions.[24]

Sentences are indeed very important, but, according to Wittgenstein, we are easily led to etherealize them:

'Remarkable things, propositions!': to say that is already to begin the subliming of all representation, *Darstellung*. The tendency to hypothesize some pure intermediary between the propositional *sign* and what is the case. Or even the desire to purify – sublime – the propositional sign itself.[25]

A gap opens up between language and reality, between the language-using animal and its world, which has to be bridged by some connecting device. The problem now is to see how language hooks up with the world. To this Wittgenstein replies as follows:

'Thought must be something unique.' When we say – *mean* – that such-and-such is the case, we do not, with what we mean, stop anywhere short of the fact – on the contrary, we mean that *such-and-such is thus-and-so*. – But this paradox (which certainly has the form of a truism) can also be expressed in this way: It is possible to *think* what is not the case.

Other illusions come from various quarters to attach themselves to the special one spoken of here. Thought, language, now appear to us as the unique correlate, picture, of the world. These concepts: proposition, language, thought, world, stand in line one behind the other, each equivalent to each.[26]

It is true that we can think what is not the case, but it does not follow that when we have thoughts of what is the case there is a gap between us and the world – our thoughts reach all the way up to the things that make them true. From the fact that our thoughts can be false we need not conclude that thoughts never reach reality.

For Wittgenstein, we may say, it was not a matter of reviving the realist *versus* idealist controversy in the hope of resolving it but rather of recovering a sense of the place of the subject in the world which would render the controversy superfluous. To put it like that, of course, is bound to remind theologians of certain strains in modern German philosophy, more likely to permeate their theo-logical reading and thus more likely to be familiar than anything in post-Fregean analytic philosophy.

It has in fact been suggested, although further exploration is required, that Wittgenstein's work between 1929 and 1933 bears so much resemblance to themes dominant in phenomenology that he must have had more than passing acquaintance with texts in that tradition.[27] It is certainly recorded that, early in 1930, in Vienna, he took part in 'spontaneous discussions of ideas of Husserl's, Heideg-ger's, and Weyl's'.[28] The term 'phenomenology' also appears quite often in *Philosophical Remarks*. Whatever he knew in detail, it is impossible not to be struck by parallels with Heidegger's emphasis on the 'world' in *Sein und Zeit* (published in 1927).

Heidegger, much more clearly than Wittgenstein, places the realism *versus* idealism dispute in the context of attempts to reconcile the Cartesian 'isolated subject' with the 'world'.[29] The idealist who alleges our inability to prove that anything exists outside our consciousness is no doubt much less sophisticated than Dummett's anti-realist, for whom verification-transcendent knowledge alone is excluded. Heidegger's realist, assuming that the existence of the outside world needs to be proved, is confident that this is capable of proof – just as Dummett's realist understands statements whose truth conditions are radically inaccessible.

Heidegger wants to put a stop to the whole project of looking for ways to reconcile the subject with the world, mind with reality. Once the gap between the subject and the world has opened up, so he argues, the only thing of which the subject can be certain appears to be something 'inner' – 'private', as Wittgenstein would say. But this is the standard Cartesian thought. This putative inner reality is pictured, in Heidegger's terminology, as something 'present-at-hand', *vorhanden*: a determinate and isolable entity, picked out of its context in life and laid out for neutral inspection. The grammar of subjectivity, in Wittgenstein's terms, is temptingly construed on the model of 'object and designator'.[30] The grip of naming as designating objects inclines us to model the inner life on a parade of immaterial objects that present themselves to private inspection. The myth of the private ostensive definition which the later Wittgenstein strove so hard to expose turns out to be another facet of the ontological orientation to *Vorhandenheit* which has isolated the subject from the world and generated the subject–object problem to which realism and idealism offer themselves as rival solutions.[31] For Heidegger, as for Wittgenstein, these 'solutions' fall away when the problem is revealed to be superfluous.

The desire for observer-independent description of reality which Dummett ascribes to the realist, and to deal with which the anti-realist project has been mounted, turns out to be the Cartesian goal of finding a prejudice-free and perspectiveless vantage-point – precisely what Heidegger is out to demolish. Dispassionate representation of isolable entities remains an enormously important activity; but it is interwoven with an immense variety of activities, practical and for the most part unreflective, which constitute the world in which we are always already situated. But if the world is always already inhabited, so to speak, and mostly by means of practices which stand in no need of theorization, the subject is no longer torn between awarding priority either to things or to ideas. The traditional basis for the realism *versus* idealism dispute evaporates.

Heidegger traces *Vorhandenheit* as a way of understanding things to our propensity to resent our contingency – what he labels *verfallen*, 'falling'. As always already situated – *geworfen*, 'thrown', as he will say – we are never in a position to choose our possibilities from the bottom up. As always having to do one thing rather than another, we can never do everything. In effect, we can never create ourselves, and we can never realize all our possibilities. In other words, we cannot be divine. The 'falling' which Heidegger finds in our way of being is a secularization of the doctrine of the Fall. But this also means that the obvious way to overcome our immersion in things is to disengage them from their context and study them as isolable and determinate entities. To view things as merely *there*, objects out of relationship, is to stop using them as equipment, as that which is (diversely) 'ready-to-hand', *zuhanden*, in Heidegger's richly 'pragmatist' understanding of our being in the world.

The Cartesian project of bracketing out our inheritance is entirely understandable, inevitable and desirable – Heidegger is not anti-scientific. The temptation is, however, that, in our culture at least, we have sought to generalize this way of treating things detachedly, so that the subject's epistemic detachment from the world comes to seem the natural condition. This, in turn, gives rise to repeated attempts to get mind back in touch with reality.

IV

Realism and anti-realism divide, according to Michael Dummett, over the intelligibility of verification-transcendent knowledge. For anti-realists, then, sentences have no meaning if we have no means of verifying them. In terms of the older story, realists and idealists divide over the intelligibility of the external world. For idealists, things only have the intelligibility that we give them. Clearly, the dispute revolves round our understanding of the place that the subject occupies in the world. Wittgenstein, and Heidegger more clearly, are out to destroy the picture of the self which sustains the whole dispute. Heidegger tries to get us to see the phenomenon of our always already being in the world: 'being-in-the-world'. Wittgenstein, much more imaginatively, devotes his later work to showing, by countless examples, that the dispute is superfluous:

When we say – *mean* – that such-and-such is the case, we do not, with what we mean, stop anywhere short of the fact – on the contrary, we mean that *such-and-such is thus-and-so*.[32]

That remark is neither realist nor idealist: the gap between the subject and the world is simply not admitted. It is not *bridged*, for it never existed in the first place.

If all this is correct, or nearly so, the realist *versus* anti-realist dispute has evaporated. This is a conclusion which one may well be strongly inclined to resist; but that would only show how powerful the grip of the great metaphysical dilemma still remains. Heidegger is commonly misread as an existentialist, just as the later Wittgenstein is treated as an exponent of anti-realism. For all the obvious differences, their two immense bodies of writing have one and the same project: to put an end to the way of thinking in which the realism *versus* idealism dispute arises. The difficulty of understanding their work is the difficulty of breaking a habit of thought that has been dominant in our tradition for at least three hundred years. The only further argument at this point would therefore be to turn either to Wittgenstein or to Heidegger and begin to work through the text.

Supposing that we had done so, and that the realism *versus* idealism dispute had begun to lose its fascination, what difference would it make? In particular, if 'jacking up the old metaphysical issue into a new semantical issue',[33] to quote Richard Rorty's inimitably elegant description of Dummett's project, finally turns out to depend for its plausibility on something like the Cartesian picture of the isolated worldless subject, how can this illuminate theologians who may, or may not, be philosophically innocent?

Charles Taylor, deliberately combining Wittgenstein and Heidegger, although never simply parroting either, has begun to develop an alternative conception of meaning which seeks to leave the realism *versus* anti-realism dispute behind.[34] In effect, he goes back to Wittgenstein's insight that we are philosophically obsessed by the habit of supposing the meaning of a word to be an object – the insight which Donald MacKinnon learned from John Wisdom in 1935. The first sixty or so remarks in Wittgenstein's *Philosophical Investigations*, for instance, explore the powerful temptation to equate meaning with *representing*. Designating objects, whether meanings in the head or the more conspicuous entities in the environment, seems singularly fundamental to human life. We are adjusted, as Wittgenstein noted elsewhere, to relate every linguistic practice to descriptions of physical objects.[35] Objective representation of processes and entities from which the observer has attained a certain independence is such a central ideal of our culture that we have come to regard it as the norm of meaningful activity. Anti-realists remain as wedded as realists to the dominance of the representation of objects, so Taylor argues. The enormous importance that designating objects of course has, as Wittgenstein shows in these early sections of his *Investigations*, depends on a whole network of activities within which connections between words and things such as reference arise in the first place. The hard thing is to give up the obsession with representation – hard, ultimately, because it means giving up the conception of the self as detached observer of the passing scene. Our very existence as rational beings, never mind our mastery of the various skills of depiction, depends upon our participation in innumerable activities which are more or less interwoven with language. By the time that Wittgenstein's writing has begun to affect us, the idea that language is essentially representational has lost its charm.

Language does not only represent things that would exist whether or not we ever named them, it enters into the constitution of many of the things that matter to us most. How much of an 'inner life' could one have without having assimilated a great deal from one's family and tradition? This need not (and is indeed unlikely to) be propositional knowledge; the communication will probably have been largely 'non-verbal'. Consider Wittgenstein's remark, one of many in the same vein:

A child has much to learn before it can pretend. (A dog cannot be a hypocrite, but neither can he be sincere.)[36]

In other words: those characteristic features of human life which we call pretending, hypocrisy, sincerity, and so on, we pick up from our elders and betters, largely by imitation and reaction, but these practices also depend on discussion and description. That makes it sound much too intellectual a development. The nuances may indeed be such as it would require Henry James to delineate, but the varieties of deception are ordinarily taught in the rough and tumble of family life, at school or at work, through mutual recrimination, tears of anger and shame, incoherent reproaches and apologies, and much else of this kind – and naming the thing comes late in the day and may well be denunciation rather than designation.

But it is not only such features of human life that are (partly) constituted by language, in the course of innumerable verbal exchanges, long before they are (partly) described. Our relations with one another, at the most fundamental level, owe their existence largely to language. How could a father distinguish his sons from some other man's but for the emergence of paternal–filial relations, hardly separable from a sense of successive generations, the passage of time, mortality, inheritance, history, and a large number of connected realities without which human life is hardly imaginable – realities that are not simply named but are to greater or lesser extent created linguistically? As Taylor insists, our emotions, aspirations, goals, our social relations and practices, are largely constituted by language.[37]

Some such view will surely appeal to theologians. It seems very likely that the people who produced the Judaeo-Christian writings, for example, accorded no special privilege to the objective description of observer-independent realities. To acknowledge this does not immediately place them outside the realm of what we can understand. If it is correct to say that detached representation of the facts had not acquired the status that it enjoys in our culture (at least theoretically), it does not follow that their writings must be classed as fiction, propaganda or forgery. It would not be surprising, however, if we found great difficulty in doing justice to texts whose characteristic ways of telling a true story long antedate the modern concern with objectivity. Once a culture has conceived the ideal of accurate representation of the facts from as detached a viewpoint as possible, and made this the primary function of language, it requires a considerable imaginative effort to read texts from a society with no such ideal. In fact, of course, much of what would commonly be regarded in our own society as 'objective reporting' has barely concealed evaluative and persuasive functions. It does not follow that we are being deceived and manipulated all the time. Nor need we conclude, when faced with texts from a very different culture, in this case one without our admiration for neutral depiction (just because that ideal had not yet emerged), that they must be totally unintelligible to us. A major part of the fascination of studying alien texts lies in the challenge that they often present to our conceptions of how to tell the truth.

It might not seem so shocking, then, that, confronted with what sounds like incipient gnosticism within the Church, some anonymous pastor, perhaps about AD 125, took the name of Peter to justify his right to castigate the heretics. This would not mean that Christians at the time lacked the concept of fraudulent writings – on the contrary, one of their principal concerns was already to sort out authentic Christian documents from the mass of gospels, letters, etc., often ascribed to apostles and other New Testament figures, but which contained more or less blatant heresy. It might mean, however, that the option insisted upon by Michael Dummett in this passage is Procrustean:

If this letter was written after the death of St Peter, then, surely, it is an imposture. If someone thinks it consistent with the Catholic faith to hold that such an imposture was included in the canon, he may say so; anyone who thinks, as I do, that it is not, must take the evidence for the late composition of the work to be misleading. The least plausible position is to attempt to have it both ways, by pretending the existence of a literary convention for which there is no shred of evidence and which is intrinsically unlikely.[38]

The logic, for all its analogy with the disciplined tread of the Welsh Guards, works with notions of truth and evidence which are easy to relate to the realism *versus* idealism dispute.

Much more importantly, however, dislodgement of the paradigm of representation leads to rediscovery of other dimensions of language, as we have noted. In particular, as Charles Taylor insists, a great deal of what matters to human beings is (partly) constituted by language. While 'a deed done', as MacKinnon says, lies at the foundation of the Christian faith, it is surely the spell of the realism *versus* idealism dispute that impels him to set the 'incarnating of the eternal in the stuff of human history' off against 'the delicate subtlety of our imaginative interpretations'.[39] That is hardly an objective description of the shocked and almost horrified process of recognition that the New Testament writings occasionally reflect.

A dead man's reappearing alive might mean almost anything. It took a whole complex of inherited aspirations, goals, social and religious relations and practices, and so on, all of them largely constituted by language, for people to say 'He has risen.' The mysterious hole I find one morning at the bottom of the garden can be puzzling to me only because the questions I can ask and the kinds of answers that would make sense all depend upon a network of habits and expectations – which may suddenly or gradually be altered and revised, but the very possibility of something obtruding as mysterious, let alone divine, gracious, healing, and so on, is determined in advance by what might be labelled, not too unfairly, as 'our imaginative interpretations'. The possibility that Christ has been raised from the dead must remain unintelligible to people whose imaginations have not been affected by the prospect of our being accountable to the God who, according to Judaeo-Christian eschatology, is to judge us at the end of time. Without such notions in our heads, and a great many more of the same kind, the 'deed done' at the foundation of Christian faith would remain unintelligible and even, as it is for most people, completely invisible. We see what we can say.

Much more needs to be said. Even if Michael Dummett's revival of the realism *versus* idealism dispute only prompted a return to such attempts as Heidegger and Wittgenstein have made to circumvent the whole dispute, nothing would have been lost. On the contrary, as Donald MacKinnon has shown, the power of the dichotomy to separate the sheep from the goats remains formidable. But the work of Charles Taylor, now that his essays have at last been collected, may have much more to offer theologians, among others, who want to get beyond what often seems a contest between hypostatized abstractions. It might be even more fruitful to return to Kant's struggle with Descartes – in MacKinnon's words, to 'his subtle and strenuous effort to have the best of both worlds, to hold together a view which treated learning about the world as a finding, with one that regarded such learning as a constructive act'.[40]

Notes

1 D. M. MacKinnon, *Borderlands of Theology and Other Essays* (London, 1968), pp. 61–2.
2 *Borderlands*, pp. 222–4.
3 *Cambridge Review*, 25 February 1956, pp. 375–8.
4 In R. Bambrough, ed., *New Essays in Plato and Aristotle* (London, 1965), p. 118.
5 D. M. MacKinnon, *The Resurrection: A Dialogue arising from Broadcasts*, with G. W. H. Lampe (London, 1966), pp. 110–11.
6 *Journal of Theological Studies*, n.s. 18 (1967), pp. 294–5.
7 D. M. MacKinnon, *Explorations in Theology 5* (London, 1979), p. 21.
8 *Ibid.*, pp. 21–2.
9 In R. W. A. McKinney, ed., *Creation, Christ and Culture* (Edinburgh, 1976), p. 105.
10 D. M. MacKinnon, 'Idealism and Realism: An Old Controversy Renewed', reprinted in *Explorations*, pp. 138–50.
11 *Explorations*, p. 27.
12 *Ibid.*, p. 29.
13 Michael Dummett, 'Biblical Exegesis and the Resurrection', *New Blackfriars*, 58 (1977), pp. 56–72.
14 *Borderlands*, p. 171.
15 R. G. Collingwood, *An Autobiography* (Oxford, 1939), pp. 44–52.
16 Michael Dummett, 'Truth', reprinted in *Truth and Other Enigmas* (London, 1978), pp. 1–19.
17 *Ibid.*, p. 15.
18 *Ibid.*, p. xxxix.
19 *Ibid.*, p. 369.
20 *Ibid.*, p. 356.
21 R. Bambrough, 'Principia Metaphysica', *Philosophy*, 39 (1964), p. 103.
22 L. Wittgenstein, *Philosophical Remarks* (Oxford, 1975), retranslated.
23 *Ibid.*, p. 86.
24 L. Wittgenstein, *Philosophical Investigations* (Oxford, 1953), Part I, section 93.
25 *Ibid.*, section 94, retranslated in the light of Roland Hall's interesting but neglected review, *Philosophical Quarterly*, 17 (1967), pp. 362–3.
26 *Ibid.*, sections 95–6, retranslated.
27 Nicholas F. Gier, *Wittgenstein and Phenomenology* (New York, 1981).
28 Brian McGuinness, ed., *Wittgenstein and the Vienna Circle* (Oxford, 1979), p. 19. Hermann Weyl (1885–1955) was a mathematician.
29 M. Heidegger, *Being and Time* (London, 1962), section 43.
30 Wittgenstein, *Investigations*, section 293.

31 Two recent books throw a great deal of light on what Heidegger is up to: Charles B. Guignon, *Heidegger and the Problem of Knowledge* (Indianapolis, 1983) and John Richardson, *Existential Epistemology: A Heideggerian Critique of the Cartesian Project* (Oxford, 1986).

32 Wittgenstein, *Investigations*, section 95.

33 In *Truth and Interpretation: Perspectives on the Philosophy of Donald Davidson*, ed. Ernest LePore (Oxford, 1986), p. 353.

34 Charles Taylor, 'Theories of Meaning', Dawes Hicks Lecture to the British Academy, 1980, reprinted in *Philosophical Papers*, 2 vols. (Cambridge, 1985), vol. 1, pp. 248–92.

35 L. Wittgenstein, *Zettel* (Oxford, 1967), section 40.

36 Wittgenstein, *Investigations*, Part II, section 11, p. 229.

37 Taylor, 'Theories', p. 273.

38 Dummett, 'Biblical Exegesis', pp. 57–8.

39 MacKinnon, *Explorations*, p. 22.

40 MacKinnon, 'Idealism and Realism', *Explorations*, p. 138.

3 Modes of representation and likeness to God

PATRICK SHERRY

In his Gifford Lectures Donald MacKinnon says that 'No modern philosopher raises more acutely than Kant the problems of the representation of the unrepresentable.'[1] A similar judgement might, I think, be applied to his own work. For few modern philosophers and theologians have been more concerned with the variety of ways in which we attempt to represent what transcends us, while yet insisting on its transcendence, than MacKinnon. In those lectures, echoing Wittgenstein, he describes the metaphysician as 'thrusting against the limits of language' and as one who

finds himself compelled to attempt the utterance of the unutterable, representation of that which cannot be represented, even, moreover, to argue the claims of one form of representation against another as less inadequately conveying the shape of what is. (p. 163)

He compares the metaphysician's task to that of a painter, as described by Cézanne in his letters. And indeed the words just quoted remind me of another painter: not Cézanne, but the aboriginal Alf Dubbs, in Patrick White's novel *Riders of the Chariot*, who struggles to express something of his religious vision on canvas.

The problem of metaphysics, for MacKinnon, is not just the difficulty of uttering, but the inevitable inadequacy of what is uttered. In the case of God, our attempts to represent Him run the risk of anthropomorphism, which he describes as 'the intellectual counterpart of the sin of idolatry' (*ibid.*, p. 15). Aidan Nichols has noted that it was Israel's abhorrence of its neighbours' idolatrous religion and its desire to protect God's transcendence that led it to

34

insist on banning all images of God. Yet at the same time Judaism taught that men are created in the image and likeness of God (Gen. 1:26–8; 9:6), a daring claim, for, as Nichols remarks, it gives to man the power of divine disclosure which, in pagan culture, was attached to the image of the god.[2] Here we have a practical illustration of the tension which MacKinnon notes, between the desire to represent what is transcendent and the need to destroy, or at least to see the limitations, of, all such representations.

In this essay I shall argue that there are two main ways in which people have sought to surmount this tension, corresponding to a distinction made by Nelson Goodman between representations and resemblances. In the case of God, the distinction is mainly between words which attempt to express something of His reality, and likenesses to Him in the world. I shall explore this distinction, and end by saying a little about the relevance of my topic to the question of theological realism.

Let me approach the distinction by showing how MacKinnon fleshes out the general remarks I have quoted by his careful attention to the variety of ways in which people try to express their glimpses of God, and to the different kinds of reflection on those ways. In the Gospels he points to the rich complexity of language and 'system of projection': historical, mythological, ironic and ontological.[3] One particular use of language singled out by MacKinnon is the parable, which may enlarge our perception of how things are, shatter self-deception, and thereby serve as an 'indirect indication of the transcendent',[4] a function similar in some respects to that of a tragedy, which is 'a form of representation that by the very ruthlessness of its interrogation enables us to project as does no available alternative, our ultimate questioning', making us 'in the end discontented with any form of naturalism'.[5] In some ways Jesus's Passion can be seen as a tragic drama;[6] and at a second-order level of reflection, a doctrine of the Atonement is an attempt to capture the sense of that drama for what it is.[7] At a further more general level of reflection, one may ponder the nature of language used both in primary religious utterances and in the Church's doctrine and theology, for instance by studying the nature of analogical predication. Here we are approaching the well-worn path of recent studies of religious language. MacKinnon does not belittle such studies; but he indirectly suggests that perhaps they have confined themselves to too narrow a compass by their neglect of the nature of novels, plays and poems. Theology needs to be fertilized by ideas growing from other areas of life and fields of study; and literature (including fiction) may be a source of revelation about humanity and a true representation of human life.[8]

If language fails, then silence may be necessary; for, MacKinnon tells us, a theologian may find sometimes that 'silence is the only adequate "system of projection" at his disposal'.[9] But other means of expression may be available, and indeed more useful. Sometimes a map of the countryside (which also involves a 'system of projection') may tell you more about it than a painting or a photograph would. In public religious practice the primary mode of expression is liturgical action, with its accompanying words: especially, for Christians, the Eucharist. MacKinnon argues that the actions of Jesus at the Last Supper had a depth of meaning which requires levels of understanding comparable to those needed to grasp the meaning of a parable or for understanding someone's self-revelation.[10]

Another way in which such disclosures may occur is, according to MacKinnon, by looking at the lives of paradigmatic religious figures, for example saints and apostles. An apostle, he says, tests his actions by correspondence, such as 'will enable men to see through him, and himself to deepen his sense of being possessed by that which has laid hold of him'.[11] Similarly, a saint's life 'is the most revealing intimation of the ultimate'.[12] Such a role is not confined to religious figures, for MacKinnon suggests that Socrates had a similar effect on Plato: the latter was guided by the 'impetus of a conviction that in the life and death of Socrates there was to be found a concretion, one might say a *mimesis*, of the way in which things ultimately are'.[13] But it is above all in Christ, particularly in the suffering and humiliated Christ, that MacKinnon finds the fullest representation of the divine glory: the condescension whereby Jesus accepted his burden can be 'interpreted as a painfully realized transcription into the conditions of our existence, of the receptivity ... that constitutes his person'.[14]

Representations and likenesses

We have in MacKinnon's work, then, a very rich account of the great variety of ways in which people discern what transcends them and try to express their glimpses of it. What I want to do now is to look at a distinction made by Nelson Goodman (in his book *Languages of Art* and elsewhere) between representations and resemblances, and to see what light it throws on our particular topic.

Goodman initially distinguishes between the relations of resemblance and representation by claiming that the former is reflexive (for objects resemble themselves) and symmetrical, whereas the latter is a matter of standing for, referring to, and being a symbol for. For him, a representation is akin to a description, in that it involves the use of a system of symbols, and is therefore subsumed along with descriptions under the category of 'denotation'[15] (the difference between them is that in his terminology 'descriptions' are of course verbal, whilst 'representations' include paintings, models and maps). Thus he assimilates the relation between a picture and what it represents to the relation between a predicate and what it applies to, and distinguishes both of them from the relation of resemblance: 'Denotation is the core of representation and is independent of resemblance' (p. 5). Representation, for Goodman, is more a matter of classifying or characterizing objects than of copying or imitating them. Non-linguistic systems differ from languages primarily in what he calls the density and lack of differentiation of their symbol systems (p. 226). But, like other denotations, representations are relative to symbol systems, for nothing is intrinsically a representation. Elements become representations only in conjunction with some correlation between symbols and what is denoted (pp. 227–8).

After making the distinction between representation and resemblance, Goodman says little about the latter in *Languages of Art*, for naturally his interest there is in methods of representation. But elsewhere[16] he has discussed the relation of similarity more fully, analysing it (wrongly, I think) in terms of two things having the same property in common. Again, he distinguishes it from the relations of representing and picturing: one coin may resemble another, one twin may be like its sibling, but we would not talk of representing or picturing in such cases. Another difference, which

Goodman does not mention here, is that a likeness may simply exist in nature and not be *meant* (at least by any human being) to convey anything, whereas representations and descriptions are products of human purposive behaviour.

Let us apply Goodman's distinction, between representations and descriptions on the one hand and resemblances on the other, to the examples which MacKinnon has given. It would seem that those examples do fall into classes corresponding to the distinction. The earlier examples which I cited are all uses of language, and are therefore 'descriptions' for Goodman. If we include liturgical actions, painting and other religious arts, then we have some non-linguistic cases which would fall under Goodman's category of 'representations'. Some of the latter examples, on the other hand, involve resemblance. Saints are regarded by Christians as those in whom the image and likeness of God, which were lost or made faint at the Fall, are being restored by the Holy Spirit (I am told by Professor Rowan Williams that in Old Slavonic the word for 'saint' is 'like' [*sc.* God]). Above all, we have in Christ 'the radiant light of God's glory and the perfect copy of his nature' (Heb. 1:3), the 'image of the invisible God' (Col. 1:15).

Having mentioned Goodman's distinction and briefly sketched its application to theology, I need to qualify it slightly by pointing out that it is not as sharp a distinction as he thinks. Common sense suggests that *some* representations are like what they represent – we talk of the likeness between a portrait and its subject. In a review article on Goodman's *Languages of Art*[17] C. F. Presley suggests that whilst in general Goodman is right to differentiate representation and resemblance, 'In representational systems that are realistic, however, one might expect symbols to look like their denotata' (p. 391). Hence he argues against Goodman that there is a distinction between 'iconic' and other signs, for picture recognition is learnt in a different way from language recognition, and reading a map differs from reading Italian. Similarly, children react differently to a picture of an orange and the word 'orange'. He concludes 'The distinction is not transitory or trivial because whether or not a symbol is iconic depends not upon our changing habits but upon our comparatively unchanging perceptual equipment' (p. 392).

There are, then, some middle cases. If we distinguish between representational and realistic art (Chagall's work is an example of the former, Courbet's of the latter), then some paintings both represent their subjects and are like them (or, better, are in their image or convey their likeness). Conversely, if likenesses are seen as created by God, they may be assimilated to pictures – I am thinking here of the way in which some Christian writers have compared the saints to pictures of Christ: in his essay 'On the Veneration of the Saints'[18] Georges Florovsky treats of icons and saints together. Of the latter he says, quoting St John of Damascus,

> God's saints ... kept uninjured the likeness unto the image of God, according to which they were created ... they became in their very nature like unto Him ... filled with the Holy Spirit...

Similarly, the Abbé Huvelin describes the saints as 'living images painted by Christ for his Church that he might recall some of his own features to her mind and console her in her widowhood'.[19]

Despite this qualification, I think that Goodman has pointed to a fundamental distinction.[20] Descriptions in language may represent reality, but they are not *like* it; similarly with diagrams, non-realistic pictures and symbolic systems. Conversely, two brothers may resemble, but do not denote or represent, each other.[21] Of course, one can think of cases which combine the two relationships: a picture may represent x, who is like y (thus an icon might represent Christ, who is the image of God), or a description of two objects may convey the likeness existing between them; and Scripture describes Christ as both Word and image. Such cases, however, do not affect Goodman's fundamental distinction.

Let us now move on to consider why people are driven to try to describe or represent God, and to search for likenesses of Him, looking at some of the particular problems raised by His transcendence.

The adequacy of words

In the case of descriptions and other linguistic uses we are dealing with the question of the relationship between language and reality (I shall not further discuss non-linguistic forms of representation). People feel driven to express what they know of God in language in various ways (and, of course, theological descriptions of His nature are only *one* such use), and yet they feel too that their words are

inadequate, and that they are 'thrusting against the limits of language'. Why is this? One common answer is that human language is
inadequate to express what transcends the world. By itself,
however, this answer tells us little, for in some sense all human
language is 'inadequate': a description of a banana will not feed you,
and, more to the point here, it will do little to convey the taste of a
banana to someone who has never tasted one. Hence people pursue
the point by arguing that human language is 'finite', that we learn
how to use it in human contexts, and that therefore in applying it to
God we are at best stretching words beyond their normal use and at
worst anthropomorphizing Him. Thus, in a discussion of St
Thomas Aquinas's theory of analogy, Fr F. C. Copleston writes:

> If we mean that God is wise in precisely the same sense that a human being is
> or can be wise, we make God a kind of superman, and we are involved in
> anthropomorphism ... the positive content of the concept in our minds is
> determined by our experience of creaturely wisdom, and we can only
> attempt to purify it or correct its inadequacies by means of negations.[22]

But this, too, is not very helpful: elsewhere I have suggested that
such an account appeals to a faulty theory of meaning (which
regards language as representing material natures through the
intermediaries of intellectual concepts), and that it anticipates non-
existent difficulties.[23] Just what is the 'precise sense' of human
wisdom to which Copleston appeals, and, if there is such a sense,
who has ever tried to ascribe it to God? Presumably Copleston is
thinking of the fact that human wisdom is limited, is acquired
slowly through experience and can be lost. But it is questionable
whether such imperfections are actually *built into* our concept of
'wisdom' and are part of its meaning. This is shown, I think, by the
fact that we can compose doublets which compare or associate
human and divine wisdom, by using sentence-frames of the forms
'x is more F than y is' or 'x is F, but y is not', e.g.:

> God is wiser than any of us
> God is wise, but I am not.

Similarly with some other perfections, like 'knowledge' and 'love';
we can say:

> God is more loving than even our closest friends
> God knows when I shall die, but I do not know.

On occasion an even closer form of comparison may seem appropriate:

> Be merciful, even as your Father is merciful.   (Lk. 6:36)

Perhaps this is why some more recent discussions of the Thomistic doctrine of analogy have stressed the importance of the transcendentals ('good', 'true', 'beautiful' and 'one') and of perfection-terms like 'knowing', 'love', and 'wise' as applied to God. Such terms, it is said, are already 'analogical' in their ordinary non-theological uses, and they have an 'openness' which makes them particularly applicable to God. Thus Fr David Burrell notes the varieties of wisdom found in the natural world and our ability to understand and use the word 'wise' in different contexts, and goes on to say of the predicates we ascribe to God:

none is adequate yet some seem more appropriate than others. The deciding factor would seem to lie in their ability to point beyond themselves, a factor already evident from ordinary use.[24]

Evaluative terms, especially those expressing perfections,

embody our efforts to communicate the richness of our aspirations; even though their descriptive side is tied to our achievements, we insist upon using the same expressions in passing judgment on those achievements.[25]

Aquinas himself, of course, had noted that terms like 'being', 'good', 'life' and 'understanding' are attributable to God because no defect is included in their definition and they do not depend upon matter (_De Ver._, II.11; _De Pot._, VII.5 _ad_ 8); similarly, he remarked that although '_sensus_' cannot be ascribed to God because it is acquired physically, through sense organs, '_cognitio_' has no such implication and so can be used of Him (I _Sent._, 22.1.2). He argued that in applying perfection-terms to God, we remove their defects or limitations and then project them to infinity (_Summa Theologiae_, 1a.13.1; this is the so-called _via remotionis_ and the _via eminentiae_). What is characteristic of writers like Fr Burrell is that they link the 'openness' of evaluative terms to the 'self-transcending' character of the human mind, shown, for instance, in our aspirations and our ability to criticize. Thus, in his defence of the use of analogical language in theology against Kai Nielsens's critique, Fr Norris Clarke links our application of the transcendentals and perfection terms to God with what he, following Karl Rahner, calls the 'implicit dynamism of our wills and minds' which reach out beyond themselves.[26] This reaching out is manifested, again, in our tendency to judge our present achievements as limited and imperfect. He concludes 'Thomistic analogy makes sense only within such a total notion of the life of the spirit as knowing-loving dynamism' (p. 93).

There is still a strong streak of agnosticism in these recent adaptations of Aquinas's teaching on analogy. St Thomas had argued that even analogical language fails to give us a full representation of God (*Summa Theologiae*, 1a.13.2). Similarly, Clarke says that God's precise mode of being remains beyond the reach of our determinate representational images and concepts, but not beyond the dynamic thrust of our spirit, which expresses its reach through open-ended dynamic concepts and flexible language. One is reminded here of the *Cloud of Unknowing* – 'By love he can be caught and held, but by thinking, never'[27] – though clearly Transcendental Thomists like Rahner and Norris see our intellectual questioning also as an aspiration akin to love, in being a 'reaching out' beyond the self.

The root of such agnosticism should not, however, be found in language. Critics of the doctrine of analogy complain that those who use analogical language do not know what they mean.[28] This is indeed true to some extent, for the use of perfection-terms of God is a projection from our ordinary uses; and defenders of analogical predication claim only that such terms are the least inadequate language to convey it. But again, this inadequacy is not, I think, primarily in language. The important facts here are that God is a mystery, that we know little of Him, and that at best we only glimpse His presence or His power. These are the real sources of our agnosticism concerning God's nature. But they are a matter of epistemology (our knowledge is very limited) and of ontology (God is a mystery, in the sense that He is a reality whose depths we cannot plumb; his existence and nature transcend the world). Analogical predication is a way of expressing what little we know of God, and not a mode of acquiring knowledge by what Pannenberg calls a 'spiritual assault'.

It is true, however, that analogical predication presupposes certain ontological considerations, for it is only in virtue of some similarity between God and creatures that we are justified in using the same terms, e.g., 'wise' and 'loving', of both. But this takes us on to the question of likeness.

The adequacy of likenesses

In the case of representations and descriptions we are concerned with the relationship between language (or pictures, symbols, etc.) and reality. In the case of likeness we are usually dealing with the relationship between two distinct realities, whether constructed by us or found in the world. In general, 'likeness' is, as Goodman notes, a symmetrical relationship: if x is like y, then y is like x.[29] To be a *good* likeness, one thing must be like another in a significant number of respects: to be told that two things are alike in that they both exist in Europe or are being much talked about today conveys little information about them.

As in the case of language about God, religious people are often anxious to safeguard God's transcendence by insisting that no earthly likeness can approach Him. Aquinas, for example, claims that God is outside of any genus and that any likeness between God and creatures is imperfect because there is no generic likeness between them.[30] One reason for such anxiety is the desire to preserve God's infinity and transcendence, but another is the desire to avoid a possible Third Man type argument: if we say that God and man are alike in their wisdom, then we seem to have a third term besides our initial two, and the beginnings of a regressive argument (see Plato, *Parmenides*, 132D–133A). Hence it is necessary to distinguish the resemblance of particulars to their universal from the resemblance of particulars to each other. Christian authors usually meet the difficulty by saying that God *is* wisdom or the perfection in question, or that the perfection is an idea in God's mind.

There is some Biblical backing for the anxiety to stress God's dissimilarity from His creatures. Isaiah, in particular, says 'For as the heavens are higher than the earth, so are my ways higher than your ways and my thoughts than your thoughts' (55:9), and 'To whom will you liken me and make me equal, and compare me, that we may be alike?' (46:5; *cf.* 40:18). But it has to be pointed out that there are far more Biblical texts which stress the likeness than ones which stress the unlikeness[31] – not surprisingly perhaps, in view of the centrality of the belief already mentioned, that man is created in the image and likeness of God. This likeness is seen as consisting in certain qualities, e.g., compassion, fidelity and mercy (Ex. 34:6; Lk. 6:36), and as being manifested in certain actions, e.g., loving widows, orphans and strangers (Dt. 10:17–19) or forgiving offenders (Mt. 5:12, 14f.). In the New Testament an even bolder idea is introduced, that of our sharing in the divine nature (II Pet. 1:4). This is seen as a possibility brought about by the divine power of Christ and by his gifts to us. Thus in the New Testament, and in later Christian tradition, a new factor has been introduced: Christ is regarded as a middle term between God and man. Since he is the image and perfect copy of God (II Cor. 4:4, Col. 1:15, Heb. 1:3), it is by imitating him that we become God-like, and it is by his redemptive work and by the Holy Spirit that whatever likeness to God was lost at the Fall is restored. Yet a further step was taken when it was claimed that not only is Christ the image of God, but actually *is* God, one in substance with the Father. Such claims, as MacKinnon says, express the belief that 'Christ's invitation to the heavy laden is not a *simulacrum* of the divine invitation but is *in fact* that invitation made concrete', and that, in the words 'I am in the midst of you as he that doth serve' (Lk. 22:27), 'Christ's *diakonia* is presented not as a parable of God's regnant service of his creatures, but as that service itself become concrete'.[32]

Thus it seems that although Christian theology warns against our anthropomorphizing God when we speak of a likeness between Him and creation, in practice it sails close to the wind. This happens for the theological reasons just noted. But in any case, there are philosophical reasons for saying that talk of likeness to God does not commit one to anthropomorphizing Him in any objectionable way. Most obviously, the relation of likeness is to be distinguished from that of equality, in that the former has varying degrees; and in the case of God His perfections are believed to be limitless. The latter consideration differentiates God from His creatures, as also does the fact that certain of His attributes are ruled out as inapplicable to creatures, for example eternity, omnipresence and the right to exact vengeance.[33] Moreover, in comparing two realities we are not committed to putting them in the same category, even in non-heological contexts, as is shown by statements like 'My headache lasted as long as the lecture' and 'Mary is more interested in men than in mathematics.'[34] It is therefore possible to speak of our likeness to God without reducing Him to what Matthew Arnold called an 'infinitely magnified and improved Lord Shaftesbury'[35] and without losing sight of the religious requirement that the object of worship far surpasses any other reality.

Words, likenesses and theological realism

In both the areas I have looked at we are concerned with relations: in the one case, a relation between words or representations and God; in the other, a relation between a likeness or image and Him. We may perhaps speak of a correspondence in both cases, provided that the term is used in a very general sense (MacKinnon, as we have seen, uses it not only of theories of truth but also of an apostle).[36] In both cases, too, theologians are on their guard against anthropomorphism, and warn against looking for much more than the least inadequate representation or likeness of the transcendent God.

A further consideration, which I shall only touch on in conclusion, is that a concern with the adequacy and inadequacy of words and likenesses naturally goes with what has come to be called 'theological realism', for the reality of God is regarded as a check on our statements about Him and on our search for resemblances. This is certainly so in the case of MacKinnon, who has firmly nailed his colours to the cause of theological realism. I do not think there is a *necessary* connection, for someone sympathetic to Don Cupitt, for example, might say that religious language is a projection whereby we attempt to represent our religious ideal, and that 'God-like' people, such as Christ or the saints, are examples of our religious ideal actualized in human form. But such a view does not give people the same incentive to examine their words and images as theological realism does: it sees such an examination as akin to an author's or artist's anxiety as to whether he has really expressed his meaning, whereas theological realism sees its task as a constant attempt to express our glimpses of divine reality and yet at the same time to check these expressions against that reality, constantly criticizing and purifying them. Moreover, if, as is usually the case, theological realism goes with a doctrine of Creation, there is again an ever-present motive to search for the footsteps of the Creator and seek His likeness in the world, for instance by scientific research, contemplation of the beauties of nature, and perhaps artistic expression. Someone like Cupitt is denied such a view of the world, for his view of the nature of divine reality obviously rules out any traditional understanding of the doctrine of Creation.

A further stage is reached if one sees creation not only as having a likeness to its Creator, but also as being a sign. Poets speak of reading the book of nature; and some have seen the beauty of creation as akin to a work of art created by God to tell us something of Himself. St Augustine said that 'God works the sensible and visible things which He wills, in order to signify and manifest Himself in them' (*De Trin.*, III.iv.10). But if created things are signs of God, then Goodman's distinction begins to collapse as far as God is concerned, for now the likenesses of Him which we discover are found to be after all representations which He has fashioned to tell us something of Himself. But that is a subject for another day!

It is sometimes said that theological realism is an over-simple view. For instance, in an article on MacKinnon's early work Paul Wignall remarks: 'Realism, perhaps, is at its best exposing the over-simplifications of others but is unable, in the end, to avoid over-simplification itself.'[37] This judgement is true perhaps of certain versions of realism, for example some forms of neo-Thomism, but not, I think, of MacKinnon's mature work. For theological realism only becomes over-simple if we neglect the variety of likenesses and representations which a theologian can explore, and if we forget about their approximate nature. It is Donald MacKinnon's achievement to have explored this variety with great subtlety and suggestiveness, and with a humble realization of our human finitude.

Notes

1 *The Problem of Metaphysics* (Cambridge, 1974), p. 57.
2 *The Art of God Incarnate: Theology and Image in Christian Tradition* (London, 1980), p. 19.
3 *Explorations in Theology 5* (London, 1979), pp. 82–3. The related phrase 'method of projection' occurs frequently in the work of Wittgenstein, where it is used of the relationship between signs, images, pictures or language, and the world. See, for example, *Blue and Brown Books*, p. 53.
4 *Explorations*, p. 181. See also *The Problem of Metaphysics*, chs. 6–7.
5 *The Problem of Metaphysics*, pp. 136, 145.

6 'Atonement and Tragedy', in *The Borderlands of Theology and Other Essays* (London, 1968), pp. 97–104.

7 'Subjective and Objective Conceptions of Atonement', in F. G. Healey, ed., *Prospects for Theology* (Welwyn, 1966), p. 174.

8 *Borderlands*, p. 50; *Explorations*, pp. 74–5; *The Problem of Metaphysics*, chs. 3–4.

9 'Theology as a Discipline of a Modern University', in T. Shanin, ed., *The Rules of the Game* (London, 1972), p. 172.

10 *Explorations*, pp. 177–8.

11 *A Study in Ethical Theory* (London, 1957), p. 261.

12 *The Problem of Metaphysics*, p. 90.

13 *The Problem of Metaphysics*, p. 110.

14 'The Relation of the Doctrines of the Incarnation and the Trinity', in R. McKinney, ed., *Creation, Christ and Culture: Studies in Honour of T. F. Torrance* (Edinburgh, 1976), p. 104.

15 *Languages of Art: An Approach to a Theory of Symbols* (2nd ed., Indianapolis, 1976), pp. 42–3.

16 See especially 'Seven Strictures on Similarity', in L. Foster and J. W. Swanson, eds., *Experience and Theory* (London, 1970). For a critique of Goodman, see J. Margolis, 'The Problem of Similarity: Realism and Nominalism', *The Monist*, 61 (1978), pp. 384–400.

17 *Australian Journal of Philosophy*, 48 (1970), pp. 373–93. For a similar point see also Göran Hermeren, *Aspects of Aesthetics* (Lund, 1983), ch. 3, section 9.

18 Reprinted in his *Creation and Redemption* (Belmont, Mass., 1976). The quotation is from pp. 204–5.

19 *Some Spiritual Guides of the Seventeenth Century* (New York, 1927), p. lxxvi.

20 C. S. Peirce similarly distinguished likeness, which he defined as a community in some quality, from signs and symbols. See the *Collected Papers of Charles Sanders Peirce*, ed. Charles Hartshorne and Paul Weiss (Cambridge, Mass., 1960), vol. 1, section 558.

21 Of course there is a sense in which one person may represent another, e.g., a barrister in court or an ambassador representing his sovereign. The relation of 'representing' is even wider than Goodman's discussion indicates (wide though it is in his usage, for he uses it to cover things as different as depiction and diagrammatic denotation; similarly, he uses the term 'denotation' to include the relationship between a score and a musical performance). He rightly sees that 'standing for' is one of the basic meanings of the term, but in confining himself to symbolic systems he deliberately disregards other uses of it (see *Languages of Art*, p. 4). Theologians use the word more widely, e.g., when they claim that in his atoning work Christ represents the whole human race or that

the Pope represents the Church (see, for example, Walter Kasper, *Jesus the Christ* (London, 1976), pp. 219–25, or Hans Küng, *Structures of the Church* (London, 1965), ch. 7).

   The etymology of the term suggests, as Henri de Lubac points out (*Catholicism* (London, 1950), p. 29), a still more fundamental meaning, that of 'making present'. In this sense the Mass, according to the Council of Trent, represents Christ's sacrifice at Calvary; see Henricus Denzinger, *Enchiridion Symbolarum* (36th ed., Freiburg, 1976), pp. 938–40.

22 *Aquinas* (Harmondsworth, 1955), pp. 129, 131.
23 'Analogy Today', *Philosophy*, 51 (1976), pp. 431–46.
24 *Analogy and Philosophical Language* (London and New Haven, 1973), p. 206.
25 *Ibid.*, p. 207.
26 'Analogy and the Meaningfulness of Language about God: A Reply to Kai Nielsen', *Thomist*, 40 (1976), pp. 61–95.
27 Penguin ed. (Harmondsworth, 1961), ch. 6, p. 60.
28 E.g., Humphrey Palmer, *Analogy* (London, 1973), pp. 141, 156.
29 Though this is not true of some cognate relations like 'being in the image of': Aquinas points out that one egg may be like another, but it is not in its image, for the latter relation adds to the idea of likeness the notions of copying and imitating (*Summa Theologiae*, 1a.93.1); nor is it always true of 'like', for when we say that a son is like his father, we regard the latter as the prototype.
30 *Summa Theologiae*, 1a.4.3 and 1a.13.5 *ad* 2. See my 'Analogy Today', p. 438, for the importance of such ontological considerations in Aquinas's treatment of analogical predication.
31 See my *Spirit, Saints and Immortality* (London, 1984), p. 94 note 6 for a list of some central texts.
32 ' "Substance" in Christology – a Cross-bench View', in S. Sykes and J. P. Clayton, eds., *Christ, Faith and History* (Cambridge, 1972), p. 290.
33 Conversely, some human perfections, for instance courage and chastity, are inapplicable to God, because as Aristotle points out (*Nic. Eth. X*, ch. 8) He cannot be threatened by risks and dangers and He has no bad appetites. Aquinas, however, claimed that courage is the mirror of the exemplar of God's unchangeableness (*Summa Theologiae*, 1a.2ae.61.5).
34 These two examples are borrowed from Fred Sommers's article, 'Predicability', p. 263, in Max Black, ed., *Philosophy in America* (London, 1965).
35 *Literature and Dogma* (London, 1873), pp. 306f.
36 *A Study in Ethical Theory*, p. 261.
37 'D. M. MacKinnon: An Introduction to his Early Theological Writings', in S. W. Sykes and J. D. Holmes, eds., *New Studies in Theology I* (London, 1980), p. 91.

4 MacKinnon and the parables

ROGER WHITE

Discussions of particular parables and of the concept of parable itself are scattered throughout the writings of Donald MacKinnon; and in one case, in the Gifford Lectures,[1] it becomes one of the central themes of a book. But my purpose in the present essay is not so much the examination of these rich and varied individual passages, as the isolation of some major themes which, it seems to me, recur in his thought about the parables – both in his writings and lectures and in informal remarks. How far I am right in seeing the ideas I shall thus set in relief as the basic ones in his thinking in this area I am unsure. What is clear to me is that the three themes that for me run through his work here are themes of great importance, and constitute, if properly appreciated, a significant corrective to a great deal of the kind of interpretation of the parables with which we are all familiar – the tradition of parable interpretation inaugurated by Adolf Jülicher and modified and developed by authors such as Dodd and Jeremias. They are also themes the depth of whose significance I believe I have learnt from MacKinnon, who indeed first stimulated my interest in the nature of the parables when I was working as a student under his supervision many years ago.

I

There is one idea that Adolf Jülicher never tires of stressing throughout *Die Gleichnissreden Jesu*:[2] an idea which is in fact far more fundamental to his thought than his celebrated opposition to allegorical exegesis and the idea of the parables as being themselves

49

allegories. This is the idea that the parables are *simple*. ' "Simplex sigillum veri": under that banner we fight',[3] he writes.

There are two reasons for believing this, rather than the opposition to allegory as such, to be the centre of his thought. First, for all the space devoted to it, he never really makes clear what he means by allegory or how allegory is marked off from other forms of figurative writing except in terms of an alleged obscurity of allegory: allegory and metaphor need interpretation or translation, whereas simile and parable are supposed to be immediately transparent in their significance. Of the two accounts of allegory he gives at various places in his discussion – one, derived from scholastic rhetoric, of allegory as a chain of metaphors, and the other of allegory as a piece of writing that needs decoding – only the second really functions in any significant way in his long discussions.

Secondly, Jülicher devotes far more polemical space in his work to his opposition to the theories of the parables he finds in the synoptic Gospels – above all in Mark – than he does to authors who have actually practised allegorical exegesis. This is true although there is no evidence that the evangelists thought of or treated the parables as allegories – apart from very occasional passages such as the Matthaean treatment of 'The Tares among the Wheat'. It certainly does not look like a major theme of the treatment of the parables on the part of the evangelists that they should be regarded as allegories. It is an idea largely imported by Jülicher himself into the account he gives of the evangelists: *at most*, it seems to me, we could say that some of the remarks in Matt. 8 suggest that it could have been an element in Matthew's thinking – and even that is not clear.

The real point of contention between Jülicher and the synoptic Gospels is that for them the parables are seen as essentially difficult to understand – indeed their obscurity is seen as integral to their very purpose. For Jülicher, on the other hand, the parables are simple and immediate in their import. They make only one point, and the purpose of the fiction is to make that point with the most immediate rhetorical efficacy. Indeed, the parables are all seen as having morals that can be spelled out with the utmost simplicity. The result of this conception, which has embarrassed all his followers, is the series of Christmas Cracker mottoes that fill Volume 2 of his work.

The argument for the simplicity of the parables is in fact amazingly thin. It is not at all based on a detailed examination of the parables: the whole theoretical stance has been fully established before there is even *any* discussion of individual parables. Looking at the features of particular parables is postponed completely to Volume 2: one could read the whole of Volume 1 without discovering any clear picture of the texts that it was meant to throw light on – the actual parables figure nowhere in the argumentation of Volume 1. The considerations adduced by Jülicher have far more the character of an *a priori* stipulation as to what parables *could be*, bringing together two different ideas.

The first is bound up with his concept of the parables as primarily rhetorical devices. He follows this up by equating what is meant by παραβολή in the New Testament with what Aristotle meant by παραβολή in the *Rhetoric*: a simple form of argument by analogy.

The second is based upon speculation about the nature of Jesus – the friend of sinners addressing simple folk. If I understand him aright, the whole pathos of Volume 1 of *Die Gleichnissreden Jesu* is that it is an affront to Jülicher's conception of Jesus that he should be portrayed as other than teaching simple messages simply, so as to be immediately comprehensible to ordinary people. He can make nothing of the austere and enigmatic figure that confronts us so disconcertingly in Mark's Gospel. He simply has no place within his *Christology* for a Jesus who could adopt a difficult mode of teaching – even less the Marcan conception of a Jesus who *deliberately* taught obscurely. When Jülicher says 'The question strikes deep – Jesus or the evangelists?',[4] meaning, is he (Jülicher) right about the parables or are the evangelists, one is taken aback by the naivety of his confidence that he knows Jesus well enough to play him off against the Gospel accounts of him: it looks more naive than blasphemously arrogant, indicating a wholly unself-conscious assumption that he already knows what Jesus is like before wrestling with the strange texts he has set himself to expound.

How *a priori* the strand of thought developed by Jülicher is – that is to say how far it is developed prior to any careful examination of the parables themselves – is shown quite simply in the way his ideas are taken up and modified in subsequent treatments of the parables, by writers who like Jeremias and Dodd take their starting point in Jülicher but with a fundamental change of emphasis. For now the idea that moves into the foreground is that the parables *as we encounter them in the Gospels* are frequently obscure and difficult to understand, and hence the task of the New Testament critic is to restore them and recover their original setting so that we may be able to see them in their full simplicity. But now something strange has happened: a cat has been let out of the bag. The simplicity and non-allegorical nature of the parables are no longer in any sense the result of an investigation. They have become the stipulated goal of one's investigation, based purely upon a reflection upon the nature of the communication seen as appropriate to Jesus teaching the crowds. There is scarcely anything surprising if the parables turn out not to be allegories, if, as with Jeremias, one uses the presence of allegorical elements in a text as evidence that it is not original.

I myself have a sort of prejudice that an investigation ought to be an investigation of something that we know about and not be an investigation of some hypothetical object produced by a speculative train of thought, and that if, in the field of New Testament studies, we wish to discover the nature of the parables, we should start with a careful study of those texts *as we find them*, and not lay down *a priori* guidelines as to where an investigation of those texts should lead us. But, be that as it may, there is one thing that is to me absolutely certain: in the particular case we are considering – the case of the parables – the parables as we find them in the Gospels are not only far more enigmatic and strange than anything we find in the results of Jülicher and his followers, they are infinitely more profound and beautiful. They are also, quite simply, more interesting. For one undoubted feature of Jülicher's work is that when he comes to interpret the particular parables the overall effect is one of systematic trivialization: the parables become a bore. This is noted on all sides, and by Dodd and Jeremias in particular; but they put the result down to Jülicher's seeking the wrong kind of message in the parables: he found moral platitudes because that is what he was looking for. However, if one actually looks at the results of their own investigations by the light of day, they seem no better than Jülicher's: an eschatological platitude is still a platitude. If one actually lists the morals derived from the parables by any of these authors, they are enormously trite when set alongside the rich complexity of the text that is actually being interpreted. To give as the meaning of 'The Good Samaritan', for example, 'Love's demand knows no limit' (Jeremias),[5] is to reduce a subtle and complex text to something banal and false, something whose falsity does not strike us only if we do not stop to consider what is actually being said ('Haply, when I shall wed,/That lord whose hand must take my plight shall carry/Half my love with him, half my care and duty./Sure I shall never marry like my sisters,/To love my father all' (King Lear, I: i, 99ff)).

There are several reasons for this trivialization, all deriving from the central conception of the simple parable. Jülicher sees the parable in purely rhetorical terms. This is construed in such a way that the parables are seen as inculcating a simple statable message in a vivid way: the task of exegesis then becomes no more than the recovery of the moral of the parable. Next, the rich subtlety of the parables is systematically under-valued in that the whole approach becomes one in which attention to the detail of the parable is feared as a sign of engaging in allegorical interpretation or eisegesis. The details are seen as no more than the fleshing out of the situation that illustrates the central point of the parable. Exegesis then has the effect of treating those details as husks to be winnowed out. There can surely be no other texts of major significance in which the rich life and vivid detail is so massively ignored by a group of commentators. But the final reason for the trivialization is more complex, and ultimately more insidious. If one approaches a text with the attitude that anything in it which is perverse, paradoxical, recalcitrant and difficult is simply to be viewed as an accretion to be eliminated, then one is continually committed to smoothing away all that is truly disconcerting and challenging. The results naturally tally with each other, and the parables come to look immeasurably dull.

II

It is against this background that I wish to introduce three strands in Donald MacKinnon's remarks about the parables that seem to me to represent a series of protests against much that is wrong with contemporary parable interpretation. I suspect he would not necessarily see the matter in these terms himself. He is certainly not, as I am, deeply antipathetic to the work of Jülicher. But at the very least what he has to say has to be viewed as a corrective to their work of the greatest significance. If, however, a corrective goes deep it may rapidly suggest that one should stop correcting, and simply overthrow the whole approach that requires such radical modification.

These strands I shall develop and interpret in my own way. That is, Professor MacKinnon would not necessarily agree with the glosses I put upon them or the ways in which I assign them significance, although I hope that what follows is at least consonant with his thought. I shall also illustrate the points with my own discussions of the parables rather than drawing upon his.

The three ideas I wish to discuss are:

1) MacKinnon lays particular emphasis upon the ways in which the parables are more than simply challenging. They are not merely initially disconcerting – the more one looks at them the more disconcerting they become. They continually seem perverse, offensive, even blasphemous in their suggestion. We are in a different thought world from that of the conventional pious homily.

2) MacKinnon invites us to meditate upon the intense human realism exhibited throughout these little fictions. If I understand him aright, his concern with the realism of the parables is very different from and goes far deeper than, say, the concern that the parables are true to life that we find in Dodd.

3) MacKinnon continually forces us to attend to the exquisite subtle detail of many of the parables. It is perhaps here that his remarks become most tentative, since he is fully aware of the dangers of *importing* significance into the text, of the dangers of the kind of allegorical interpretation which so horrified our grandfathers. But it is also here that this alertness to the significance of the details within the parables constitutes for me his most important challenge to writers such as Jülicher, who, even when they do discuss details of the particular parables, are so intent on seeing the parable as a simple whole that they neglect the full import of precisely these details.

These three ideas are closely inter-related, and come together in the idea of the parable as the profoundest possible vehicle for exploring the relation of God and man. For the tentative and *exploratory* nature of so many of MacKinnon's remarks here is, I think, in part a recognition of the fact that to be engaged with a parable is not simply to register a message: it is to be challenged fundamentally to explore many of one's most fixed ideas about God and one's relation to him, so that everything one had previously thought can be thrown into disarray, and even then never altogether satisfactorily reassembled.

III

When we read the parables, we are continually being confronted with that which is completely disconcerting, which is bewildering in its near-blasphemous overtones, which is grimly at odds with conventional, pious, received opinion.

There is a kind of grim humour at work in many of the parables that one sees all too often being explained away by commentators. Whatever else they are meant to do, parables such as 'The Unjust Judge' (Luke 18:1ff) are surely meant to disturb our complacency. All too frequently authors simply gloss over what is shocking about such a comparison. It simply will not do to say, as Quick does, 'The point is not that God answers in the end; but that, if even the Unrighteous Judge will yield in the end, then God must answer the prayers of His saints immediately.'[6] It is not merely that it is difficult to see how this parable can possible be meant to point up this 'safe' lesson; it simply castrates the grim irony at work, and makes the parable lifeless: why tell *this* story if that is what it is all about? That surely is to convict Jesus of fanciful perversity. Theologians continually engage in fast talk when confronted by examples like this. Obviously, when we make a comparison, the comparison is never intended to hold in every respect. But in the cases before us, we should not be over-hasty in saying that the comparisons do not hold in the respect which we find offensive.

In the parables, we find God compared to:

> A judge who fears neither God nor man.
> A hard man who reaps where he has not sown.
> A man who, being comfortable in bed, doesn't want to be
>   bothered to help a friend.
> An absentee landlord.
> A woman frantically searching for a coin she has lost.

and so on.

Now of course one may sidestep what is shocking about such comparisons merely by insisting that every comparison has to be taken aright. But to do so would be to overlook what is crucial: each of these comparisons makes a deep point that is missed if we neglect the aptness of the 'shocking' elements within them. We do not understand these parables at all if we ignore the extent to which their analogies contain a grim truth about the nature of life in this world in its relation to God. We *are* in a world where justice and virtue are not naturally triumphant, where the wicked flourish and the saints' causes founder. For the man in need turning to God for deliverance from his sufferings, praying that the cause of justice and peace should prosper, hungering and thirsting after righteousness, it *is* very much as if he is confronted in his prayers by an utterly corrupt magistrate who has no particular concern to see that justice prevails. In such parables, Jesus continually presses beyond the conventionally pious, inviting us to explore the full reality of life before God without sheltering behind platitude: inviting us actually to *look* at it.

When confronted by these embarrassing analogies it is all-important that we should not attempt to resolve the paradoxes by a neat application of dialectic and substitute something bland for the full enormity of the parable.

This is the first major point. If we are not to remain content with a facile and complacent faith, we must allow ourselves to be challenged by the way in which the parables insistently point to that which is truly disconcerting and which remains so: it is not as though, after profound soul-searching, we will come to find the comparison between God and an absentee landlord easy and acceptable. That comparison, which is recurrent within the parables, is and remains disconcerting in its aptness: it disconcertingly keeps before our eyes features of life before God that we might rather avoid or dilute in our theological reflection, features that in the end we do not know how to think about properly and so prefer to disguise.

We have sections in our Dogmatic Theologies entitled 'God as Shepherd', 'God as King', or 'God as Judge', exploiting the safe analogies. There are no sections entitled 'God as magistrate who ought to be struck off the bench'. It is an embarrassment to have to preach on such a parable as any I have mentioned, or, for instance, 'The Unjust Steward'. And it appears that at least one fundamental purpose of the parables is to lead us precisely to such embarrassment.

Consider, for instance, a major theme of Jülicher's work – the notion of the parable as an argument by analogy. Although it is not nearly as frequent as he would suggest, clearly many of the parables do have the form of such an argument. But what turns out to be the case is that, far from our considering the simple little arguments that we encounter in Aristotle's *Rhetoric*, we have what seems continually to be a parody of such arguments: our attention becomes focused on the wholly bizarre nature of the analogy we are being asked to argue from. A very clear example is indeed 'The Unjust Judge', which we have just considered. But even in less apparently offensive parables this happens over and over again.

Consider for instance Luke 12:22ff, where the disciples are invited not to be anxious about the necessities of life because the flowers and birds flourish without all the human busyness:

Consider the lilies, how they grow; they neither toil nor spin; yet I tell you, even Solomon in all his glory was not arrayed like one of these. But if God so clothes the grass which is alive in the field today and tomorrow is thrown into the oven, how much more will he clothe you, O men of little faith!

The first thing about this is that when we attend to the whole passage, the dysanalogies, the contrasts are what are most striking: we are being invited to argue from plant life to human life in respects in which they *obviously* differ. Far from this being a straightforward argument by analogy, even to consider this argument is to be invited to ignore much that we do not know how to ignore. The enormity of the initial suggestion comes out if one imagines, say, going to a dole queue and inviting the men there not to be worried about how they are going to cope with their rents and their families' upkeep by reflecting that plants flourish – and they don't go to work either. The parable does not work in the same way as a straightforward argument by analogy at all; it confronts one with an utterly disconcerting challenge to think in a totally new way, to adopt the foreign and disconcerting perspective from which this *would* be a good analogy to argue from.

Now what are we to say of all this? What account can we give of the perversity which appears to run through so much of the recorded parabolic teaching? I do not think we should hasten to give an answer, any more than we should hasten to explain away the recalcitrant elements in particular parables. We should in the first instance simply note the facts here, and reflect on the inadequacy of most of what passes for theories of the parables to begin to accommodate them. To emphasize these facts adequately is far more important here than to attempt an explanation of them, since any explanation is going to fall far short of what is to be noted here, and may distract attention from it. But with this proviso, there are suggestions to be made: suggestions which it seems to me imply the parables to be totally different from what Jülicher sought to show them to be.

We could say that the parables give us a direct image of divine transcendence: that is to say, they continually offer us analogies for God that simply do not fit comfortably with our ideas about Him. If there is an appropriateness in such comparisons then that may be an index of the inadequacy of our normal patterns of thought to comprehend the true nature of God. The pious pictures we form of God do not accommodate the possibility of these parables, and so we are continually thrust by them against the limits of the adequacy of any of our thinking about God. Our idea of how an all-good, all-wise God would rule may be crassly inadequate; and one function of these little fictions offering analogies for the way God rules, for the Kingdom of God, may simply lie in that: to point up the inadequacy of our version of how God may be expected to act – how, if you like, we would act if we were God.

The account of the parables in Mark's Gospel is immensely subtle, and it would be hopeless in an essay of this length to spell it out in any detail, but if I understand him, then we could say that in a particular way, for Mark, the parables were instruments of conversion. Of all the evangelists he places most stress on the incomprehensibility of the parables, not merely as a theoretical point, but also to make it clear that Jesus's hearers – including the disciples – found them bewildering enigmas. It was bewildering to them that Jesus should teach like this, and bewildering to imagine what the teaching could possibly mean. But within the structure of Mark's Gospel, chapter 4 is counterbalanced by chapter 8. In chapter 4 we see Jesus teaching in parables and the disciples bewildered and lacking in understanding of what is meant; but in chapter 8 we see Jesus teaching 'plainly' – παρρησία – verse 32, and once again the result is bewilderment and lack of comprehension, here erupting as direct opposition. The transition from the enigma of the parable to direct speech does nothing here to ovecome the barrier to understanding – for Peter's thoughts are still the thoughts of men, not of God.

Jesus is seen here above all as the *unexpected* Messiah, who confounds men's expectations as to what the Lord's anointed should be like and what he should do, because he is the Messiah of a Lord whose ways are not our ways and whose thoughts are not our thoughts. Any direct showing forth of such a Messiah, whether at Caesarea Philippi or at the Transfiguration, just meets bafflement, misunderstanding or even offence. To come to understand such a Messiah and accept him as such is to undertake a strange and arduous pilgrimage, following strange paths of thought and having many of one's most profoundly held convictions about God and His purposes overturned. It is a pilgrimage surrounded by bafflement and misunderstanding all along the line. But that which is baffling and offensive is leading the disciples beyond themselves to a point where, after the Crucifixion and beyond the confines of Mark's Gospel, they will be enabled to declare the revelation they have received. Within the discipline of that pilgrimage they are necessarily confronted over and over again with ideas that they can do nothing with, with enigmas, with offence. Hence it is – if I understand Mark's intention aright – that the primary form of Christ's teaching is the parable, the enigmatic riddle, the saying that Christ's hearers can do nothing with as yet, but which, like a seed growing, will eventually grow into a complete transformation of the understanding. But for Mark, within Christ's earthly ministry such a transformation of the understanding of the disciples had not yet occurred: they were following someone they did not as yet understand at all, and within the confines of that ministry Jesus's teaching was and remained enigmatic, only to be understood, if at all, after the Crucifixion and the Resurrection. Within this context the parables become instruments of conversion, precisely because they cannot be understood by unconverted man.

To follow this up any further would require a most extensive treatment of Mark, chapter 4, which is as far removed as could be imagined from the simplistic crudity it is often made out to be: it is one of the subtlest pieces of sustained theological reflection in the whole New Testament. All I can do in this essay is indicate a line of thought, and I will turn to rather more straightforward but related considerations concerning the 'offensiveness' of much of what we find in the parables.

The most famous example of a 'parable' from the Old Testament – the parable of 'The One Ewe Lamb' told by Nathan to David – has one clear and obvious purpose: to overcome and bypass David's self-deception. David is confronted by the reality of what he has done by being made to pass judgement upon it without realizing that is what he is doing. Because he is concerned with the hypothetical case of the fiction he is not concerned to take offence at Nathan's accusation or to put up defences for his action. Only when he has passed judgement is the case presented as his own, and his defences have been completely undermined.

It is one of the major functions of a fiction to force us to consider matters afresh by presenting cases in such a way that our normal prejudices, self-deception and complacency are not allowed to operate. In the Gifford Lectures, MacKinnon says, about the parables, 'the crust of custom must be broken'. Kafka describes a book as 'an axe to break up the ice which is frozen around the heart'. One way in which this occurs is for the fictitious medium to force us to judge a case on its own merits and not according to the standard reactions our prejudices bring forth. Our normal pious platitudes, self-deception and pride are not allowed to operate. The strangeness, the perversity of the fiction is to take us away from a region where our defences are safe and in order.

Consider a familiar example here: the parable of 'The Good Samaritan'. The context that Luke provides for this parable provides us with a key to its understanding. A lawyer who regards Jesus as a suspect figure is putting him to the test. He asks him a question, 'What shall I do to inherit eternal life?', to which Jesus gives the impeccably orthodox answer of directing the lawyer to the law, and the lawyer answers his own question. The lawyer then presses his question by asking for an interpretation of that answer at one specific point: 'Who is my neighbour?' Now we may ask, why is this specifically a test question *for Jesus*? Why does the lawyer expect *this* question to trap him? Within the context of Luke's Gospel, the answer to this is clear: it is because Jesus 'feasted with publicans and sinners'. That is to say, it is clear that within the law, within the context of Leviticus 19, the neighbour who is to be loved is the fellow-member of the covenant people. In consorting with those who have put themselves beyond the pale of the law – with people who, from the lawyer's perspective, could no longer be considered as people of the covenant – was not Jesus himself disregarding the law? Was he not treating obedience to the law as a matter of no consequence by disregarding the lawlessness of those with whom he was prepared to associate? Who was the neighbour the law required us to love?

In reply to this train of thought Jesus tells the parable. Now, the whole standard interpretation of the parable, in effect, that loving your neighbour consists in going to the help of those in radical need, has remarkably little to do either with the parable or with this context.

What is most striking about the parable and which seems purely gratuitous from the standpoint of the standard interpretation is that it is a *Samaritan* who is shown as going to the help of the man in need. Why a Samaritan, if the whole point is to inculcate a message of practical love?

Furthermore, the question that the lawyer put, 'Who is my neighbour?', is to be answered according to Jesus not by the answer one would expect from the normal interpretation – 'Look at the Samaritan: he didn't ask who was his neighbour, he simply saw who was in need and went and loved him. Whoever you see in need is the man you should love without worrying about theological niceties' – but by an answer that is at first strange: the neighbour whom one should love is the *Samaritan*. For the lawyer's question, 'Who is my neighbour?', the answer is that for the man fallen among thieves, the Samaritan is the neighbour. The neighbour who should be loved is 'Him who showed mercy'. That is to say, the command to love the neighbour here is seen, not as the command to help those in need, but as the command to recognize and love those who minister to our need. And this is in line with the Pentateuch itself. Deuteronomy and Leviticus of course know a great deal about commands to help those in need – the orphans and the widows – but the formulae which surround such commands always relate them back to the command to love God. Part of one's love for God is to help those in need. ('You shall remember that you were a slave in the land of Egypt; therefore I command you to do this.') But alongside this first major theme, that as the people of the covenant they should love the Lord of the Covenant, emerges a second theme, that as people of the covenant they should recognize that they do not live alone but together with their fellow covenant people – that they are not as individuals in covenant with God, but as members of a covenant people. Just as they now exist with God, they no longer exist alone, and as they must respond with love and gratitude to the God who has delivered them, so too they must respond with love to those with whom their existence has now been bound up.

It is against this background that we must understand the parable in which Jesus introduces a Samaritan as the obvious candidate for the title of neighbour. The force and offence of this can clearly only be understood in terms of the deep sectarian hostility between the Samaritans and Jews. We regain the shock involved if we imagine, say, a Northern Irish Protestant asking about Christian fellowship – 'Who is my brother in Christ?' – and being told a story of his being mugged, and afterwards being taken to hospital by a Roman Catholic passer-by while the fellow members of his congregation ran away when the incident happened. That *such* a story should be used to clarify the meaning of having someone as one's brother in Christ perhaps reactivates something of the potential offensiveness of the parable, which has been dulled for us by the remoteness of the rivalry of Samaritan and Jew.

Once again, confronted by a complex text like this a full interpretation of the significance of this offensive story is impossible in the space at my disposal, but we can see the parable as being directed at pushing beyond the pride implicit in the lawyer's vantage-point. He is one of the Chosen People and concerned to defend his purity by keeping aloof from those he deems not to be, and he is in a position to test the orthodoxy of a suspect figure like Jesus who goes among those whose way of life prevent them from full obedience to the law. From such a vantage-point Jesus is seen as treating the law and the covenant lightly. Is he not treating as his neighbours those who put themselves outside the covenant?

The parable then radically challenges the assumed privileged position of the lawyer. The question 'Who is my neighbour?' is no longer the question, 'From within my assured position within the covenant to whom should I extend the privilege of also being regarded as within the covenant?', but is instead turned into the question 'If I am in radical need, who is that man whom I should value as I value my own life, love as myself?' For the standpoint of the man fallen among thieves the question 'Who ought I to love?' is profoundly unproblematic, and the question 'Who is my neighbour?' is similarly unproblematic if one can see one's own standpoint as one of being radically in need in ways which are ministered to by others – expected or not, welcome or not. This radical change of perspective is forced by Jesus on to the lawyer by the offence implicit in the parable, by taking the last man the lawyer would contemplate as a possible neighbour and forcing the lawyer to acknowledge him as such.

IV

I turn next to a particular kind of concern with the realism of the parables which I discern in MacKinnon's writings. Now of course, to say that he stresses the realism of the parables does nothing to mark him off from a great deal that has been written about the parables in the twentieth century. Is it not central to the conception of both Dodd and Jeremias that the parables are realistic – are true to life? But in fact their concern for the realism of the parables is significantly limited. They see the parables as offering us a form of argument by analogy from the world of nature to the world of grace. It is simply for that reason that they are concerned to show that what happens in the parable corresponds with what actually happens, in this way validating the argument to the conclusion that is the point of the parable. (Indeed in Jeremias this takes the curious form that the parables are almost supposed not to be fictions but to be based on incidents which actually occurred.[7]) What this means is that once one has recognized the situation of the parable as the kind of thing that happens and appreciated the principle embodied in that happening, one's concern for the realism of the parable is exhausted. The parable has only one point and once that is grasped one's interest ceases.

It is significantly different in the approach which we find in MacKinnon's explorations of the realistic features of the parables, in a way which is difficult to spell out though easy to recognize in the concrete case. We could put it this way: for Dodd and Jeremias the realism of the parables is put in the service of using human stories to *illustrate* the divine, whereas in MacKinnon it is time and again put in the service of *exploring* the divine.

Despite their brevity, what we continually find in the parables is a human situation of high complexity where every detail is chosen with superb economy to bring out the subtleties inherent in that situation. If we consider, say, a parable such as 'The Prodigal Son' it would be hard to imagine greater psychological subtlety and accuracy contained in such a brief compass. We have a familiar human transaction in which the full psychological dynamics of the family come to life. In most accounts of the parable known to me remarkably little is made of the fact that the brothers are *brothers* – even in those accounts which do pay proper attention to the elder brother, who is every bit as significant for the force of the parable as the father and younger brother. And yet we have here a human transaction which is quite recognizably one between *brothers*. We all know not only the type of brother who kicks over the traces, rebels against his family and goes 'into the far country', but also the type of 'good' child who seeks always to earn the approval of his parents through obedience, and the fierce hostility of the latter towards the former. Whatever else it is, this parable is a story of sibling rivalry and jealousy, in which one brother sees in the acceptability of the other a profound threat to himself and his own position. If he has earned his father's love by his obedience, what becomes of all this activity if his brother is so readily accepted without any such obedience? Crucial, it seems to me, to the whole situation is that the elder brother perceives the acceptance of the younger brother as a threat to him, making a nonsense of his whole life of obedience to his father. Unless we see the parable as concerning the relation between brothers we do not understand at all what is going on here. (The final exchange between the elder brother and the father is exquisitely nuanced: 'This son of yours . . .', says the elder brother, 'this your brother . . .', replies the father.)

Now the parable as it appears in Luke occurs as a reply to the murmurings of the Pharisees and scribes – 'This man receives sinners and eats with them' – and this is surely a highly intelligible context for it. Their reaction is here being compared to the reaction of the elder brother. The parable clearly rests on the standard analogy between God and a father, but develops it by exploring relations within the covenant as relationships within a family, where the family is seen, for all the brevity of the parable, in its full depth. What is the moral of this story? Does it have a moral? It is surely in some sense saying that, just as the elder brother has misconstrued the situation, so too the Pharisees have got things wrong, and in the same way. To that extent we may see the parable as at least implying the argument by analogy seen as crucial to the parables by Jülicher.

But to treat that as though that were all that was achieved by the parable is surely to diminish it: here the central concern of Jülicher to reduce a parable to one point emasculates what is going on. For writers like Jülicher, once one has found the point of the comparison, to pay attention to the details of the parable as having their own meaning is to flirt with allegory. But here the whole situation is explored with extraordinary sureness of touch and delicacy; and this seems to me to be one of the hallmarks of the parables: one situation is *explored* by means of a comparison. As the situation within the family is unfolded and seen with ever greater precision, so the relations within the covenant are explored. Not that this is a matter of a point by point comparison, but the parable is an invitation to an open-ended examination of the relations within the covenant that is far from exhausted by any single point.

If this is right, then the realism of the parable has far greater significance than is implied by the formulations that Dodd gives. By coming to see the full human reality of the situation before us in its full detail, and by being made to contemplate and reflect on what that detail amounts to, we are embarked on a subtle investigation of the dynamics of relations within the covenant. The elder brother has got things wrong. But how? If we consider the human situation, fraught with powerful anger and jealousy, inevitably we are led to say that he is not only wrong to be horrified by his father's acceptance of the younger brother, but that horror is an index of the fact that there is something already wrong in his own relation to his father. It is because he treats his father's love as something to be earned, and something that he has earned, that he feels a violent threat in the way his brother receives the love for nothing. We may say he does not *trust* his father's love – he apparently does not trust it enough to ask his father if he can invite friends in for a party. The love is for him only to be guaranteed by his working for it. If the younger brother gets his father's love wrong by abusing it, the elder brother gets it just as wrong. Both have failed to grasp the nature of love within the family. This is all superbly true to life. But the parable invites us to explore that life in order better to understand God's relation to the covenant people, and the ways in which both the 'sinners' and the Pharisees and scribes who murmur against Jesus have got that relation wrong.

V

This leads naturally on to the other stress that I associate with MacKinnon's writings about the parables: an attention to the precise detail of the parable and a reflection on its significance, an attention to detail that has nothing to do with allegory.

If when we read a parable, we are not merely concerned with an illustration of a religious truth but with an exploration of God's relation to man, then attending to the precisely observed detail of the human situation is part of that exploration. Let us continue to look at 'The Prodigal Son': this is described by Jeremias as 'a joyful message of repentance and forgiveness'. But that is, it seems to me, a highly inaccurate register of what we are actually given. Above all, in what sense does the younger brother repent? To talk of 'repentance' here carries with it all the wrong overtones for the actual detail of what happens that we are given. He spends all the money and finds himself in a mess. He has reduced himself to desperate straits. 'He came to himself' in this context means far more 'he came to his senses', than what we ordinarily mean by 'he repented': he simply recognized that he had set himself on a course that led to disaster and set about extricating himself. What prompts him to decide to go to his father and say, 'I have sinned against heaven and against thee' is not some profound conviction of wrongdoing but the simple necessities of his situation. Even if we do not say he is insincere in wishing to use this formula, the quality of this repentance is to say the least questionable. The centre of the situation is that out of desperation he returns home – he has nowhere else to go. The use of the formula is not so much a manifestation of a recognition of guilt, as an attempt to say the right thing to extricate himself from his predicament.

And he does not actually say it: it all turns out to be irrelevant, since regardless of his attitude or what he says, before he has had a chance to explain himself the father takes compassion and simply accepts him back. We may imagine the young man rehearsing what he has to say as he travels back uncertain as to what reception he will have, when everything is brushed aside by the father's simply treating this as a homecoming of his son. Just as repentance hardly comes into it, 'forgiveness' seems to me to give the wrong suggestion as to what transpires. The father does not so much forgive as regard the son's homecoming as wholly unproblematic. Certainly the son has done great wrong, has done great harm to his family, and so we may say the father forgives him, but that suggests a wrong emphasis. The father simply accepts the son as his son and behaves in such a way that the son's wrongdoing does not enter into his calculations at all.

The point at stake here is far from minor. When Jesus is engaged in polemical confrontation with the Pharisees, the point at issue is not that he is accepting 'penitent' sinners; he is simply feasting with prostitutes and tax-gatherers without waiting for their penitence. The Pharisees would themselves have willingly accepted a penitent sinner who resolved to abandon his former ways and return to life under the law. But, like the father in the parable, Jesus does not wait to hear the profession of guilt. He simply accepts them where they are: it is that which is offensive in his behaviour.

It is instructive here to compare this parable with *Antigone*, where the points at issue have striking resemblances to our present concerns. One idea to which Sophocles recurs is the idea of the great sinner, the man who has broken fundamental laws of his homeland, who must be treated as an outcast from his own people, but who is now dead. Is such a man to be accorded burial rites by his people or not? This idea occurs in its simplest form in *Ajax* and its most complex form in *Oedipus at Colonus*, but perhaps its most intensely dramatic treatment is the confrontation between Creon and Antigone. Polyneices, in raising an army against his own homeland, has clearly for both of them put himself absolutely in the wrong. Not one word is said in defence of his action. We might judge Eteocles to have provoked Polyneices's action, and to have been equally in the wrong but there is no suggestion of this within the play. Antigone and Creon are both completely agreed that Polyneices has died in his sins – there is certainly no question of a penitent sinner. But the issue between Antigone and Creon is clear. For Creon, Polyneices was the man who had committed the ultimate crime – raising an army against the polis; he was simply an outcast and to be treated as such, with his corpse allowed to rot. For Antigone this was her brother and as such to be honoured in his death.

Hegel saw in this opposition a basic form of tragic conflict, a conflict of right with right, between the public and the private, the political and the personal. But this is a great over-simplification.

There is nothing within Sophocles's treatment to suggest that for him there was any right on Creon's side: his action was intelligible, but disowned by the gods and, in the end, his people. But more to the point, it seems to me that the divorce between the political and the personal is only imported into the play by us. Antigone's concerns could be seen as 'political' too. Does the polis defend itself and maintain its integrity by showing, with Creon, utter opposition to those who fight against it, and by disowning and denying burial to Polyneices? Or can it be seen as defending its integrity when finally, when Polyneices is no longer a threat, the polis, with Antigone, acknowledges its own as its own by burying Polyneices as a brother and a member of the house of Thebes? Antigone can be seen as defending the polis every bit as much as Creon.

It is, I suggest, this conception which informs the details of the parable of 'The Prodigal Son'. Jesus is *affirming* the covenant by going among its law-breakers. The covenant is more fundamental than their sin, and to suppose that being within the covenant is dependent upon the keeping of the law is to misconstrue the covenant in precisely the same way that the elder brother misconstrues love within the family.

In the course of the recent British miners' strike, Len Murray was interviewed and asked whether the Trade Union Congress ought not to disown the National Union of Mineworkers in view of some of the recent excesses and abuses of the strike. He said simply that that was out of the question – 'They're family.' In saying that he was not saying anything sentimental, or blindly ignoring the questionable nature of much that happened during the strike. It was a sober political statement, a statement of the loyalty that sustains the Trades Union Movement. So too on an infinitely higher plane we have a parable, of God's faithfulness sustaining the covenant regardless of the sins of its members. To bring into this a picture of penitence and forgiveness is not only to blur all its significant details, to throw out of focus the actual nature of what we are told; it is also to trivialize the full thrust of what the story actually would wish us to contemplate.

Once we think of the realism of the parables as a way of exploring the divine, rather than as a truth to life necessary to establish the basis on which the parable argues its *one* point, we will over and over again find that the slightest details of the parable have been placed with the greatest precision to further a highly complex investigation.

VI

In conclusion I would like to consider a suggestion made by Donald MacKinnon in his Gifford Lectures, as a way of bringing together the different elements within this essay. In effect he invites us to contemplate the possibility that the father in 'The Prodigal Son' is a silly old fool.[8]

Why does such an outrageous possibility even arise? One's natural initial reaction is to think 'piously', to think automatically of the father as God, and approve of what he does. And yet, how automatic a reaction is it to approve of the father in the human situation of the parable? To say the least, the reaction of the elder brother is highly intelligible and the father's disregarding of the gross wrongs his son has done him is not even the obviously right thing to do from a moral standpoint. The father is shown to be swept along by emotion – running with undignified haste to greet the son, putting on a party in his honour, while his brother grumbles that no such parties have been available for him. Will not even the younger brother regard his father as 'soft'?

Now, we may in the end reject such an interpretation. But what is significant here is that if we engage ourselves seriously with the parables, we are continually invited to tread strange and offensive paths of thought. The parables are very far from the innocuous little anecdotes that Jülicher made them out to be: if we are to say something better about them than he did, then we must be prepared, with Donald MacKinnon, to confront them in their strangeness, to embark on an exploration, and exploration which leads to the heart of the divine even if it goes along routes that we would not of ourselves have dared to take.

The parable of 'The Prodigal Son' seems to me to end most significantly on a question – a question in the end addressed to us. The future life within the family is entirely open. Will the elder brother persist in his hostility and rejection of his father? Will the younger brother regard his father as a soft touch and continue to abuse his love? Nothing in what we are told begins to settle such questions.

At most the father has provided the opportunity for restoration within the family; the outcome of his doing so is left completely unclear. The question 'Is the father a silly old fool?' is a question directed to us as we contemplate the story just as much as it is one to the protagonists within the story. It is on to such strange paths that MacKinnon in his reflections on the parables continually points us, and in so doing, it seems to me, he is responding to one of their most basic features.

Notes

1 D. M. MacKinnon, *The Problem of Metaphysics* (Cambridge, 1974).
2 A. Jülicher, *Die Gleichnissreden Jesu*, 2nd ed. (Freiburg i.B., 1899).
3 *Ibid*, vol. 1, p. 322.
4 *Ibid*, vol. 1, p. 148.
5 J. Jeremias, *The Parables of Jesus*, E. T. (London, 1963), p. 205.
6 O. C. Quick, *The Realism of Christ's Parables* (London, 1931).
7 *Cf.* for example *The Parables of Jesus*, pp. 49 and 203.
8 MacKinnon, *The Problem of Metaphysics*, pp. 137f.

5 Trinity and ontology

ROWAN WILLIAMS

I

Donald MacKinnon's writings from about the mid-1960s onwards, at least, return regularly not simply to the fundamental theme of 'realism *versus* idealism', but to the treatment of this issue by G. E. Moore in a classical essay on 'External and Internal Relations'.[1] This, along with certain other writings by Moore and Russell in their assault on idealism,[2] sets the terms of the problem for MacKinnon; and it is important to remember this when, as is sometimes the case, the words 'realism' and 'idealism' seem to become impossibly loose in their scope. Behind all the discussion of the question of fundamental ontology in MacKinnon's maturest work stands a set of rigorous arguments in logical theory, in the light of which this work requires to be understood; and without this perspective the heart of MacKinnon's theological achievement remains opaque.

Moore's target is primarily Bradley's contention that every relation in which a specific term is involved enters into the being of that term, so as to be intrinsic to it. Moore's first clarification (pp. 281–2) is to note that, strictly speaking, it is 'relational *properties*' that are in question, not relations – i.e., Bradley's claim is one about relations to particular and distinct terms that are truly predicated of another single term ('*A* is the father of *B*', not '*A* is a father' only). The claim then amounts to saying, 'Without the relational property *p*, *A* would not necessarily be *A*' (p. 284); not-*p* entails that the subject of *p* is qualitatively and numerically different

71

from *A*. But there are clearly relational properties of which this cannot hold (a materially discrete or discernible part in a composite whole, for instance, may or may not possess the relational property of being part of the whole; it would not necessarily be numerically different if it did not): thus it *may* follow that if *x* is not *p*, it is not *A*, but there is no necessity, no *deducibility* of not-*A* from not-*p*. There is, Moore proposes (p. 291), no *entailment* of not-*A* by not-*p*, no logical relation, that is, comparable to the deducibility of '*B* is less than *A*' from '*A* is greater than *B*'.

If not-*p* always and necessarily entailed not-*A*, every true proposition would entail every other true proposition. (*p.q*) would be analytic of *p*; with the unpalatable consequence that every *false* proposition would entail every other proposition, true and false (p. 285). This is manifestly absurd, and there are obvious examples of conjunctions of true propositions neither of which can in any accessible sense be deduced from the other (pp. 300–1, 304–5). Relational properties thus cannot all be internal in the sense of belonging necessarily to their terms: some are, but some are not and cannot be. Even if we allow (p. 309) that a relational property entails some quality in the term that makes it capable of having that property, such a quality does not entail the property. Thus – though Moore does not so express it – there are contingently true propositions not deducible from others.[3] To know the truth of *p* does not mean knowing the whole scheme of true propositions; there are things we *come* to know, so that a certain attitude to the timebound nature of our knowing is involved here. If *A* is not necessarily *p*, *A* must be knowable as changing, as 'entering into' relations and ceasing to be involved in them. Granted what has been said about the *conditions* in *A* for *p*, it is not true that *A* is made to be *A* by *p*; and this is what is meant by asserting the existence of *external relations* – not, crudely, the chance juxtaposition of intact atomic subjects, but simply the fact that there are some non-constitutive relational properties.

If there really are 'external relations', Bradleian idealism must be fatally confused; its flaw lies in the assimilation of all relations between true propositions to entailment, which is (to say the least) counter-intuitive. At best, this assimilation is a kind of eschatological myth; at worst, it is simply a muddle about the language we actually speak. Of this demonstration of the flaw in such an epistemology, MacKinnon writes: 'What Moore establishes in this paper is something about the world . . . a fact of a peculiar order; indeed, one is hard put to it at first . . . to say clearly what sort of fact it is.'[4] I am not sure that it is helpful or intelligible to speak of 'a' fact here; if Moore is right, what we actually have is something more like a definition of what facts are, a grammatical stipulation, or (lest that be thought to sell the pass again) an ontological framework. If p and q can, independently of each other, be known to be true, they are known to be *contingently* true; $(f)x$ does not have to be so. The functional variable does not shift according to a necessary law-governed pattern. x is now this, now that, and what it is cannot be predicted as if it were the end of a mathematical operation of a certain kind.

But this means also that there is one distinction that is somehow ontologically positive: that between the constant and the variable terms of propositions, between the processes of change and that which changes (without which, of course, we could have no notion of change at all).[5] 'The concept of the thing is the concept of the way in which various sorts of event are organisable or constructible', as MacKinnon puts it in an essay published in 1972:[6] we cannot do without the notion of self-continuous subjects in talking about the world, since there is no other way, it seems, of making sense of the flux of perceptions. But even that is a profoundly misleading way of putting it, suggesting that there might *first* be perceptions of something like 'events', which we subsequently carve up into things. We should need to revise and intensify MacKinnon's 1972 phraseology to do justice to what he is attempting to say: the concept of the thing is what is presupposed in the very concept of a perceived world.[7] The world could not show itself in our thought and language as an intelligible, utterable, discussable continuum did we not know 'first' (the word should not be taken with chronological literalness) what a thing was.

Here we are in very deep waters indeed. MacKinnon rightly repudiates the 'crudities of the picture-theory of the proposition',[8] and regards straightforward logical atomism as mythological.[9] It sounds from much of his writing as though it is in fact impossible to give a satisfactory account of what a thing *is*; we are certainly not being invited to see the world as divided into discrete lumps answering to nouns in our language. Correspondence is not a scrutable relation between words and things, but something more like a controlling *image* for our understanding of understanding.[10] I suspect that the emphasis on the ontological irreducibility of the thing, the self-continuous subject, actually represents a kind of 'negative metaphysics'. If the truth of $(f)a$ and the truth of $(f)x$ can be independently known, we can at least know that a and x are neither of them part of the definition of the other. We cannot but treat them as subjects of their distinct histories, even though neither is real *apart* from those histories:[11] there is no Lockean substrate to be excavated. But if this is how we speak and are constrained to speak, we also know, from the reciprocal non-entailment of p and q, that we recognize as true what *comes to be true* and whose coming to be true is not predictable; and if it is not predictable, it is nonsense to say – in extreme idealist fashion – that it is 'made to be true' by the knowing mind. The unpredictable is, necessarily, that whose truth is a matter of question and puzzlement (we *come* to know it), to which understanding must adjust:[12] it is what changes the very scope of the knowing mind. We may not be able to give a clear answer to the question, 'How are objects of experience possible?', but we must ask it in order at least to register the fact that our speech is marked by the pressure of 'experiential constants', place, date, continuity of subject, causal agency.[13] 'If these constants are expressive of the form of the world, they are so expressive as realizing the inescapable limits of our understanding.'[14] The idealist temptation is to foreclose the issues raised in this remark by treating its unavoidable anthropocentrism ('*our* understanding') as a solution rather than a problem[15] – i.e., by turning the notion of 'inescapable limits of understanding' into a theoretical prohibition on considering what understanding actually understands, and ultimately into a denial that this latter consideration has any meaning.

Some of the difficulty and unclarity in all this is, I think, due to the fact that MacKinnon tends to elide various kinds of anti-realism, producing an implicit portmanteau scheme which no one philosopher has held or could logically hold. There are several targets for his polemic that need to be distinguished. As we have seen, the first and perhaps most basic of these is the doctrine Moore sets out to refute, that there are no propositions that are contingently true; the rejection of this implies the primitivity of discrete subjects ('things') in our language, and MacKinnon thus turns to attack the idea of the reducibility of things to events or event-clusters. He is wary of the pitfalls of crude atomism, yet insists that the 'constants' of our speech are not arbitrary; and this leads him to reject the suggestion that all we know is how our language works. But the rejection of arbitrariness in the sense of non-determination by extra-linguistic reality involves him equally in dismissing the idea that what can and shall be thought, known or spoken is up to us, is our 'creation', resting on our 'decision'.[16] This last point is both the weakest and in some respects the most important in MacKinnon's polemical outline of realism – weakest because least related to any serious idealist views and involving him in what seems a rather contentious, even distorting, account of Wittgenstein on the foundation of mathematics, most significant because it brings out the *moral* force of the first and strongest part of the polemic, the assertion of the reality of external relations. One could perhaps represent this by saying: if the world is not a system of necessary inter-connections, and if knowledge is therefore genuinely historical,[17] coming to know what comes to be true, then the will can have no finally determinative role in our relation to the world. To suppose that it can is not only a lie, but a destructive (and self-destructive) lie. Logically, the universality of internal relations and the primacy of the will as a 'world-causing' reality have nothing to do with each other, but for the practical reason both may serve to secure the ego a kind of invulnerability from interruption,[18] challenge, resistance; both may reinforce the idea that the hidden, immutable essence of subjectivity is limitlessness, and that there can be no genuinely diminishing injuries to the subject, no real defeats. The indeterminate depths of selfhood abide.

We are back with what earlier I called a 'negative metaphysics'. Filling it out, without destroying its negative character, is a programme of daunting proportions which MacKinnon himself only hints at, and which is beyond the compass of this essay. One or two things, though, might be said, in a kind of parenthesis, at this juncture. First of all, it is important to keep in sight the possibility that the 'correspondence' metaphor might be edged away from its focal position without thereby sacrificing the concerns of realism. If we are prepared to jettison picture-theories of propositions, the correspondence we can speak of becomes a far more elusive thing: it is not the correspondence of photograph to scenery or physiognomy, nor yet that of, say, a chemical formula to a specific chemical reaction in the laboratory. Is it, then, more like the *appropriateness* of a move in chess? The exhibiting of a proper and conventionalized but not totally determined skill in responding to what is presented? This sails very near the pragmatist wind, but cannot be accused of covert voluntarism, at least. If picture-theories must go, are we left with any option but something like this: a realism which 'shows itself' in the halts and paradoxes, shifts and self-corrections of language itself as a material and historical reality? Following on from this: MacKinnon certainly hints that the concept of a 'thing' is analogical, but does not fully tease out the implications of this. There have been those who suggest that if the idea of self-continuous substance is analogical, the prime analogate is the concept of human subjectivity. But lest this should turn into an appeal to the justly unpopular notion of separable (disembodiable) selves, we must insist that what is in question is the self as embodied agent. If language expresses irreducible discontinuities, this has something to do with the fact that what we ordinarily count as consciousness involves assuming the difference between our bodily presence and what acts upon it or resists it. To be conscious is to be 'placed' in respect of bodily limits. It is also to be (at least potentially) a speaker, defining oneself in saying 'I' and presenting – in response to the address of what is materially other (including words) the construct of a self-continuous subject. The intertwining factors of body and speech *oblige* us to be in the world as individual subjects: that is how we speak, think, and so are. And it is on the basis of this that we are able to learn to give names, to acquire the skill of identifying 'things'. Regular patterns of interaction between body and other can only be formulated in the language of 'things' if the body is first located as 'addressed' and required to organize or present itself in response, so that there is a constant in respect of which patterns can be established as regular.

This is no more than an attempt (indebted in some ways to von Balthasar's metaphysical sketch in *Herrlichkeit*;[19] less obviously, to some of the recent work of Fergus Kerr,[20] and with a cautious glance in the direction of Lacan) to indicate how MacKinnon's central concerns about the avoidance of the mythology of the knowing self's illimitability might be pursued and discussed further, once realism is detached a little more from atomism and picture-theories. It is meant to allow (i) that the sentient individual is more than a 'logical construction out of events'[21] without involving us in speculative fancy about naked individual subjects existing prior to relation and perception; (ii) that while there is no way in which the individual is graspable without seeing that it is constituted in and by the material fact of bodily limit and the relation of being – as I have put it – 'addressed', and formed as a speaker in and by the linguistic community, this does not and cannot mean the kind of relational determinism in all aspects of its particular history that Moore repudiates;[22] (iii) that the concept of a thing is indeed indispensable, primitive, but is ultimately dependent on the condition of continuous perception – or, in plain English, things exist as continuing subjects of change because speakers do. The fact that (iii) depends on a particular analysis of the material–linguistic conditions of perception itself may rescue it from the charge of vulgar Berkleianism.

This has been a laborious prologue to the consideration of strictly theological issues; but MacKinnon's own insistence that theology cannot neglect the questions of ontology makes such a preliminary exploration necessary. It will be clear that I have some misgivings about MacKinnon's residual tenderness towards an 'atomist' realism and about the degree to which varieties of idealism are – I think – too hastily assimilated to voluntarism; and I have tried to see whether MacKinnon's concerns can be preserved in a reconstruction that gives more ground than he would to strategies associated with constructivist and coherentist accounts of truth – to the idea of 'reality without reference'.[23] However, the determination to demythologize a free, triumphant, endlessly resourceful, sovereign willing self remains focally important: MacKinnon's *moral* interest in realism is one of his most valuable contributions to the whole of this tangled debate, and I share his conviction that it is a crucial dimension for our philosophizing and theologizing. We must turn next, then, to what exactly is involved in this moral interest, and to its theological import.

II

If the world is our creation, or even if the world is masterable as a system of necessities, the idea of irreparable and uncontrollable *loss* ceases to make sense: there are no tragedies. But in brute fact, human disaster does not submit itself to a calculus of perceivable necessities in this or any imaginable world (Ivan's challenge to Alyosha about torturing a single child to secure the happiness of the world is perhaps the starkest of familiar expressions of this).[24] All explanation of suffering is an attempt to forget it *as* suffering, and so a quest for untruthfulness; and it is precisely this kind of untruthfulness that is served (in MacKinnon's eyes) by anti-realism. It is pointless to ask whether the moral failure of anti-realism leads us to seek for a logical critique, or whether its logical muddles help to make it a moral delinquency to hold it: chickens and eggs. Both the moral and the logical criticisms of anti-realism involve a certain appeal to the counter-intuitive character of the idea of the world as a necessary system; and, for MacKinnon, the most important aspect of such an appeal is that it reminds us that we do speak of and experience tragic loss, senseless, inexplicable, unjustifiable, unassimilable pain. 'People change and smile, but the agony abides.' The resolution of the sheer resistant particularity of suffering, past and present,[25] into comfortable teleological patterns is bound to blunt the edge of particularity, and so to lie; and this lying resolution contains that kind of failure in attention that is itself a moral deficiency, a fearful self-protection. It is just this that fuels the fantasy that we can choose how the world and myself shall be.

MacKinnon's Gifford Lectures[26] return more than once to the Kantian principle of the primacy of the practical reason; and it is in a very clearly Kantian way that the transition from these observations about the unassimilably particular to theology is realized. The world is such – *is*, independently of our choice and our fabrication – that we cannot think away particulars into comprehensive explanatory systems; the world is such that attention to particularity is demanded of us. If we are to speak of God, can we do so in a way that does not amount to another evasion of the world? There is a way of talking about God that simply projects on to him what we cannot achieve – a systematic vision of the world as a necessarily inter-related whole. Trust in such a God is merely deferred confidence in the possibility of exhaustive explanation and justification; and deferred confidence of this sort is open to exactly the same moral and logical objection as any other confidence in systemic necessity of this kind in the world. A God whose essential function is to negate the 'otherness' and discontinuity of historical experience, and so to provide for us an ideal *locus standi*, a perspective transcending or reconciling discontinuity into system, is clearly an idol, and an incoherent one at that: if he is the negation of the reciprocal negations or exclusions of worldly subjects, either he is the completion of the process of historical dialectic (in which case he cannot strictly provide a *locus standi* outside it for us *now*, as there is no alternative to living through that dialectic); or else he is simply a further object, of a rather unusual kind, standing in opposition to the rest of the objects that there are (in which case there is no ultimate overcoming of discontinuity). These are familiar cruces in monist ontologies, from Plotinus and Iamblichus to Hegel, Marx and beyond.

Apart from this threatened incoherence, though, there is also the fact that no content can be given to the concept of such a God, let alone to the 'explanation' he is meant to provide – except that a Hegelian might reply that the 'content' is the whole rational process of the universe. However, even if such a form of theism were capable of intelligible statement and defence, it would hardly be compatible with the Christian doctrine of God as loving and active 'in his own right', irrespective of there being a world. Between God and the world is a relation which approaches the limit of 'sheer externality',[27] in that God is in no sense *made to be* what he is by the sum total of worldly fact. The Christian problem then becomes one of elucidating the sense in which God *is* related to the world, most particularly in Jesus Christ. If God is neither a quasi-Hegelian organizing principle, nor an abstract postulate, nor yet an agent among other agents, what *is* to be said of him?

Christian practice begins to answer that question by repeating the story of Jesus: what is to be said of God is that Jesus of Nazareth was born, ministered in such and such a way, died in such and such a way, and was raised from death. This is an odd statement, in that it treats the narrative of a human being as predicated of a substance or subject which is God; and all sorts of qualifications must at once be introduced in order to avoid the obvious pitfall of failing to allow that we are, after all, speaking of a human individual.[28] But what is being claimed is that the substantiality, the 'subjecthood', the continuous identity of this individual is so related to the substantiality of God that it cannot be grasped in its full reality without allusion to God as *constitutively* significant for it: this human individual's relation to God is 'internal to the term assumed', so that the humanity of Jesus as independent of its assumption by God is abstract or 'impersonal' (anhypostatic)[29] – a feature of classical Christology normally so misunderstood and distorted in contemporary discussion that MacKinnon's presentation of it must itself be accorded something of a classical status.

God is what is constitutive of the particular identity of Jesus; that is what can be said of him, and it is what the *homoousion* of Nicaea endeavoured to say. If we say less than this, the identity of Jesus becomes external to God and so 'parabolic' in its significance: it is one determinate thing pointing to another. Jesus is 'like' God in certain respects, and presumably not in others, which licenses us to leave out of account in our theology what in the story of Jesus is held on some prior grounds to be unassimilable for language about God. Thus we are swiftly brought back to the question of the authority by which we may say anything at all of God. Christ as parable relieves us of Christ as paradox; and it pushes back towards the purely negative characterization of God once more, as that which is not involved in the world's discontinuities. MacKinnon's repeated insistence that we attend to the *tragic* in the narrative of Jesus[30] belongs with this rejection of parabolic status for this narrative: only that to which the *homoousion* points can hold before us the full human particularity of Jesus, and so prevent us from yet another variety of fantasy and avoidance of the truth. For Jesus to have been a temporal individual at all is for him to have changed and learned and made decisions whose full consequences he did not control; for him to have been *responsible*, as all adult persons are, for the injuring and diminution (even if it was also the self-injuring and self-diminution) of others. His innocence or sinlessness becomes a dauntingly complex matter if it is not to be taken as a complete alienation from the realities of temporal existence. It must be something compatible with the experience of what we would have to call 'moral limit':[31] MacKinnon speaks of an 'historically achieved innocence',[32] implying that sinlessness can only be a judgement passed on the *entirety* of a life in which the inevitable damage done by human beings to each other has not sealed up the possibility of compassionate and creative relationship (even to those most deeply injured: what could one say here of the relation between the figure of Jesus and post-Holocaust Judaism, as perceived by modern Jewish writers? does this give a hint of what the content of 'sinlessness' might be?).

If, then, we are serious about the constitutive character of God's relation to Jesus, we are saying that we speak and cannot but speak of God in the context of *limit* – the limits of particularity, of bodiliness and mortality, of moral capacity, of creatureliness. For Jesus is also a creature who prays to God, someone addressing a Father in heaven; and what is more, he is shown to us – in Gethsemane and in the Johannine farewell discourses – as interpreting, at starkly painful cost, the final 'limit' of his approaching torture and death as the moment, the 'hour', in which the act of the Father in and through himself is to be accomplished.[33] The otherness, the final unmasterable otherness of the world present to all of us as our approaching death, is for Jesus inseparable from the otherness to him of God. So the paradoxes are sharpened: if we affirm that God's relation to Jesus makes Jesus to be what he is, we move on inexorably to saying that God constitutes in Jesus a life which is – so to speak – paradigmatically *creaturely*, distanced from God. The God who is the ground and form of Jesus's particular history is also the God to whom Jesus calls through the mortal darkness of Gethsemane and Calvary. The God present *in* Jesus is present *to* Jesus in the enduring of his comfortless death: sheer externality.

It is this that compels us to the trinitarian enterprise; not to find a resolution for all this, but to continue with the question of what is to be said of God, to find a language for the proclaiming of Christ that does not break down into nonsense or presage retreat into abstract theism (God as ideal negation). In the conclusion of his 1976 essay on 'The Relation of the Doctrines of the Incarnation and the Trinity',[34] MacKinnon writes: 'If we suppose that in the theology of the Trinity an *analogia personarum* can be complemented by an analogy of *limits* (in the pregnant sense of the Greek *peras*), it may go some way towards grounding within the eternal the essentially human element of temporality, the sense of inescapable limitation.'

If we are to speak of God in terms of Jesus, we must say that in God there is that which makes possible the identity-in-difference – indeed, identity in distance or in absence – of Jesus and who or what he calls Father: something approaching the 'externality' of creator and creation, yet decisively not that, but a mutually constitutive presence, an internal relation of terms. What is to be said of God must be 'expressive of a total spontaneity and absolute mutual response'.[35] Creation in its 'externality' to God and its 'externality' within itself can be so because the life of the creator is what it unchangingly is in a relation we only perceive as something teasingly and disturbingly like self-negation; but *not* that.

This is, I think, what MacKinnon means by saying,[36] in the wake of von Balthasar, that the presence of God in Christ is a 'putting at risk' of the unity of the divine life. I do not believe that MacKinnon is flirting here with any kind of residual Valentinian mythology – the fall of Sophia – or with any of the less intelligent and intelligible versions of process thought. The point is surely this: we cannot say what God is in himself; all we have is the narrative of God with us.[37] And that is a narrative of a 'journey into a far country' (to borrow Barth's powerful image,[38] itself of normative importance to MacKinnon), a story of God's Son as a creature and a mortal and defeated creature: the unity of God and his Son in this story is not, in the actual detail, moment by moment, of the story, desert temptation, Gethsemane, dereliction, realized for us as an unshakeable, already achieved thing. It emerges at last, when Christ goes to his Father risen and glorified, as the issue of a temporal process, with all its ambiguity, the uncontrolledness of its effects ('moral limit' again), the precariousness of its growth. That is what temporal process *is* for us. In other words, it is a story of 'risk'; and only at Easter are we able to say, 'he comes *from* God, just as he goes *to* God', and to see in the contingent fact of the resurrection – the *limited* events of the finding of an empty tomb and a scatter of bewildering encounters – that which is not contingent, the life of God as Father and Son together.[39] We cannot start from this end-point in the sense of treating it as the given framework for making complete and satisfying sense of the angular, specific and untidy narrative of ministry and Cross, because the sense of *this* ending emerges only from the telling of *this* story. Bultmann's kerygma, 'The crucified is risen', stops short of that decisive key to

speaking about *God* offered in the proclamation that 'The risen one –
the exalted Lord, the heavenly and eternal Son – is the crucified.'

We have, then, no concrete language for the unity of God but this
story of risk and consummation, of unity forged through absence
and death between God as source (Father) and the created life of
Jesus of Nazareth (as Son). We are left with only the most austere
account of God's life as such: that it must be what makes this
possible. Even if we say, for instance, that this establishes God as
free to be what he is even in dialogue and difference, to be himself in
the other, we are no further forward, except in so far as we have
thereby done away with the idea of God as an individual all of whose
relations to what is not himself are in the crudest sense external to
the other term of the relation as much as to himself, the relation of
one atomic individual to others – an idea hard to reconcile with any
serious doctrine of creation as well as with any theology of grace as
divine indwelling or 'information'.

We do not avoid the pressure of the negative by speaking of God
in trinitarian terms; but this apophaticism is at least not merely
abstract, not a matter of articulating God's life solely as the opposite
of temporal *altérité*. As MacKinnon fully allows, negative theology
of this sort is an indispensable element in the whole enterprise, so
that we should not delude ourselves that God's difference is merely
that of one thing from another: we need to put down those formal
markers (immutable, impassible, omnipotent, etc.) as a way of
insisting that we cannot write a biography of God. As has already
been said, his history is Jesus. If anthropomorphism is always
perilously close in the kind of trinitarian pluralism which the life of
Jesus seems to enjoin upon us,[40] it is still finally deflected by the
recognition that the 'essential' or 'immanent' Trinity can finally be
characterized only as that which makes this life (and death and
resurrection) possible and intelligible. Without reference to the
immanent Trinity, we are liable to idolatrous 'trivialization of the
divine';[41] but MacKinnon is well aware that there can be a trivialization no less disastrous and idolatrous in a kind of mythological
pluralism, projecting on to God the limits of created identities with
no sense of *metabasis eis allo genos* in our speech.

It could be said, perhaps, that in this perspective what is wrong
with an Hegelian view of the Trinity is that it projects the 'achieved'
character of Christ's union with the Father as enacted in history on

to eternity (and so destroys the proper contingency and unresolved or tragic limitedness of that and every history). And – although MacKinnon can write appreciatively of Moltmann[42] – it is clear that the same kind of projection is at work in the kind of pluralist doctrine that gives to the *historical* encounter of Jesus with the God of Israel a constitutive role in the life of the Trinity as such. God would not be God were he not the God who is such as to be the ground and 'form' of this encounter; but this is not the same as to say that God would not be God were it not for a set of contingent events in the first century of our era. Both Hegel's and Moltmann's trinitarian models are controlled by the desire to take history seriously, to bridge the gap between a remote eternity and the concrete temporal world; but they end in evasions of the temporal – Hegel by generalizing Good Friday into a necessary moment in the universal dialectic, Moltmann by weakening the force of the recognition that Jesus's suffering is humanly inflicted, through his concentration on the Cross as the Father's giving-up of the Son, a transaction in a mythical rather than historical space.

These two models, so apparently – and in many ways really – close to MacKinnon's, fail because they reverse the *ordo cognoscendi* of revelation. We do not begin with the trinitarian God and ask how he can be such, but with the world of particulars, Cross, empty tomb, forgiven and believing apostles, asking, 'How can this be?' Hence MacKinnon's image of 'transcription':[43] what we first know is the reality we subsequently come to know as derivative, transposed from what is prior. Kenosis is defined as the common form of Jesus's earthly life (as service, acceptance, authority in and through dependence) and the life of God (as gift or commitment to an other and the simultaneous imaging and returning of that act). The self-abnegation of Jesus in its specific form of active and transfiguring acceptance of the world's limit is not at all a mere paradigm for conscienceless obedience or resignation;[44] it is what puts to us the question of how God can be if this is how he is historically. Thus the abiding importance of the language of self-emptying is salvaged without recourse to the clumsy Apollinarian mythologies of some of those writers associated with 'kenotic theories' of the Incarnation.'[45]

The trinitarian theology thus sketched by MacKinnon represents an impressively balanced 'retrieval' of a number of classical themes;

but its greatest significance lies, I believe, in the thorough integration of trinitarian language with the over-riding concern for a truthful moral vision. The connections may not be at once obvious, but there is in fact a close link in this scheme between the evasion of the tragic and the denial of the relational character of God. However, we need also to note that MacKinnon's account of the tragic and of its reinterpretation in the language of Trinity and Incarnation has aroused some suspicion lately. In the final section of this paper, I propose to look briefly at these suspicions and to attempt a response based on indications offered in MacKinnon's own writing.

III

The problem is said to be this:[46] that any emphasis on the acceptance and interpretative transformation of moral or spiritual defeat is dangerously open to an ideological use that amounts to a commendation of passivity. What is absent from the 'tragic' orientation is a proper seriousness about the imperative to transformative *action*, and thus to protest: as Marx understood, interpretation is not enough. The Christian commitment is to a world of reconstructed relationships, not to a venture merely of 'reading' or 'rereading' the world. This is a weighty charge, and it must be allowed to possess some degree of plausibility. Christ as an exemplar of unresisting suffering is undoubtedly an ambivalent symbol; even Christ as the enactment of divine *solidarity* in suffering can be distorted in similar ways. And if – as MacKinnon many times insists – divine solidarity is a shocking and unmerciful judgement upon human and specially ecclesiastical power relations, what does this judgement *change*, other than ways of seeing and speaking? How shall we avoid being left with moralistic recommendations to abjure earthly power?

One point that needs making at once is that the tragic *by definition* deals with human limit; that is, with what is not to be changed. There is pain in the world that is, so to speak, non-negotiable. The suffering that *has* happened and cannot be made not to have happened (the irreversibility of time) is, in spite of various kinds of vacuous, insulting and brutal rhetoric, religious and political, unchangeably there for us. And there is present suffering, terminal illness or irreversible brain damage or what you will, that is equally, as a matter of bald fact, beyond us to change.[47] There can be a paralysing obsession with the tragic, but there can also be an attempt to evade the limits of time and particularity through an attempt to bypass or rationalize pain and death. Lionel Trilling's remarkable and under-rated novel, *The Middle of the Journey*, memorably shows us a man, recovering from a near-fatal illness, who realizes that his devoted and courageous socialist friends see him and his experience as a threat: death is reactionary. And this dread is shown in the novel to be as destructive and untruthful as the tragedy-soaked rhetoric of Gifford Maxim, the hypnotically eloquent ex-Communist and apprentice neo-conservative.

In the *Guardian* of 10 February 1986, the playwright Howard Barker offered '49 asides for a tragic theatre'. Among these theses were the following:

> Ideology is the outcome of pain . . .
> Tragedy liberates language from banality. It restores the power of expression to the people.
> Tragedy is not about reconciliation. Consequently it is the art form for our time.
> Tragedy resists the trivialization of experience, which is the project of the authoritarian regime . . .
> In the endless drizzle of false collectivity, tragedy restores pain to the individual.
> You emerge from tragedy equipped against lies. After the musical, you are anyone's fool . . .
> . . . Only tragedy makes justice its preoccupation.

It would be impertinent to gloss these remarks, except to point out that the tragic here is not simply the order of the world that must be accepted (tragedy is not accident, says Barker): it is *one's own* appropriation of the limits of possibility, in protest against a polity and a culture that lure us to sink our truthful perceptions in a collective, mythologized identity that can shut its eyes to limits (and so can talk of mass annihilation without pain).

No one acts without perceiving something. And if that is so, the disjunction between interpretation and transformation becomes less absolute. If interpretation is not an explanatory reduction, but the gradual formation of a 'world' in which realities can be seen and endured without illusion, it is not alien to the only kinds of transformation that matter, transformations of what is actually present, without prior distortion or trivialization. Tragic theatre forms such a world, and so is a point of reference over against claims to final resolutions of our condition. But we need to take the question further: interpretation does not happen because an individual or individuals invent a set of symbols. The possible world of truthful perception depends on what has been concretely *made* possible, however precariously and impermanently, for actual persons in communication with each other. How do you learn to confront the fact, say, of racism in British society? Not by information, not by words. They produce the kind of pain we cannot handle, and we take refuge in ideological denial of the facts of power in Britain. To confront both the suffering of the victims of racism and my own *de facto* involvement in and responsibility for this, without fantasizing and self-lacerating guilt, requires specific encounter and the possibility of its continuance; not reconciliation, but a kind of commitment without evasion. The 'reading' of our situation in certain terms rests on existing small-scale transformations – and also, of course, assists in the creation of further transformation.

Tragedy is capable of being lived with and articulated because – once again – of the particular, the narratively specific, out of which certain kinds of new language grow. So, to return to the strictly theological frame of reference, if we see the Cross as the identification of God with the limits of time, and learn from this a different reading of the temporal world, this 'seeing' of the Cross, and through it of the world, is concretely made possible through the existence of 'reconstructed relationships' – not an internal shift of attitudes but the coming into being of a community with distinctive forms of self-definition. This is relatively seldom explored in MacKinnon's work; and this near-silence helps to explain why it is possible to suspect his scheme of stressing interpretation at the expense of change. But it is also related to another near-silence: in common with so many contemporary writers on the Trinity, he has little to say of the Holy Spirit. The Spirit as that which forms or sustains the new world of perception through the constant re-creation of the Church as it is judged by its foundational charter in the paschal event[48] is the condition of the Christian reading of the Cross; once this is granted, the essential unity of interpretation and historical, public transformation is theologically grounded.

Putting it another way: trinitarian reflection begins in the recognition that the encounter of Jesus with the God of Israel 'transcribes' the encounter that is intrinsic to the life of God, but it does not finish there. God is constitutive of the identity of Jesus; God is also constitutive, in a different sense, of the process of the Church continually coming to judgement – the encounter of believers with the encounter of Father and Son. God is 'other to himself' or 'himself in the other' not only in the difference of Father and Son, but in that 'second difference' (borrowing the term from John Milbank's admirable recent essay)[49] that enables the communication of the *Gestalt* of Jesus's life in the Church. Not only Jesus's distance from the Father, but our distance, our critical 'absence', from Jesus is included in the eternal movement of God in and to himself. Without this, we should indeed be able to do no more than look at Jesus as exemplar, with the ideological risks that implies, making the life of God once again undialectically external in its realization to our present history.

If, then, we extend MacKinnon's methodology in this way to secure a serious doctrine of the Spirit as the divine condition for truthful 'coming to judgement' in the Church's life, some of the doubts raised about ideological ambivalence can be turned aside. The encounter of the Spirit with Christ is potentially an encounter with our own complicity in the Cross, and so with the crosses of our own making in the present and past; it should, then, if it is what it claims to be, form a central strand in Christian protest and the articulation of such protest in transforming *action*. But it must also hold us to penitence, the acknowledgement that our present possibilities are shaped by our past, that limit remains inescapable; and so it can save us from facile and shallow utopianism, which so readily spills over into authoritarian expression. MacKinnon's relentless insistence on attention to the costliness of historical action[50] and the unconsoled nature of historical pain remains the most disturbing and important lesson he has to teach – when all the necessary qualifications or reservations have been raised. 'When society is officially Philistine,' writes Barker (and he is not making a preciously aesthetic judgement, but speaking of moral insensibility), 'the complexity of tragedy becomes a source of resistance.' 'Complexity as a source of resistance' is no bad summary of MacKinnon's theological project; what he has done is to help us see that the need for resistance, so passionately spoken for by Barker (and a good many more), ultimately looks to a theology that can deploy, publicly and critically, its central, classical doctrinal resources of trinitarian and incarnational language in a time of false and would-be painless consciousness. Can we do this? If not, and if MacKinnon is right, there is no point in pretending to be theologians at all.

Abbreviations

ACS   'Aristotle's Conception of Substance', in Renford Bambrough, ed., *New Essays on Plato and Aristotle* (London, 1965), pp. 97–119

SA   *The Stripping of the Altars* (London, 1969)

SP   'The Problem of the "System of Projection" Appropriate to Christian Theological Statements' (1969), reprinted in *Explorations in Theology* (London, 1979), pp. 70–89

ARH   'Absolute and Relative in History: A Theological Reflection on the Centenary of Lenin's Birth' (1971), reprinted in *Explorations in Theology*, pp. 55–69

SC   ' "Substance" in Christology: A Cross-Bench View', in S. W. Sykes and J. P. Clayton, eds., *Christ, Faith and History: Cambridge Studies in Christology* (Cambridge, 1972), pp. 279–300

PM   *The Problem of Metaphysics* (Cambridge, 1974)

IT   'Some Notes on the Irreversibility of Time' (1975), reprinted in *Explorations in Theology*, pp. 90–8

IR   'Idealism and Realism: An Old Controversy Renewed' (1976), reprinted in *Explorations in Theology*, pp. 138–50

IncT   'The Relation of the Doctrines of the Incarnation and the Trinity', in Richard McKinney, ed., *Creation, Christ and Culture: Studies in Honour of T. F. Torrance* (Edinburgh, 1976), pp. 92–107

RI   'The Conflict between Realism and Idealism' (1977), reprinted in *Explorations in Theology*, pp. 151–65

PC   'Prolegomena to Christology', *Journal of Theological Studies*, 33 (1982), pp. 146–60

Notes

1 *Philosophical Studies* (London, 1922), pp. 276–309. This is referred to in *ACS, PM, IR* and *RI*. I have generally restricted myself in this paper to those of MacKinnon's works published after 1965.

2 E.g., Moore's 'The Refutation of Idealism', *Philosophical Studies*, pp. 1–30, and Chapter 5 of Bertrand Russell, *My Philosophical Develop-*

ment (London, 1959), quoting at length (pp. 55–61) from a 1907 paper dealing largely with the logic of relations.

3 Compare *SC*, p. 287.

4 *ACS*, p. 99.

5 *ACS*, p. 101.

6 *SC*, p. 287.

7 This is clearly implied in *ACS*, p. 114.

8 *RI*, p. 154.

9 *IR*, p. 142.

10 As suggested in *IR*, pp. 142 and 145–6, and *RI*, p. 154.

11 *SC*, pp. 284–8, *ACS*, pp. 103–5.

12 *IR*, p. 146.

13 *IR*, pp. 140–1.

14 *IR*, p. 140.

15 *IR*, pp. 149–50.

16 E.g., *IR*, p. 143 (on Wittgenstein), *RI*, pp. 156–7.

17 Compare the remarks on knowledge and *learning* in Rowan Williams, 'Trinity and Revelation', *Modern Theology*, 2 (1986), pp. 197–212, especially 197–8.

18 On 'truth as interruption', compare Eberhard Jüngel, 'The Truth of Life: Observations on Truth as the Interruption of the Continuity of Life', in Richard McKinney, ed., *Creation, Christ and Culture: Studies in Honour of T. F. Torrance* (Edinburgh, 1976), pp. 231–6.

19 *Herrlichkeit. Eine Theologische Ästhetik. III. 1. Im Raum der Metaphysik. II. Neuzeit*, 2nd ed. (Einsiedeln, 1965), pp. 943–83.

20 I have in mind particularly the sequence of articles on the soul in *New Blackfriars*, 64 (1983), pp. 76–85, 124–35, 188–98, 225–34.

21 *SC*, pp. 284–5.

22 *SC*, pp. 287–8.

23 The title of an influential and important study by Donald Davidson, reprinted in *Inquiries into Truth and Interpretation* (Oxford, 1984), pp. 215–25.

24 *The Brothers Karamazov*, vol. 5, ch. 4 ('Rebellion').

25 See, for example, *IncT*, pp. 90–3.

26 *PM*; see especially ch. 5.

27 *RI*, p. 161, *PC*, p. 157.

28 The dangers are spelt out in *PC*, pp. 149–53.

29 *PC*, pp. 149–50, 153.

30 See *IT passim* and especially pp. 96–8, *IncT*, p. 104, *ARH*, pp. 65–6, the short piece on 'Theology and Tragedy' in *SA*, pp. 41–51, and several of the earlier articles. The recurrent themes are the responsibility of Jesus for the damnation of Judas, and the connection between the events of redemption and the history of Christian anti-Semitism.

31 See the fine essay by D. Z. Phillips, 'Some Limits to Moral Endeavour', in *Through a Darkening Glass: Philosophy, Literature, and Cultural Change* (Oxford, 1982), pp. 30–50.

32 *IncT*, p. 97.

33 *ARH*, pp. 63–4, *SC*, p. 290, *PC*, pp. 158–60, etc.

34 *IncT*, p. 104.

35 *IncT*, p. 104; compare *ARH*, p. 68, and the remarks in *SP*, p. 85, on the 'contingency' of the proposition that the Father raises the Son – given that this is a profoundly unsatisfactory word, 'necessity', MacKinnon insists, is no better.

36 *IncT*, pp. 101–2; compare *ARH*, p. 67, *PC*, pp. 157–8, and MacKinnon's introduction to Hans Urs von Balthasar, *Engagement with God* (London, 1975).

37 For a particularly lucid exposition of this, see Herbert McCabe, 'The Involvement of God', *New Blackfriars*, 66 (1985), pp. 464–76.

38 Karl Barth, *Church Dogmatics*, 4.1, section 59.1.

39 See, for example, *SP*, pp. 75–9, 81–3.

40 *IncT*, p. 103.

41 *IncT*, p. 100.

42 *IncT*, p. 105. The parallels would be worth exploring in more detail, as would the important divergences. It is perhaps surprising that MacKinnon has never undertaken a fuller discussion of Moltmann.

43 *IncT*, p. 104.

44 The whole question of the ethics of obedience is one that has long preoccupied MacKinnon; see, for example, the essay on 'Moral Objections' in *Objections to Christian Belief*, by D. M. MacKinnon, H. A. Williams, A. R. Vidler and J. S. Bezzant (London, 1963), and 'Authority and Freedom in the Church', *SA*, pp. 52–61. Both show signs of bitter hostility to any conception of obedience that relieves people of the risk and responsibility of choice.

45 The Apollinarian risk is certainly present in Gore. More recently, David Brown's skilful apologia for pluralist trinitarianism and kenotic Christology (*The Divine Trinity* (London, 1985)) fails to avoid the pitfall of treating the Incarnation as an episode in the history of a divine subject, though it is not clear that he is guilty of a simple confusion between the Word and the psyche of Jesus of Nazareth.

46 See Philip West, 'Christology as "Ideology" ', *Theology*, 88 (1985), pp. 428–36, for a strong statement of this case.

47 West's article appears in the same issue of *Theology* as Margaret Spufford's 'The Reality of Suffering and the Love of God' (pp. 441–6), which offers a profound and moving reflection on suffering that we *cannot* change.

48 See the essay on 'Parable and Sacrament', *Explorations in Theology*, pp. 166–81, on the focusing of this judgement in the Eucharist.

49 'The Second Difference: For a Trinitarianism Without Reserve', *Modern Theology*, 2 (1986), pp. 213–34.
50 On the question of cost, see 'Lenin and Theology', *Explorations in Theology*, pp. 11–29, among other more fragmentary discussions.

6 Some aspects of the 'grammar' of 'incarnation' and 'kenosis': reflections prompted by the writings of Donald MacKinnon

KENNETH SURIN

In his so far unpublished 'Introduction' to the (also unpublished) lectures given by Oliver Chase Quick during his tenure as Regius Professor of Divinity at Oxford, Donald MacKinnon speaks favourably of Quick's treatment of the doctrine of the Incarnation. Describing the approach adopted by Quick in these lectures, MacKinnon says that

> Quick does not there offer a last word; rather he gathers together, in the form of a question, the work which he believes next requires to be done; but it is a considerable part of his achievement that . . . the refined delicacy of the writer's analysis of a number of absolutely fundamental problems . . . has enabled [the reader to] receive that concluding query as at once insight and incentive.[1]

Acquaintance with this particular essay and other writings of MacKinnon on the subject of 'incarnation' will, I believe, soon convince the reader that the above estimation of Quick's work is one that is just as applicable to MacKinnon's own *œuvre*. It will also be just as evident to our (hypothetical) reader that MacKinnon does not have anything amounting to an elaborate and comprehensive 'doctrine' of the Incarnation. Rather, he provides the reader with a series of clues which point to those features that would have to be present in any account faithful to the Gospel narratives and the christological traditions of the Church. But no attempt is made to press these clues into any kind of systematic framework. MacKinnon's is very much a method of 'indirection', and an expository and analytical presentation like the one attempted in this essay will inevitably make his

93

views seem somewhat 'tidier' than they in fact are. Having sounded this cautionary note, I shall begin by outlining some of the salient features which characterize MacKinnon's understanding of how the treatise *De Verbo Incarnato* is properly to be approached.[2]

I   Some clues

It must be stressed that the following 'themes' extracted from MacKinnon's writings are very much a series of headings which serve as prolegomena to further christological reflection: they are perhaps best seen as a *preliminary* to the kind of systematic christological formulation associated with, say, Wolfhart Pannenberg's *Jesus: God and Man* or Jon Sobrino's *Christology at the Crossroads* (as we have indicated in note 2).

(1) Since Christianity is, in Whitehead's well-known phrase, 'a religion in search of a metaphysic', any remotely adequate attempt to reflect on the nature and person of Jesus Christ will require the theologian to '[do] justice to some of the complexity of that quest . . .'[3]

(2) Christology pivots on the recognition that 'the unique Christian ultimate is acceptance of a movement from God to man, and not of one from man to God'.[4] It is a corollary of the foregoing that 'ultimate significance shall be received, not imposed'.[5]

(3) Christology cannot be articulated from a divine standpoint. The mystery of the divine self-donation in Christ 'happened at a depth which must hide from us its reality'. Hence, even if the theologian benefits from the insights afforded by ontological analysis, she has 'still to receive, as far as possible in its own terms', the mystery of this divine self-bestowal.[6]

(4) In christology we are enjoined to be epistemological 'realists', for 'perceiving [is] a finding rather than a fashioning' and truth '[resides] in the correspondence of proposition and fact'.[7]

(5) In christology we have to engage – inescapably – with the concrete and the particular: 'In the Word made flesh, we have to reckon not with the disclosure of a principle, but with a human history that, in virtue of its origin, grounds, and issue in eternity, is in its concrete particularity decisive for all who went before, who were its contemporaries, and who came after.'[8]

(6) While 'faith in Christ is not simply one more recognition of the presence of God to his creation', the theologian 'must also allow . . . our knowledge of Christ to illuminate for us the rich complexity of the natural and human worlds in which our ways are set'.[9] This dialectical tension has to be sustained by any christology concerned seriously to reflect on the reality of Jesus Christ: the doctrine of the Incarnation and the doctrine of creation are each inextricably bound up with the other.[10]

(7) 'Adoptionism' in christology, and 'exemplarism' in soteriology, are pitfalls that the theologian must guard against, for 'the ministry of Jesus is not an instance or an example of the love of God, but rather its very substance'.[11]

(8) The starting-point of christology is 'the relation of Christ to the Father, realized for our salvation in flesh and blood', and the abiding characteristic of this relation is 'a final, a haunting receptivity' on the part of the Nazarene.[12]

(9) The 'most fundamental task of christology . . . is the one of reconciling the use of the category of substance in the articulation of the christological problem with the recognition that it is the notion of kenosis which more than any other single notion points to the deepest sense of the mystery of the incarnation'.[13]

(10) The indispensability and the centrality of the category of *substance* for christological formulation has to be counterpoised by Kant's insight that this category is of an 'inherently limited character'. This insight in turn suggests 'immediately . . . that theology must fall with the tradition of negative theology'.[14]

(11) MacKinnon's endorsement of the Kantian *bildervorbot* has implications not only for the doctrine of God, but also for the way in which the theological 'task' is undertaken. For if God is 'incomprehensible', then theology – as 'speech about divinity' – has to allow this recognition to penetrate all its characteristic procedures. It has, necessarily, to proceed by a way of 'indirection', a way which involves a negative doubling back on every affirmation ventured. This, in fact, is MacKinnon's own way of 'doing' theology (though MacKinnon, as far as I know, has never given a systematic account of how he conceives the theological task). This way of doing theology sometimes prompts the complaint, which I have heard on more than one occasion, that MacKinnon seems unwilling to 'come straight out and say just what he means'. The person who makes this

complaint, however, fails to appreciate that for this kind of theologian, the 'point' of theology is not so much to *convey* certain items of 'information' (about God or the Holy Spirit or the Trinity or whatever), as to *enact* certain recognitions, or perhaps more appropriately, certain (unavoidable) *failures* of recognition, in the very sentences that one employs in the course of theological formulation. If God is fundamentally 'incomprehensible', then the difference between God and everything else is not patient of 'description': this difference can only be enacted or 'shown' (to use Wittgensteinian parlance).[15]

The foregoing brief and cursory headings – which only hint at the range and subtlety of MacKinnon's writings on christology in general, and on the Incarnation in particular – indicate quite clearly that the category of 'substance' (as it features in the *homoousion* and the 'hypostatic union') and the notion of 'kenosis' are absolutely decisive for MacKinnon's approach to christology.

II The *homoousion* and the 'hypostatic union'

Recalling Whitehead's dictum that Christianity is 'a religion in search of a metaphysic', MacKinnon is quite emphatic that '[it] was only when we had (and here I am drawing my own lesson, from Quick's teaching) made our own the great intellectual achievement of the *homoousion* that we could go on to approach the ultimate mystery of the divine self-giving that lay beyond it'.[16] When it comes to appropriating 'the great intellectual achievement of the *homoousion*', MacKinnon proposes that we use the distinction, made in the philosophy of logic, between first- and second-order propositions. First-order propositions express 'the simpler, more direct, more immediately moving christological affirmations of the gospel'.[17] The *homoousion*, by contrast, is a second-order proposition which ranges over these basic evangelical affirmations. More simply, first-order propositions are 'about' *Christ*, whereas second-order propositions are about *propositions 'about' Christ*. Another way of specifying the difference between the two orders of propositions is to say that the first-order propositions constitute something approximating to a 'theology of Jesus of Nazareth', whereas second-order propositions constitute christology *per se*.[18] This proposal has at least a couple of merits. Firstly, it could be said to have a basis in exegesis because it does seem to be the case that the Gospel traditions were in the first place 'theologies of Jesus', out of which grew more elaborate and complex patterns of christology. Secondly, the use of this distinction enables us to circumvent a minefield of problems expressed in questions concerning the omniscience, omnipotence, omnipresence, passibility, etc. of the incarnate Logos. It enables us to affirm both the true humanity of Jesus of Nazareth and the total involvement of divinity in his life, death and Resurrection. Unfortunately, this proposal of MacKinnon's is somewhat defective, inasmuch as it seems to confine christology to the noetic order, by construing the ascription of divinity to Jesus Christ on the basis of a *human* understanding of the relation between Christ and the Father, rather than on the basis of the mode (*per se*) of Jesus's relation to the Father. A disturbing element of subjectivity and abstraction is introduced into christology, and this is the very thing that MacKinnon has ceaselessly enjoined us to avoid. How can this element of subjectivity and abstraction be avoided? In an earlier article, I argued that the 'answer' to this difficulty lay in a different area of philosophical logic.[19] In a well-known paper criticizing Russell's Theory of Descriptions, P. F. Strawson has argued that the assignment of a truth-value to a proposition in certain cases *presupposes* the truth of other propositions. A proposition Q is said to presuppose a proposition P if and only if Q is neither true nor false unless P is true. For example, the truth of the proposition 'There is a country called "Oman" ' (P) is a *necessary condition* for the proposition 'Mrs Thatcher had a chance meeting with her son in Oman' (Q) to be either true or false. In short, the proposition 'Mrs Thatcher had a chance meeting with her son in Oman' *presupposes* the proposition 'There is a country called "Oman".'[20]

Using the notion of a *presupposition* it could be argued that it is preferable to construe 'incarnational' propositions not as second-order propositions, but precisely as instances of propositions whose truth must be presupposed in order that we may assign a truth-value to other more abstract theological propositions. Thus, for example, it could be argued that the proposition 'In Christ God reconciled all things to himself' (Q) presupposes the 'incarnational' proposition 'Jesus Christ is of the same substance as God (the Father)' (P), because it is a necessary condition of determining whether or not humankind is saved that God salvifically identifies with humanity by 'becoming incarnate' in Jesus of Nazareth. Only by God's direct and 'fleshly' engagement with the depths of human evil can our salvation be wrought.[21] Its *prima facie* plausibility notwithstanding, the proposal that 'incarnational' propositions be regarded as semantic presuppositions has one serious flaw: it does not pass the so-called 'test of negation' which is a defining characteristic of *semantic* presuppositions. According to this test, a proposition is genuinely a semantic presupposition if it is true even when the proposition of which it is the presupposition can be shown to be false. Thus 'Mrs Thatcher had a chance meeting with her son in Oman' presupposes 'There is a country called "Oman" ', *and* 'Mrs Thatcher did not have a chance meeting in Oman with her son' (also) presupposes 'There is a country called "Oman".'[22] But the denial of the soteriological proposition 'In Christ God reconciled all things to himself' does *not* presuppose the 'incarnational' proposition 'Jesus Christ is of the same substance as God (the Father)'. For, according to the Christian faith, if it is *false* that God reconciled all things to himself, then it is likewise *false* that Jesus Christ was God incarnate. There is no way for a Christian to affirm Christ to be God incarnate *and* to affirm at the same time that God's work of salvation was somehow 'unsuccessful'.[23] So our 'incarnational' proposition fails the 'test of negation'. The failure of 'incarnational' propositions to pass the 'test of negation', however, only disqualifies them from being *semantic* presuppositions: it may be possible to see them as belonging to another category of presupposition, viz., the *pragmatic*.[24] Robert Stalnaker characterizes a *pragmatic* presupposition thus:

> To presuppose a proposition in the pragmatic sense is to take its truth for granted, and to assume that others involved in the context do the same. This does not imply that the person need have any particular mental attitude toward the proposition, or that he need assume anything about the mental attitudes of the others in the context. Presuppositions are probably best viewed as complex dispositions which are manifested in linguistic behaviour. One has presuppositions in virtue of the statements he makes, the questions he asks, the commands he issues. Presuppositions are propositions implicitly *supposed* before the relevant linguistic business is transacted.[25]

Applying the notion of a *pragmatic* presupposition to christological discourse, we could argue that in principle 'incarnational' propo-

sitions are propositions which must be true in order that christological discourse may properly be transacted; they are propositions
which must be true if christological utterance is to be 'appropriate'.[26] Opponents of this proposal – among whom must surely be
numbered the authors of *The Myth of God Incarnate* – will of course
dispute its tenability. It will be impossible to resolve this issue in a
paper of such limited scope, but here the 'incarnational' theologian
has little alternative but to advert to soteriology – just as our patristic
forebears took the divinization of Christ's human nature to be the
foundation of our redemption, the 'incarnational' theologian today
will find herself being compelled to endorse the following 'axioms':
(i) that God redeems all things by breaking into the continuum of
(unredeemed) history; (ii) that our healing is accomplished only
when God allows our sin to *interrupt* his own life in and through
Jesus of Nazareth; and (iii) that this 'interruption' is possible only if
the very *being* of God engages and identifies with the human
condition to its very depths in and through Jesus of Nazareth.[27] Our
justification for upholding (i)–(iii), however, can ultimately come
only from Scripture. Scripture does not of course sponsor (i)–(iii) in
exactly the way we have formulated them, but it does speak about
Jesus Christ in a quite specific way, and to espouse (i)–(iii) is thus to
have a theology which professes to conform to the *modus loquendi* of
Scripture. We allow our discourse about Jesus Christ to be constrained by (i)–(iii) because Scripture requires us to speak of him in
just this (and not another) way.[28] It is being argued here, in other
words, that theological utterance is 'appropriate' when 'incarnational' propositions are (pragmatically) presupposed by those
who engage in such utterance, and that what 'justifies' the
deployment of such propositions as (pragmatic) presuppositions is
the *modus loquendi* of Scripture.

The centrality of the *modus loquendi* of Scripture for theological
discourse brings this discourse, with its controlling metaphor of
'incarnation', into the sphere of ecclesiology. For the Church is the
community which consents to be interrogated by the Scriptures in
such a way that it learns – slowly, laboriously and sometimes
painfully – to live the way of Jesus.[29] 'Incarnational' propositions are
thus the indispensable underpinning of the ecclesial community's
'pedagogy of discipleship', a 'pedagogy' which is inaugurated when
the believer enters the Church's Gospel-shaped narrative 'space'. She

is baptized – 'linguistically' or 'textually' – when she consents to be 'interrogated' by these narratives (which, of course, have 'incarnational' propositions as their pragmatic presuppositions). The ecclesial community's origin is thus irreducibly 'incarnational'.[30] The so-called 'hermeneutical circle' is in evidence at this juncture: 'incarnational' discourse is justified by the christological *modus loquendi* of Scripture, and yet Scripture exercises its interrogative function in the 'pedagogy of discipleship' precisely because 'incarnational' propositions are 'pragmatically' presupposed by the narratives which motivate and ground this 'pedagogy'. This is hardly surprising: Scripture demands that we speak of Jesus Christ in this 'incarnational' way, and at the same time we begin to 'make sense' of Scripture by speaking of Jesus in just this ('incarnational') way.

The claim that the scriptural 'narrative' operates explicitly and canonically in the believing community's 'performance' of the Scriptures should not be taken to imply that it is the narratives *themselves*, as opposed to the process of *entering* into the narratives, which are of real and ultimate significance for the Church's 'pedagogy of discipleship'. To 'perform' a narrative one has to learn to 'read' it, and the Church *can* be the community which 'performs' the Scriptures because it *also* happens to be the community which determines the 'shape' of our reading, but it first does this by enabling us to undergo what is best described as a narrative 'baptism'. The Church prepares us for an immersion into narrative, an immersion described by Fredric Jameson (in his characterization of a kind of 'realism' which he calls 'magic realism') as

the shock of *entry* into narrative, which so often resembles the body's tentative immersion in an unfamiliar element, with all the subliminal anxieties of such submersion: the half-articulated fear of what the surface of the liquid conceals; a sense of our vulnerability along with the archaic horror of impure contact with the unclean; the anticipation of fatigue also, of the intellectual effort about to be demanded in the slow apprenticeship of unknown characters and their elaborate situations, as though, beneath the surface excitement of adventure promised, there persisted some deep ambivalence at the dawning sacrifice of the self to the narrative text.[31]

The Church is the community which enables this baptism – 'the dawning sacrifice of the self to the text' – to take place and to be lived through. This inaugural immersion into the scriptural narratives frees the Christian to 'read' and 'live' these texts (with their controlling metaphor of 'incarnation') in a 'self-sacrificial' way, that is, in a way which places her in that 'slow apprenticeship of unknown characters and their elaborate situations' which is the Church's 'pedagogy of discipleship'. The Church, it could be said, is (at least in part) the 'event' of this narrative 'baptism'.[32]

But does such an ecclesially-centred 'grammatical' reading of 'incarnational' propositions capture everything that MacKinnon wishes to affirm when he embraces the 'hypostatic union' and the concomitant notion of the *homoousion*? What about the Platonic and the Aristotelian metaphysical frameworks which constitute the typical, and perhaps even the essential, background for these notions? Does not MacKinnon accord the ontologies of Plato and Aristotle a centrality with which we have simply failed to reckon? These questions advertise complex matters which cannot be dealt with in a paragraph or two. But here we should heed Christopher Stead's salutary reminder, made with reference to the deliberations of the fathers of Nicaea, that '[there] is ... no question of "an" orthodox or "a" heretical use of *ousia*; the case is rather that *within* this generally accepted and little-discussed structure of usage certain differences of meaning and application acquired importance or began to be recognized'.[33] And these applications and discriminations of the term *ousia* were from the beginning theologically constrained; indeed, as Stead again points out, Athanasius (whose views are decisive for any specification of christological orthodoxy), in his desire to distance himself from the Origenism of Alexander of Alexandria, used *homoousios* in a way that marked a clear asymmetricality between the Father and the Son:

> Athanasius never says that the Father and Son are *homoousioi*; still less, of course, that the Father is *homoousios* with the Son. Nor does he ever connect the term with a noun referring to the Godhead as a whole; he does not speak of the 'consubstantial Trinity' (as he does of the 'indivisible Trinity'), nor of the 'consubstantial Godhead' (as he does of 'the one Godhead').[34]

It is fairly clear, therefore, that from the beginning the term *homoousios* was used heuristically to secure explicitly *theological* objectives, objectives which derive their ultimate force and inspiration from the conviction of redemption, i.e., the determinative conviction which receives expression in the paradigmatic 'axioms' (i)–(iii). Our terminological preferences notwithstanding, I cannot see how any deployment of the notion of 'substance' in the sphere of christology can do anything more than safeguard these paradigmatic 'axioms'. There is thus no real need, in christological reflection, to set absolute store by the category of 'substance' in (say) its identifiably Aristotelian gloss: as long as our christological discourse guarantees the paradigmatic 'axioms' (i)–(iii), we have a *prima facie* warrant for espousing our particular christological 'grammar' (even if it does not happen to employ terminology of a recognizable Aristotelian provenance). The main consideration here must surely be to 'save' the truths vouchsafed by the christological *modus loquendi* of Scripture and by the tradition of the Church; certain special cases apart, once our paradigmatic 'axioms' have been secured, there can be no real warrant for demanding that we should commit ourselves to all the historically-conditioned 'surface' forms used traditionally to convey these 'truths'.[35] Thus George Lindbeck is right when he says that

[the] terminology and concepts of 'one substance and three persons' or 'two natures' may be absent, but if the same rules that guided the formation of the original paradigms are operative in the construction of the new formulations, they express one and the same doctrine. There may ... be complete faithfulness to classical Trinitarianism and Christology even when the imagery of Nicaea and Chalcedon have disappeared from the theology and ordinary worship, preaching, and devotion.[36]

It is in this ecclesially-focused way, and in this 'grammatical' sense, therefore, that the notions of *homoousios* and the 'hypostatic union' find their proper employment.

III   'Kenosis'

Speaking of Oliver Quick's treatment of the divine self-limitation in the act of creation, MacKinnon says:

God is related to his world, and though the world depends asymmetrically upon him and its creation is an act of his sovereign freedom, it exists as something with which (to speak anthropomorphically) God has to come to terms. This coming to terms with the world is focused in the Incarnation, and if we are prepared to approach the kenosis of the divine condescension by finding limitation self-imposed by God on himself as creator, it is through the kenosis we come to understand that limitation for what it is.[37]

The clear implication of this passage is that, unlike the category of 'incarnation', the notion of kenosis belongs to a first-order language: this notion does not merely 'regulate' speech about 'godness'; it tells us, in a suitably qualified way, what the 'divine condescension' in creation is 'about'. But not only does the doctrine of kenosis indicate to us what 'godness' is about (at least *vis-à-vis* creation); it also has implications for our understanding of Christ's consciousness: 'Kenosis is an ontological mystery . . . it is one that has a profound bearing on the way we represent . . . the manner of Christ's consciousness as incarnate.'[38] In addition, we 'see kenosis as in effect the principle that bids us measure the Logos–Christ by the *Christus-patiens*'.[39] Here we get to the heart of MacKinnon's understanding of the divine kenosis. What MacKinnon, seemingly, wants to do is to 'qualify' the divine Logos by the *Christus-patiens*, albeit without subscribing to the patently 'mythological' and metaphysically problematic idea of a 'depotentiated' Logos. The 'strange, haunting alternation, even interpenetration of humility and authority, receptivity and confident demand' displayed by Jesus of Nazareth are thus the 'only key we have to the inner ways of God, and the only sure guide to the posture befitting us in the world he has fashioned'.[40] The advantage of upholding a kenotic theory which, somewhat like MacKinnon's, eschews talk of a 'divestment of divine attributes' on the part of the incarnate Logos is that it goes a long way to enabling the kenoticist to avoid the strictures of her opponents, who charge her theory with being 'clearly incoherent' (Don Cupitt); a 'joke' (Brian Davies); and an 'unacceptable . . . temporary theophany' (D. M. Baillie).[41] But does MacKinnon really have a cast-iron exemption from these strictures? In order to safeguard himself from these criticisms of the kenotic theory he would perhaps need to reformulate the theory in a somewhat different way – a way which bypasses all talk of the 'consciousness' of Christ, and so forth – by seeing it in terms of what Ray S. Anderson has called 'the question of historical transcendence', that is, the question 'Can the transcendence of God be understood in an utterly historical form?'[42] By framing the so-called 'kenotic' question in the way recommended by Anderson we can be far more confident of avoiding the problematic 'empiricism' which bedevils so many – some would say, all – versions of the kenotic theory.[43]

The potential fruitfulness of Anderson's rethematization of the

'kenotic' question becomes evident when we scrutinize his deline-
ation of what he calls the 'inner logic of historical transcendence'.
According to Anderson, there are two strands to this 'inner logic';

first of all, the transcendence of God is God's *placing* of himself into
concrete, historical relation to man as the limiting reality of man's authentic
existence. As the Logos becomes increasingly identified with Israel, the
transcendence of God becomes increasingly ... material ... When man
comes up against this limit of transcendence, his existence is qualified by the
'God who is for man'. Secondly, the transcendence of God acts as the
'covenant response' which is made possible by the transcendent limit itself.
Because this covenant response is intrinsic to the creation–covenant, it is
man's original affirmation of his own authentic humanity in terms of
response in freedom towards God. Thus, from the human side, God's
transcendence works out the covenant response through the humanity of
Israel, pointing towards the 'Man who is for God'. This logic of Incarnation
converges upon the person of Jesus Christ and seeks its concrete fulfilment.
He is the 'God who is for man', and at the same time, the 'Man who is for
God'.[44]

Anderson then asks whether the kenosis can be understood as the
transcendence of divinity in both these ways. He answers in the
affirmative, but rejects the suggestion that this divine 'self-
emptying' takes the form of a surrendering of the attributes of
divinity on the part of incarnate Logos:

This 'way of kenosis' which we see as the movement of the Son towards the
Father in the Spirit, is not a kenosis or a self-emptying in the form of a
renunciation of the nature of God himself, but is a self-emptying precisely
because self-renunciation is the very nature of God himself ... It is the
renunciation of a negative self-existence, in the form of a 'separate' kind of
existence, which constitutes the eternal relation of Father, Son and Spirit.
Thus, the Incarnation of the Son is the same Spirit of positive self-renunciation which is the very nature of divine existence. It is actually the dynamic
dimension of love as activity.[45]

This statement of the 'inner logic of historical' transcendence is beset
by at least three weaknesses, a couple of which are minor and the
third somewhat more severe. Firstly, and less importantly, Anderson's elucidation of this 'inner logic' implies a theological anthropology too much afflicted by the resonances of an existentialist
'jargon of authenticity'. Secondly, and again less importantly, it seems
to imply that God is 'placeable', thereby threatening not only the

transcendence of divinity, but also the very 'logic' of the dynamism of divine love. Anderson, to his credit, is all too aware of this second problem, and warns us that

our language, with its 'opticizing' tendencies, becomes too rigid for the dynamic and fluid inner logic of the transcendence of God, which is an *intra*-active personal reality of love and not just an *inter*-active force. When the eternal Subject prays to the eternal Subject, as a son talks with a father, we can hear what we cannot see – the intra-action of divine communion with one of the voices speaking out of history.[46]

The transcendence of divinity can perhaps be better safeguarded by pushing Anderson's suggestion that God is not a self-enclosed Absolute in a more explicitly 'Thomist' direction, and seeing the divine creative act as the opening out of a dynamism *within* God, so that the mystery of God 'creates' by emptying itself out 'kenotically', in this way making room 'within' itself for the non-divine.[47] As long as Anderson retains the 'difference' between two (or three?) apparently self-positing, separate, eternal Subjects (one of whom – a kind of positive *datum* – 'speaks out of history'), and continues to posit a dialectical *unity* between an 'intra-active' (i.e., inner-trinitarian) reality and an 'inter-active' (i.e., extra-trinitarian) force, his otherwise profound characterization of God's historical transcendence will be vitiated by a deficiently personalist trinitarianism.[48] Thirdly, and most seriously, the anchoring of the divine kenosis on a unique act of divine 'self-renunciation' gives Anderson's divinity the form of a fathomless, but somehow '*wilful*', plenitude.[49]

How then is the divine kenosis to be thematized? Anderson is not wrong to transpose the so-called 'kenotic' question into the question of God's 'historical transcendence'. Indeed, he is right – for, 'semantics' (as opposed to 'syntax') apart, the 'grammar' of the divine kenosis is no more, and no less, than the 'grammar' of 'incarnation'. In working out the 'grammar' of 'kenosis', we have to bear in mind that since 'kenosis' (like 'incarnation') requires us to speak of God, we cannot hope to use this term *descriptively*.[50] Hence, we have no adequate way of 'representing' the divine kenosis, and therefore have no alternative but to construe it as a 'logically primitive' notion, i.e., a notion that we 'pragmatically presuppose' in our christological discourse. We discourse 'appropriately' about

Jesus Christ only in so far as we employ this notion (and use it exclusively of him), and we derive our justification for using it from the christological *modus loquendi* of Scripture.[51] It should be noted, however, that while the 'syntax' of 'kenosis' is the same as the one for 'incarnation', its 'semantics' is somewhat different. It was seen in the previous section that 'incarnational' propositions have the regulative function of safeguarding the conviction of redemption, i.e., the paradigmatic 'axioms' (i)–(iii). 'Kenosis' does not have this regulative function: to do so it would have to connote – in the way that '*homoousios*' does – a generic identity between the 'being' of God and the 'being' of Jesus Christ, and this of course it does not do. To grasp the 'semantics' of the divine kenosis we have therefore to advert to a different context – that of creation – and see 'kenosis' in terms of God 'making room' within the mystery of the divinity for the order of finite things. In creation we are, as it were, summoned to think of all things in their proper relation to God. In so doing, we see ourselves as creatures, as terminating a relation of radical dependence on that from which we have our being.[52] By seeing the matter thus – that is, by seeing all things as themselves standing in a transcendent relation to God – we see our own relation to the world and its Creator in a different light. To have a sense of the 'logic' of creation is therefore to perceive the 'need' to change our thinking, speaking and doing. It is to engage with the world and its Creator in a new and different way. To seek to do this in a Christ-shaped world, to acknowledge that the world has this shape, is to begin to grasp the 'logic' of the divine kenosis. It is a 'logic' which invites us to embark on, or to recognize that we are already embarked on, the Church's 'pedagogy of discipleship'.[53]

Notes

1   Donald MacKinnon, 'Oliver Chase Quick as a Theologian', unpublished manuscript, p. 1. Hereinafter referred to as 'Quick'. Underpinning all of MacKinnon's writings on christological themes is the question whether the figure of Christ remains determinative for christological reflection, or whether one resorts to a religious epistemology for a framework with which to 'understand' the Incarnation. MacKinnon rejects the latter alternative, and stresses the unique importance of christology as the route to 'theological realism'. On these themes, cf. ' "Substance" in Christology: A Cross-Bench View', in

S. W. Sykes and J. P. Clayton, eds., *Christ, Faith and History: Cambridge Studies in Christology* (Cambridge, 1972), pp. 279–300 (hereinafter referred to as 'Substance').

2 As is the case with most kinds of christological reflection, MacKinnon's understanding of 'incarnation' can be seen to contain two quite separate strands. The first pertains to a christology *per se*, that is, a substantive explication of the 'nature' and person of Jesus Christ. The second takes the form of a '*meta*-christology', that is, a second-level discourse which attempts to specify the appropriate procedures and norms which govern a first-level christological language. A scrutiny of MacKinnon's writings will show that he accords primacy to the second of these two strands. MacKinnon's preponderant concern, seemingly, is with the christological agenda set before us by Scripture and tradition, and also the philosophical and theological constraints which operate on christological reflection. Where the first strand is concerned, he is generally content to accept the accounts of the Gospel writers (while of course giving due regard to the findings of New Testament scholarship) and the formulations of the Church tradition (especially the christological 'definitions' promulgated at Nicaea and Chalcedon). It goes without saying that 'modern' theologians – such as Gore, Weston, Scott-Holland, Quick, von Balthasar, Moltmann and Jüngel – also feature prominently in MacKinnon's writings.

3 The invocation of Whitehead's dictum is in fact Quick's, though MacKinnon reports it in 'Quick' without any qualification or dissent. Cf. 'Quick', p. 2, from which the quotation is also taken. MacKinnon, though, would certainly dissent from Whitehead's resolutely 'pre-Kantian' suggestion that God is 'the chief exemplification . . . [of] all metaphysical principles'. For this claim, which is foundational to Whitehead's metaphysical system, see his *Process and Reality* (New York, 1929), p. 521.

MacKinnon's affirmation of the necessity of 'ontological analysis' is to be found in the following works: 'Substance', *passim*; 'The Relation of the Doctrines of the Incarnation and the Trinity', in Richard W. A. McKinney, ed., *Creation, Christ and Culture: Studies in Honour of T. F. Torrance* (Edinburgh, 1976), pp. 92–107 (hereinafter referred to as 'Incarnation and Trinity'); and 'The Problem of the "System of Projection" Appropriate to Christian Theological Statements', in Donald MacKinnon, *Explorations in Theology* (London, 1979), p. 78 (hereinafter referred to as 'The Problem of the "System of Projection" ').

4 'Quick', p. 3. Cf. also 'Incarnation and Trinity', p. 98; and the early, 'Barthian', work *God the Living and the True* (London, 1940), pp. 18ff. On MacKinnon's relation to the 'early Barth', cf. Richard Roberts, 'Theological Rhetoric and Moral Passion in the Light of MacKinnon's "Barth" ', pp. 1ff. above.

5 'Kenosis and Establishment', in MacKinnon's collection of essays The Stripping of the Altars (London, 1969), p. 40. MacKinnon takes the reception (as opposed to the imposition) of 'ultimate significance' to '[belong] to the heart of the idea of kenosis' (ibid.).

6 'Quick', p. 8.

7 Cf. MacKinnon's contribution to the Barth festschrift, 'Philosophy and Christology', reprinted in Borderlands of Theology and Other Essays (London, 1968), pp. 55–81. Quotation taken from p. 63. A fuller treatment of the role of the correspondence theory of truth in christological reflection is to be found in 'The Problem of the "System of Projection" ', pp. 79ff. Cf. also 'Idealism and Realism: An Old Controversy Renewed', in Explorations in Theology, pp. 138–50; and 'The Conflict Between Realism and Idealism', Explorations, pp. 151–65.

8 'Subjective and Objective Conceptions of Atonement', in F. G. Healey, ed., Prospect for Theology: Essays in Honour of H. H. Farmer (London, 1966), p. 173. Cf. also 'Absolute and Relative in History: A Theological Reflection on the Centenary of Lenin's Birth', in Explorations in Theology, pp. 55–69, and 'Philosophy and Christology', pp. 58, 64, 67, 75, 78 and 81.

9 'Quick', p. 20. MacKinnon thus welcomes Teilhard de Chardin's and Charles Raven's stress on the need to employ a cosmic perspective when it comes to expressing the significance of Christ's saving work. On this see also 'The Future of Man', in Explorations in Theology, pp. 4–5.

10 For MacKinnon's insistence that 'the doctrine of the incarnation assumes a doctrine of creation', cf. 'Prolegomena to Christology', The Journal of Theological Studies, 23 (1982), p. 156. The stress is MacKinnon's. Cf. also 'Incarnation and Trinity', p. 99.

11 'Philosophy and Christology', p. 68.

12 'Incarnation and Trinity', p. 98. On 'receptivity' as a trinitarian attribute, see also MacKinnon's review of Edward Schillebeeckx's Jesus and Christ books, in The Scottish Journal of Religious Studies, 1 (1980), p. 60.

13 'Substance', p. 297. As will soon be indicated, with this affirmation we get to the very heart of MacKinnon's understanding of the christological task. My essay will therefore take the form of a 'grammatical' exploration of the homoousion and the 'hypostatic union' (in section II) and the divine 'kenosis' (in section III).

14 For MacKinnon's stress on the importance of the Kantian version of the via negativa for theology, cf. The Problem of Metaphysics (Cambridge, 1974), p. 9; 'Kant's Philosophy of Religion', Philosophy, 50 (1975), p. 141; and 'Some Aspects of the Treatment of Christianity by the British Idealists', Religious Studies, 20 (1984), pp. 143–4. The principle that there can be no 'ratio' or 'order' between finite and infinite lies at the heart of MacKinnon's 'The Inexpressibility of God', Theology, 79

(1976), pp. 200–6. More generally, MacKinnon would, I suspect, be inclined to endorse von Balthasar's claim that modern dogmatics gives virtually no place to the theme of God's incomprehensibility. *Cf.* Hans Urs von Balthasar, 'The Unknown God', in M. Kehl and W. Löser, eds., *The von Balthasar Reader* (New York, 1982), pp. 181–7. MacKinnon's relation to Kant is perceptively examined in John Milbank, ' "Between Purgation and Illumination": A Critique of the Theology of Right', pp. 161–96 below.

15 The problem of style as enactment is raised not only by MacKinnon's 'theological' deployment of the Kantian ban on conceiving the Absolute but also by works as diverse as Derrida's *Of Grammatology* and Fredric Jameson's *The Political Unconscious*. In Derrida's eyes, we cannot 'tell it straight' because the movement of language is that of an unlimited semiosis, an infinite series of deferrals and displacements which collapses the 'real' into the (erasable) 'trace'. In Jameson's case, the question of style as enactment is raised by his (Marxist) refusal to sanction a bourgeois ideology which professes to uphold the stylistic values of 'lucidity' and 'simplicity' while simultaneously obscuring its role in legitimizing the existing unjust social order. Cf. Jacques Derrida, *Of Grammatology*, trans. Gayatri Chakravorty Spivak (Baltimore, 1974); and Fredric Jameson, *The Political Unconscious: Narrative as Socially Symbolic Act* (London, 1981). I am indebted to William C. Dowling's *Jameson, Althusser, Marx: An Introduction to 'The Political Unconscious'* (London, 1984) for an illuminating discussion of the problem of style as enactment as it arises in the work of Derrida and Jameson; see especially pp. 10–12.

16 'Quick', p. 6. The so-called 'hypostatic union' – i.e. the doctrine that the divine Logos is the unique subject in which the humanity of Jesus subsists – calls for the *homoousion* as its presupposition, though obviously in the christological tradition the latter does not connote the former: the Council of Nicaea (325) not only antedates but also precedes, in terms of christological development, the Council of Ephesus (431). This asymmetricality apart, I will use the terms 'hypostatic union' and *homoousion* interchangeably. Thus, when MacKinnon argues that the 'hypostatic union' is the statement of a problem, and not a 'solution', he must, by extension of logic, say the same of the *homoousion*. For this statement of MacKinnon's, cf. 'Prolegomena', p. 151.

17 'Substance', pp. 291ff. A similar proposal is to be found in Edward Schillebeeckx, *Jesus: An Experiment in Christology*, trans. Hubert Hoskins (London, 1979), p. 549; and *Interim Report on the Books JESUS & CHRIST*, trans. John Bowden (London, 1980), pp. 93–7.

18 It is not being implied here that the later christologies are an 'advance' on what was there before, so that the authors of, say, the fourth-century *De*

Incarnatione or the eleventh-century *Cur Deus Homo* are in the happy position of being more 'knowledgeable' about the nature and person of Jesus Christ than the four evangelists. For criticism of this 'incremental' theory of the genesis and growth of christology, see C. F. D. Moule, *The Origin of Christology* (Cambridge, 1977), pp. 2ff. A similar disavowal of such evolutionary accounts of the rise of christology is implict in Martin Hengel, *The Son of God: The Origin of Christology and the History of Jewish–Hellenistic Religion*, trans. John Bowden (London, 1976), pp. 66ff.

19 Kenneth Surin, 'Atonement and Christology', *Neue Zeitschrift für Systematische Theologie und Religionsphilosophie*, 24 (1982), pp. 131–49.

20 Here I follow the line of argument adumbrated by P. F. Strawson in his 'On Referring', *Mind*, 59 (1950), pp. 320–44.

21 Here I am seeking to provide a logico–linguistic explication of Pannenberg's dictum that '[the] divinity of Christ remains the *presupposition* for his saving significance for us'. Cf. his *Jesus: God and Man*, trans. L. L. Wilkins and D. A. Priebe (London, 1968), p. 38. The stress is Pannenberg's. I shall not undertake the very important (and 'grammatically' prior) task of specifying what exactly is involved in professing the truth of 'incarnational' propositions such as 'Jesus Christ is one in being with God'. It will not be necessary to make such a specification at this juncture because the account of 'incarnational' propositions just given cannot be accepted as it stands (as we shall see shortly). It is important to acknowledge that Pannenberg restricts the presuppositional role of the divinity of Christ to the realm of soteriology. He criticizes Barth for using the divinity of Christ as the presupposition for christology *simpliciter*, arguing that '[instead] of presupposing it, we must first inquire about how Jesus' appearance in history led to the recognition of his divinity' (p. 34). This criticism is repeated in Alister E. McGrath, *The Making of Modern German Christology: From the Enlightenment to Pannenberg* (Oxford, 1986), p. 114. The strictures of Pannenberg and McGrath are misplaced. Firstly, 'divinity' is fundamentally such that it is not something that we can ever hope to 'recognize' or 'pick out'. Secondly, the assumption behind this criticism – viz., that the invocation of the divinity of Christ as the ('absolute') presupposition for christological discourse necessarily prescinds from any kind of *historicizing* appropriation of the nature and person of Jesus Christ – is one that is easily discredited by locating the concept of *presupposition* in a formal pragmatics. This will be attempted shortly.

22 For the 'test of negation', see Paul and Carol Kiparsky, 'Fact', in D. D. Steinberg and L. A. Jakobovits, eds., *Semantics* (Cambridge, 1971), p. 351; and George Lakoff, 'Linguistics and Natural Logic', *Synthese*, 22 (1970), pp. 175–6. This test does not work for certain kinds of presup-

position. On this cf. F. R. Palmer, *Semantics* (Cambridge, 1981), pp. 167ff.

23 In this connection, the following remarks of R. H. Fuller are germane: '[in] the New Testament men are first confronted by the history of Jesus of Nazareth – by what he said and did – and they respond to it in terms of a Christology ... Through what he does they come to see who he is.' Cf. his *The Foundations of New Testament Christology* (London, 1969), p. 15. A similar statement is to be found in P. T. Forsyth, *The Person and Place of Jesus Christ*, 4th ed. (London, 1930), p. 220. Likewise, Pannenberg insists that '[the] confession of faith in Jesus is not to be separated from Jesus' significance for us'; cf. *Jesus: God and Man*, p. 38. However, Pannenberg immediately goes on to say of Christ that '[the] soteriological interest cannot ... be the principle of Christological doctrine ... [The] saving significance of his divinity is the reason why we take *interest* in the question of his divinity.' The stress is Pannenberg's. Pannenberg understates the relation between christology and soteriology by maintaining that it is (merely) one of 'interest'. While the affirmation of Jesus Christ as Saviour is in no sense the *presupposition* of the affirmation of his divinity (and to this extent Pannenberg is right), the connection between the two affirmations is not merely heuristic: *pace* Pannenberg, it takes the form of what H. P. Grice has termed a 'conversational implicature' (or what we shall later call a 'pragmatic presupposition'). Cf. Grice's 'Logic and Conversation', in P. Cole and J. L. Morgan, eds., *Syntax and Semantics, 3: Speech Acts* (New York and London, 1975), pp. 41–58; cf. also James D. McCawley, *Everything that Linguists have Always Wanted to Know about Logic* (Oxford, 1981), pp. 215–34.

24 For the distinction between semantic and pragmatic presupposition, see E. L. Keenan, 'Two Kinds of Presupposition in Natural Language', in C. J. Fillmore and D. T. Langendoen, eds., *Studies in Linguistic Semantics* (New York, 1971), pp. 45–54; Robert C. Stalnaker, 'Pragmatics', *Synthese*, 22 (1970), pp. 272–89; and McCawley, *Everything that Linguists have Always Wanted to Know*, pp. 251–8. In what follows I shall rehearse ideas presented mainly in Stalnaker's article.

25 Stalnaker, 'Pragmatics', pp. 279–80. Another way of distinguishing between semantic and pragmatic presupposition is to say that the latter is a relationship between an utterance and a proposition, whereas the former is a relationship between two propositions. On this, cf. McCawley, *Everything that Linguists have Always Wanted to Know*, pp. 237–8.

26 Here I am paraphrasing McCawley, *Everything that Linguists have Always Wanted to Know*, p. 238.

27 I take (iii) to express the nub of the patristic axiom (which lies at the heart of the 'physical' theories of the atonement formulated by Athanasius and Gregory of Nyssa) that 'the unassumed is the unhealed'. Maurice Wiles

has argued that this axiom has no plausibility for modern men and women because it belongs to a Platonic anthropology in which human nature is problematically regarded as a universal in which all individual human beings participate. Cf. his essay 'The Unassumed is the Unhealed', in *Working Papers in Doctrine* (London, 1976), pp. 122–31, especially p. 117. I do not have the space to attempt it here, but it seems to me that Wiles's objection to this patristic axiom *can* be overcome by resorting to the theory of ideas developed by Walter Benjamin in the 'Epistemo-Critical Prologue' to his *The Origin of German Tragic Drama*, trans. J. Osborne (London, 1977), pp. 27–56. In this 'Prologue', Benjamin maintains that there are universals, but that these can be grasped only within (empirical) particulars. In this process of conceptual ordering, (particular) objects *become* their (universal) ideas, and so although ideas are 'eternal' they none the less are objective significations of 'historical crystallizations' which emerge from the 'process of becoming and disappearance' that constitutes history. On this, see *The Origin*, p. 45. There is no reason why the patristic axiom criticized by Wiles cannot in principle be explicated in the neo-Platonic (and yet historicizing) epistemology developed by Benjamin. Wiles, it seems, has failed to acknowledge the possibility that even the Platonic Forms can be located in a historicizing and historicized account of cognition.

28 Here I follow the procedure adumbrated by St Thomas Aquinas in his *Summa Contra Gentiles*, IV, 39, 1–3. Cf. the translation of C. J. O'Neil (Notre Dame, Indiana, 1975), Vol. 4, pp. 189–90. I have so far spoken of *homoousios* as generic, though it should be borne in mind that MacKinnon is anxious to note that it is possible for more to be at issue than this. For this cautionary note, cf. 'Substance', p. 291.

29 A similar perspective on the role of the Scriptures is to be found in Nicholas Lash, 'Performing the Scriptures', in his collection of essays *Theology on the Way to Emmaus* (London, 1986), pp. 37–46. My proposal differs from Lash's in two respects: I possibly place greater stress on the 'interrogative' aspect of the performance, and, as we shall see shortly, my account gives emphasis not just to the Scriptural narratives, but especially to the point of *entry* into these narratives.

30 My remarks here accord in principle with Rowan Williams's account of 'the generative significance' of Jesus Christ for the ecclesial community; cf. his 'Trinity and Revelation', *Modern Theology*, 2 (1986), pp. 197–212. The attention given in this essay to the nexus between Christ and Church should not be taken to imply that there is no place for an identification of the Church with the Spirit. Leonardo Boff is surely right when he maintains that the Church's origin is both christological *and* pneumatological; cf. his *Church: Charism and Power (Liber-*

ation Theology and the Institutional Church), trans. J. W. Diercksmeier (London, 1985), pp. 144–53.

31 Fredric Jameson, 'On Magic Realism in Film,' *Critical Inquiry*, 12 (1986), p. 304.

32 On the Church as 'event', see Leonardo Boff, *Saint Francis: A Model for Human Liberation*, trans. J. W. Diercksmeier (London, 1985), p. 129. The Church of course does more than simply regulate the 'reading' of texts – it also 'forms' them when it evolves its tradition. But the notion of a 'textual' or 'narrative' baptism can also be extended to include texts associated with tradition (as opposed to Scripture). The background 'theory' of religious and theological language presupposed by the notion of a 'textual' (and *ex hypothesis* 'linguistic') baptism is provided in my 'Is it True What They Say About "Theological Realism"?' in my collection of essays, *The Turnings of Darkness and Light: Essays in Philosophical and Systematic Theology* (Cambridge University Press, 1989).

33 Christopher Stead, *Divine Substance* (Oxford, 1977), p. 225 (Stead's emphasis).

34 *Divine Substance*, p. 260.

35 Hence it is no surprise to find so 'orthodox' a figure as Charles Gore maintaining that '[if] we would justify [the Chalcedonian definition] we must recognise very frankly that the purpose of the dogmas was negative – to exclude certain fundamentally misleading interpretations of the person of Christ'. Cf. his *The Incarnation of the Son of God: Bampton Lectures 1891*, 2nd ed. (London, 1909), p. 228. My remarks need to be heavily qualified in two respects. Firstly, what we take to be the 'surface' expression of a theological truth may have penetrated very deeply into the practice of the liturgy, thereby becoming an indispensable source of what Theodore W. Jennings calls 'ritual knowledge'; cf. his 'On Ritual Knowledge', *The Journal of Religion*, 62 (1982), pp. 111–27. In his case, the deeper ritual or 'practical' resonance of a particular 'surface' formulation will certainly enjoin that we retain it. Secondly, it should be clear that our paradigmatic 'axioms' are only intended to regulate a specifically *christological* discourse. It is highly likely that quite different 'axioms' will become paradigmatic once we move beyond such a discourse into other areas of theological language.

36 George A. Lindbeck, *The Nature of Doctrine: Religion and Theology in a Postliberal Age* (London, 1984), p. 95. Our paradigmatic 'axioms' are intended as a christological and soteriological complement to Lindbeck's principles of 'monotheism', 'historical specificity' and 'Christological maximalism'. For these principles, see p. 94.

37 'Quick', p. 10a.

38 'Philosophy and Christology', p. 80. In saying this MacKinnon professes to follow 'men like Gore, Scott-Holland and Weston' (*ibid.*).

39 'Scott-Holland and Contemporary Needs', *Borderlands*, p. 114.

40 'Prolegomena', p. 153, and 'Scott-Holland', p. 111. MacKinnon's work on the kenotic doctrine can be seen as a corrective to the tendency, displayed by Gore and Illingworth among others, to valorize the Incarnation at the expense of the doctrine of reconciliation. MacKinnon has learnt well from Barth; hence his ability to administer this corrective. On this valorization on the part of Gore and Illingworth, see Thomas A. Langford's illuminating study, *In Search of Foundations: English Theology 1900–1920* (New York, 1969), especially pp. 187ff.

41 Cf. Don Cupitt, 'Mr Hebblethwaite on the Incarnation', in Michael Goulder, ed., *Incarnation and Myth: The Debate Continued* (London, 1979), p. 45; Brian Davies, *Thinking About God* (London, 1985), p. 306; and D. M. Baillie, *God Was in Christ: An Essay on Incarnation and Atonement*, 2nd ed. (London, 1961), pp. 96–8. Cf. also J. M. Creed, *The Divinity of Jesus Christ: A Study in the History of Christian Doctrine Since Kant* (London, 1964), p. 135.

42 Ray S. Anderson, *Historical Transcendence and the Reality of God: A Christological Critique* (London, 1975), p. 148.

43 For a recent example of such an 'empiricism' in formulating a kenosis-christology, see David Brown, *The Divine Trinity* (London, 1985), and the exchange between us in *Modern Theology*, 2 (1986), pp. 235–76. Nowhere is this 'empiricism' more evident than in Brown's discussion of the 'coherence' of the Incarnation in *The Divine Trinity*, when he weighs up the respective merits of the Chalcedonian and the kenotic patterns of christology and says: 'The force of the arguments either way thus seems to me to be finely balanced, and a definitive choice impossible, though obviously to God the Son something swung the balance and he became incarnate in one way rather than the other' (p. 271). Brown insists that all his statements are to be construed analogically, but it is hard to avoid forming the picture of a Son confronted by two 'models' – one articulated by the Council of Chalcedon and the other based on a certain reading (or misreading!) of, say, the christological hymn in Philippians 2:5–11 – and then having to decide which of these two 'models' contains the better prescription for 'taking flesh'. To avoid such a problematic 'empiricism' in addressing the 'standard' form of the kenotic theory, one has to be insistent in facing up to the patently mythological character of the notion of kenosis. MacKinnon certainly evinces such a determination. But adopting Anderson's recasting of the 'kenotic' question affords us the luxury of not having to be quite so much on our guard against this theory's obviously mythological elements.

44 Anderson, *Historical Transcendence*, p. 151.

45 *Historical Transcendence*, p. 179; cf. also p. 167.

46 *Historical Transcendence*, p. 179.

47 Since only objects are 'placeable', the 'Thomist' proposal – precisely because it does *not* imply that 'godness' is such that it can be 'placed' (albeit 'self-placed') – better safeguards the transcendence of divinity. For my understanding of the role of the metaphors 'without' and 'within' in St Thomas's doctrine of creation I am indebted to William J. Hill, *The Three-Personed God: The Trinity as a Mystery of Salvation* (Washington, 1982), p. 76.

48 For criticism of such a problematic personalism in reflection on the Trinity, made with specific reference to the views of Walter Kasper, see John Milbank, 'The Second Difference: For a Trinitarianism Without Reserve', *Modern Theology*, 2 (1986), pp. 213–34.

49 For criticisms of this 'voluntarism' in the sphere of trinitarian reflection, see again the article by Milbank cited in the previous note.

50 This is the view of Aquinas, who espouses the principle that 'all human examples fail to represent divine things'; see his treatise *de Rationibus* 6, section 984: 'Sed tamen haec exempla a praedicta unionis representatione deficiunt, sicut et cetera exempla humana a rebus divinis'. Cited in Bruce D. Marshall, *Particular Identity and Method in Christology* (Oxford, 1987), p. 182. I am indebted to this work for its fine study of Aquinas's treatment of reduplicative propositions in christology.

51 The suggestion that the metaphor of 'kenosis' is part of a discourse congruent with Scripture's *modus loquendi* might attract the objection that this metaphor is already to be found in Scripture (e.g., in Philippians 2:7). Not being a biblical scholar, I can only rely on the judgement of more competent individuals. Summarizing the views of Ernst Käsemann, J. S. Lawton, E. R. Fairweather and M. Jones, Ralph P. Martin says that 'there is nothing in ancient Christian thought which provides a substantial precedent for the theory of Christology which goes by the name of Kenosis'. See his valuable study *Carmen Christi: Philippians 2:5–11 in Recent Interpretation and in the Setting of Early Christian Worship*, revised ed. (Grand Rapids, Michigan, 1983), p. 67. James Dunn argues that the christological hymn of Philippians 2:5–11 (which is commonly regarded as the *locus classicus* of kenotic theory) does not imply any kind of belief in a pre-existent Christ – this belief of course being integral to a 'kenotic' reading of this passage. See his *Christology in the Making: An Inquiry into the Origins of the Doctrine of the Incarnation* (London, 1980), pp. 114–21 and 125–8.

52 This, of course, is Aquinas's understanding of what is involved in accepting that God is Creator. Here (and in what follows) I am deeply indebted to the discussion in David B. Burrell, *Aquinas: God and Action* (London, 1979), p. 139. Burrell does not give an explicitly christological focus to his neo-Thomist characterization of affirming God as Creator. It

is not impossible, however, to augment his account with an *analogia Christi* – for Christian faith, after all, God's relatedness to the world receives its decisive 'utterance' in the taking flesh of his Son.

53 I am indebted to Peter Sedgwick for his very helpful comments on an earlier draft of this paper. He is not of course responsible for the inadequacies that remain.

7 Tragedy and atonement

DAVID F. FORD

Only there is no escape from contingency. Donald MacKinnon[1]

One of the striking things about Donald MacKinnon's speaking and writing is the way he interprets the Bible. Frequently a passage is focused on, taken up into a discussion, and shown to be fruitful in ways that go beyond the horizons of most scholarly commentaries. Take, for example, his treatment of John, chapter 20 in 'The Problem of the "System of Projection" Appropriate to Christian Theological Statements'.[2] At the culmination of a complex argument involving logical implication, the relation of various types of language to reality and the status of the Resurrection of Jesus in Christian faith, John, chapter 20 is introduced as 'one of the classical Christian documents concerning the relation of perceiving (and especially visual, auditory and tactile perception) to faith'.[3] What happens in the interpretation that follows is worth noting.

The main thing going on is what might be called conceptual redescription of the text, like the German *Nachdenken*. The details of the story in all their complex inter-relationships are described in philosophical language, and thought tries to keep closely to the particularities of this text while also exploring its logic. The result is both to sharpen appreciation of the thrust and nuances of the text and to connect its narrative with some perennial philosophical issues. Yet for all the apparent neutrality of the attempt simply to describe, the implications of this approach can be considerable. Treating the author of the fourth Gospel seriously, as a thinker whose subtlety can stretch the best of contemporary philosophers, shocks us out of tendencies to paternalism towards him or her. And the consequence of this respectful engagement may be to have our most important conceptions transformed or challenged by the unique nature of what we come to recognize. As MacKinnon concludes:

> One must use these models; yet what one seeks to capture is unique. One's use is part of the way in which one takes hold of the system of projection involved in the Christian faith; the taking hold of a problem from which one continually retreats, preferring the *ersatz* of an allegedly formal orthodoxy, or the security of an absolutely autonomous faith, unbound by the factual, and creative of its own objects, or the greater manageability of more tractable presentations of the fusion of complexity and simplicity character-istic of the evangelists' portrayal of the central figure. Philosophy, whether metaphysics, descriptive or speculative, or logic, is never master in theol-ogy, but its indispensable servant, never however giving a service that can be construed after a formula but one that throws light, now in one direction, now in another.[4]

In this chapter I want to see how this sort of approach can be followed through further in exploring one of MacKinnon's main themes, tragedy and atonement. Earlier in the essay quoted above he says that the Christian system of projection is one 'in which one form of expression complements the deficiency of another'.[5] In that essay he demonstrates this in relation to John's narrative and philosophical discourse. In discussing atonement he often adds a third genre, that of tragic drama. My main reference-points will be his writings that combine those three, and I will add three other main partners: Paul's second letter to the Corinthians, Dame Helen Gardner's T. S. Eliot Memorial Lectures of 1968 on 'Religion and Tragedy', and the philosophy of Emmanuel Levinas (joining the discussion in that order).

I   2 Corinthians and atonement

The doctrine of atonement has found many of its favourite texts in 2 Corinthians. In particular, chapter 5 has provided them:

> For the love of Christ controls us, because we are convinced that one has died for all; therefore all have died. And he died for all, so that those who live might no longer live for themselves but for him who for their sake died and was raised.   (5:14–15)

Therefore if anyone is in Christ, he is a new creation; the old has passed away, behold, the new has come. All this is from God, who through Christ reconciled us to himself and gave us the ministry of reconciliation; that is, in Christ God was reconciling the world to himself, not counting their trespasses against them, and entrusting to us the message of reconciliation. So we are ambassadors for Christ, God making his appeal through us. We beseech you on behalf of Christ, be reconciled to God. For our sake he made him to be sin who knew no sin, so that in him we might become the righteousness of God. (5:17–21)

Yet the doctrine that has quoted these has often failed to learn from their setting. In MacKinnon's terms, their sense is inseparable from the way they are related to the contingencies of history. The importance of contingency is even clearer in this letter than it is in the Gospels. Paul's Gospel is not necessary or general truths but news of a particular person and events. It is itself communicated through involvement in all the contingencies of life, and people have to be appealed to and persuaded to respond to it so that its history is contingent on their responses. The letter itself is part of this, sent into a particular situation as an appeal that tries to change the way the Church in Corinth is behaving. It is full of references to the joyful and the painful contingencies of Paul's ministry and his relationship with the Corinthians, seen in the light of the Gospel: and this reaches its climax in Paul's account of what he learnt about God's own involvement in contingencies: 'my power is made perfect in weakness' (12:9).

There is a family of metaphors that Paul uses which captures something of this sense of the contingent, the practical and the relational quality of atonement or reconciliation. The doctrine of the atonement is notorious for its inextricability from metaphors – legal, military, medical, social, cultic and financial – and many doctrines seem like the systematization of a central metaphor. Yet the abuse of metaphor is just the other side of its importance, and it has to be thought through. In the passages just quoted from 2 Corinthians a key metaphor is that of exchange. This clearly has cultic resonances in relation to sacrifice, but it also has financial and economic connections, and the rest of 2 Corinthians reinforces this latter line of inquiry. The Holy Spirit is a down-payment or guarantee (1:22, 5:5), the Gospel is 'this treasure' (4:7), Paul sees himself as a poor man who makes many rich (6:10) and his activity is characterized as *diakonia*, a basic form of work in the economy of the time. Corinth was a major commercial centre, Paul himself was a craftsman who manufactured, bought and sold and probably integrated his ministry and his daily work, so it is not surprising that his Gospel was expressed partly in economic language about resources, work, money, production, distribution, promises, value and exchange, together with the processes and relationships that these involve.

But it is what he does with this family of metaphors that is most significant. The content of the Gospel transforms the concept of economy that is taken up. One obvious feature is its theocentricity. God has set up this economy and has produced a resource comparable to the most fundamental resource, creation (*cf*.4:6, 5:17). The nature of this Christ-centred work of God is the key theme of Paul's Gospel, and the most astonishing fact about it is that it is simply given by God. God has done something and offered it freely, and this availability of grace, life, the Spirit, glory, reconciliation, freedom, wealth, or however else it is described, determines both Paul's work and the new state of affairs of the world. The distribution of this resource is now the most urgent priority, and Paul calls this 'co-working' with God (6:1; *cf*. 1 Cor.3:9).

The generative event in this economy is the Crucifixion and Resurrection of Jesus Christ characterized as an exchange which enables a new economy of exchanges. There is no competition between 'objective' and 'subjective' atonement: intrinsic to the event is its purpose 'that those who live might live no longer for themselves but for him who for their sake died and was raised' (5:15). Believing the Gospel means participation in the exchanges of the economy in all the contingencies of life:

For as we share abundantly in Christ's sufferings, so through Christ we share abundantly in comfort too. If we are afflicted, it is for your comfort and salvation; and if we are comforted, it is for your comfort, which you experience when you patiently endure the same sufferings we suffer. Our hope for you is unshaken; for we know that as you share in our sufferings, you will also share in our comfort.   (1:5–7)

One striking feature of that is the repeated note of abundance. It runs through the letter, expressed in thanks, praise, joy, hope and above all glory, summed up in 4:15: 'For everything is for your sake, so that grace abounding through more and more of you may cause thanksgiving to overflow to the glory of God.' The economy of the Roman empire was a 'limited good' economy, with a roughly stable, limited amount of resources. This divine economy was in contrast symbolized by 'grace abounding', 'more and more'. The unit of value was the whole person (Paul says: 'I will gladly spend and be spent on your behalf', 12:15) and the language of the measuring scales in the market is used to reckon cost-effectiveness: 'For this immediate trifle of an affliction produces for us, in extraordinary quantities, an eternal weight of glory' (4:17).

Perhaps the most remarkable thing, however, is what happens in chapters 8–9. There Paul writes about the collection for the Jerusalem Church. He takes the economic language which has already been transformed by the Gospel content and he refers it back to literal finances. Financial attitudes and relationships are reconceived, and the literal and divine economies are shown as inextricably interwoven. Paul's terminology is astonishing – Dahl says it is untranslatable.[6] One key 'theological' word after another is applied to the collection. It is called *charis* (grace, gift of grace), *koinonia* (partnership, fellowship, sharing), *eulogia* (blessing, liberality), *leitourgia* (service, voluntary or priestly), *haplotes* (single-minded commitment, generosity) and *perisseuma* (overflow, abundance), among other terms. As Dahl shows, Greek and Jewish economic ideas and ethics are here taken up into something new.

The key theological statement puts a kenotic concept of the atonement in financial terms: 'For you know the grace of our Lord Jesus Christ, that though he was rich, yet for your sake he becomes poor, so that by his poverty you might become rich' (8:9). This is a redefinition of the Gospel with very practical implications. The Gospel has, in MacKinnon's words, provided 'the terms in which men and women . . . engage with the fundamental problems of their existence'.[7] For Paul the living reality of atonement is represented by the Macedonians:

We want you to know, brethren, about the grace of God which has been shown in the churches of Macedonia, for in a severe test of affliction their abundance of joy and their extreme poverty have overflowed in a wealth of liberality on their part. For they gave according to their means, and, as I can testify, beyond their means, of their own free will, begging us earnestly for the favour of taking part in the relief of the saints – and this, not as we had expected, but first they gave themselves to the Lord and to us by the will of God.   (8:1–5)

There is the note of abundance and overflow again, yet without any forgetfulness of the Cross, and it reaches a crescendo in a string of hyperboles: 'in fact, God enables every grace to overflow into you, so that in every way and all the time you have total self-sufficiency to overflow into every act of goodness . . .' (9:8).

Through the economic metaphors and also in many other ways[8] this letter attempts to do justice to the crucified and risen Jesus Christ. MacKinnon has written of the letter:

. . . its background is ontological; what Paul speaks of is not something that he records as 'the contents of his consciousness', but a sense of his mission and its significance that he has won through daring to see it in the light of the Cross. He knows that the ground of his mission, to which it belongs, is all. So there is a deep movement in his language between what is almost autobiographical description, what is theological interpretation, and what is, in effect, the expression of a deepened understanding of the mystery of the Cross through the refraction of that mystery, in the arcana of his own spiritual life and suffering. And yet, because all is under the sign of kenosis, the final note is of a radical self-abandonment.[9]

Yet one question that the letter prompts one to ask MacKinnon is whether he has done justice to the joyful note of abundance. Paul describes himself and others as 'sorrowful, yet always rejoicing' (6:10); can MacKinnon's emphasis on tragedy fully affirm the second half of the paradox? Or, putting another side of the question, is there any sense of tragedy that can go with 2 Corinthians as a whole? This brings us to the next contributor to our discussion.

II   Tragedy and 2 Corinthians

Dame Helen Gardner[10] agrees with the common view that a characteristic mark of tragedy is the embracing of contraries in tension. There are various ways of formulating the tension: between ultimate sense and nonsense, between two ideals (a conflict in the very ethical nature of reality), between contradictory aspects of human nature, between the Dionysian and the Apollonian, between protest and acceptance, or between the contingencies of life and their meaningful coherence. From this joining of contraries comes the ambiguity of tragedy, which is notably seen in the vastly varied interpretations that the great tragedies have been able to sustain. Other key marks of tragedy are the stature and dignity of the chief character or characters, the unavoidability of distress and suffering, and the plot, the logic of events which has some sort of resolution.

Paul's Gospel, and the drama of which his life, according to 2 Corinthians, is a part, could fit such criteria (one can see contraries in tension, ambiguities, suffering, characters of stature and a plot with resolution), but the pivotal issue is the relation of Crucifixion to Resurrection. Surely that resolution is untragic? I think not. Indeed, I want to argue that 2 Corinthians show the tragic being taken into a transformation which sharpens rather than negates it, while yet rendering the category of the tragic inadequate by itself. The genre of tragedy remains a helpful way to illuminate 2 Corinthians and its concept of atonement while yet being unable to do justice to all that is there.

The case is as follows. Paul is as acutely aware as MacKinnon of the dangers of a triumphalist understanding of the Resurrection. In 1 Corinthians he had had to reassert the continuing centrality of the Cross, and in 2 Corinthians he pursues the theme with a more personal focus. The major issue is his own authority, and he sees the mistake of his opponents being to conceive power and authority in terms that divorce the Resurrection from the content of Crucifixion. The Resurrection is not simply the reversal of death, leaving death behind it. Paul 'carries in the body the death of Jesus' (4:10): the Resurrection message has sent him even more deeply into contingency, weakness and suffering. It is an atonement whose power is to allow him to stay close to, even immersed in, the tragic depths of life.

But there is a purpose in this: it is to communicate the Gospel. Here is the clue to the new possibility of tragedy. The Gospel is the new contingency. It relativizes all the old contingencies of suffering and death. But it does not end contingency; rather, it intensifies it terrifyingly. Paul can hardly bear the tension this means for someone with a responsibility like his: 'For we are the aroma of Christ to God among those who are being saved and among those who are perishing, to one a fragrance from death to death, to the other a fragrance from life to life. Who is sufficient for these things?' (2:15–16). There is the new contingency, the new mystery. Paul even says: 'And even if our gospel is veiled, it is veiled only to those who are perishing. In their case the God of this world has blinded the minds of the unbelievers, to keep them from seeing the light of the gospel of the glory of Christ, who is the image of God.' (4:4. 'The god of this world' is how the Revised Standard Version actually reads, with God in lower case, but I think this is a shying away from the apparently intolerable meaning of the Greek.)

This means that there is no guaranteed happy ending. There is a continuing possibility that can only be called tragic. There is a temptation to resolve this in predestinarian terms (4:4 could be taken like that), but that would make nonsense of the urgency and responsibility of Paul's ministry. Its urgency is only comprehensible if the things he does and says are significant, if tragic disobedience is a possibility, if in some sense the future is open while yet in God's hands. (I will take up this problem in relation to eschatology in the final section.)

Helen Gardner says: 'Tragedy displays causes in calamities and shows design, but in so doing reveals what remains mysterious and inexplicable.'[11] That fits Paul and his Gospel. She also argues that what is conceived as calamity changes in emphasis from Greek to Elizabethan tragedy. For the Greek tragedians tragic suffering was connected with the changes and chances of life, the possibility of pollution, and the tensions between arbitrariness and law and between the jealousy and the justice of the gods. For the Elizabethans there was rather the tension between mortality and immortal longings, and between undeserved suffering, guilt and the need for justice. What is calamity for Paul? For him the concerns of both Greeks and Elizabethans are taken up to some extent, but they are relativized by the Gospel, and the sense of touching the deepest mystery surrounds the Gospel itself. Calamity is rejection of the Gospel, or unfaithfulness to it. In this drama ultimately significant events happen, and because contingency, justice, death and suffering are part of them, tragedy continues to illuminate them.

This is intensified by what at first sight may seem to weaken the sense of tragedy in 2 Corinthians: the extraordinary reality of *shared* suffering in the Christian community. Paul draws continual comfort from his joint membership in Christ with others who share both his joy and his suffering. Is it not the case that suffering taken up into this mutual comfort and even rejoicing can hardly be called tragic? And in MacKinnon's treatment of the Church, is there again a failure to maintain that combination of 'sorrowful yet always rejoicing' that Paul's grasp of atonement enabled him to affirm?

Helen Gardner's lecture on Shakespearean tragedy concludes with a remarkable comment on *Lear*:

King Lear presents an extremity of suffering, physical and mental, falling on man from the hostility of the natural world, the cruelty of others, the visitations of fortune, and the burning shame the thought of his own sins and follies brings. It displays suffering as the universal law of life with all the heightening of common experience that tragedy gives. But without in any way diminishing agony and pain it shows men discovering through their suffering truth, and beyond its demonstration of learning by suffering, the *to pathein mathein* of the Aeschylean tragedy of suffering it displays most movingly the fellowship of suffering, that men are bound to each other in their pain. As the play proceeds the prosperous fall apart; the outcasts draw together, sharing each other's burdens and bearing their griefs.[12]

She sees such mutuality, and the overall ethical temper of Shakespeare's plays, with their valuing of mercy, gentleness and conscience, as signs of their being deeply Christian, usually in a secular way. She also shows how the fellowship of suffering and even the possibility of renewed joy are not incompatible with the greatest tragedy.

The fellowship in *Lear* is hardly comparable with that seen in 2 Corinthians, but yet one can see how the latter does not rule out the tragic either. The focusing of what one might call Paul's concept of the tragic around the Gospel means that the community called into being through the Gospel is also subject to the threat of tragedy. Indeed, it is almost as if in Paul's dramatic conception of history the spectacle of the people of God, whether Israel or the Church, is what chiefly evokes his pity and fear. 'The corruption of the best is the worst', and he is acutely aware of how the place of greatest glory is also the place of greatest responsibility and temptation. MacKinnon, coming after nearly 2,000 years of Church history, has even more appalling evidence that the Gospel, far from making the category of tragedy less important, both illuminates new ways in which it is relevant and makes possible new forms of communal evil. There is again a heightening or deepening of the tragic even as its ultimate content is transformed by the Gospel.

But now we have to ask about that transformation. As MacKinnon says, referring to his philosophical concepts, tragedy has to be used but not allowed to dominate or obscure the uniqueness of what is here. What is this uniqueness?

III   The face of Christ

We have already tried to show that any uniqueness is not to be found in such characteristics as taking contingency and evil with ultimate seriousness, or in leaving behind, in the interests of a happy ending, the tensions between contraries, or in sharing the tragic reality of life in a community that is itself somehow the answer to tragedy. The question symbolized by Paul's phrase 'sorrowful, yet always rejoicing' has also been raised about MacKinnon's way of relating tragedy to the Gospel. I have defended him against any simplistic accusation in these terms, such as Paul's opponents in Corinth might have made, but a question remains. How do we identify the *in*adequacy of tragedy as a genre through which to understand the Gospel whose climax is the Resurrection joy, but without falling into the traps which MacKinnon has so insistently pointed out?

2 Corinthians suggests a possible answer. Its most powerful and original theology does not come in the passages already quoted in chapter 5 but in the previous two chapters, in the light of which the explicit statements about atonement need to be understood. In chapters 3–4 Paul sets his own ministry in the context of Moses at Sinai and the distinctive content and effects of the Gospel. The climactic verse is 4:6: 'For it is the God who said, "Let light shine in darkness," who has shone in our hearts to give the light of the knowledge of the glory of God in the face of Christ.' That verse could inspire a whole systematics, but the phrase I want to explore is 'the glory of God in the face of Christ'.

Could this be one way of beginning to develop the 'radicalized and transformed' notion of the contingent that MacKinnon suggests is required by christology?[13] This face has been through historical contingencies, it is not separable from them yet also not reducible to them. It has also been dead. Yet it is seen as the manifestation of the glory of God, so that in future the glory of God and this death cannot be thought of without each other. It has also been raised from death, and represents the unity beyond paradox of the Crucifixion and Resurrection. The face of Christ calls for christology as well as soteriology. And for all its definitiveness it also allows one to conceive of continuing involvement in contingency, the sensitivity of a living face to events and people, and a mode of interaction which respects the freedom and randomness of creation while yet continuing to suffer and confront it.

Yet an important thing to note about the phrase 'the face of Christ' is that it is also eschatological (*cf.* 1 Cor. 13:12 – 'but then face to face'). It can help us to rethink many ideas of eschatology. If the ultimate is recognized in a face, we glimpse a way out of the dilemma of eschatology which so often seems unable to conceive of a definitive consummation of history without also seeing it as predetermined. The face of Christ is definitive, but it does not predetermine. Rather it is the counterpart of a new history of freedom and responsibility, involving a new notion of what glory and freedom are, as the rest of 2 Corinthians makes clear.

What about tragedy? In Helen Gardner's attempt to redefine tragedy with all its apparent paradoxes she eventually chose the analogy of a face:

> I have left to last a formula that for me comes very near expressing the nature of tragedy: the words that Beethoven scrawled, perhaps only in jest, above the opening bars of the last movement of his last quartet: 'Muss es sein?' 'Es muss sein.' He wrote above the whole movement the words 'Der schwer gefasste Entschluss', 'The Difficult Resolution'. The affirmation is in the same words as the question; only a hair's breadth, hardly more than an inflection of the voice separates them. Protest and acceptance are like expressions on the same face. According to their convictions and beliefs men attempt to conceptualize the protest and the affirmation; and according to temperament and even to mood the balance between question and answer quivers. Some find the essence of tragedy in the power with which the question cried out; others in the difficult final resolution.[14]

Perhaps in the light of 2 Corinthians the face could be more than an analogy. The Gospel is about someone who has done justice to the tragic. This face, beyond all categories and syntheses, embodies both the powerful question and the difficult final resolution. And it is a resolution that does not fall into triumphalism or cheap joy when it enables the overflow of thanks and Paul's 'always rejoicing'.

At this point MacKinnon's question might be: but what sort of face is this face? In 2 Corinthians it is one of a historical succession of faces, from Moses through to the Corinthians. It is not just an idea or a future ideal but belongs to one who was 'made sin' and crucified. In its affirmation there is an inescapable element of trust in testimony. Yet the shining of this face in the heart is not simply a matter of perception or believing someone else's testimony. The matter is just as complex as in John, chapter 20, and for the same reason: the relationship of faith to sight is extremely difficult to formulate appropriately. What MacKinnon's brilliant redescription of the issue by reference to John 20 does is to leave open the space for such a strange concept as the face of Christ. This face is heard of and anticipated, but not yet seen face to face; it is unsubstitutably identified not by identikit or photofit but by the events of Crucifixion and Resurrection; it fits no category short of the glory of God; and it is only appropriately recognized in a context such as that in which 2 Cor.4:6 places it – that of the complete prevenience of the God who said 'Let light shine in darkness', and of the transformation of selves in community that happens when this face is allowed to shine *kata pneuma* in our hearts. In other words, the trinitarian structure of the verse testifies to the incomparable fact of this face.

This leads into the question of ontology. What sort of metaphysics can do justice to the ultimacy of a face? The philosophy of Emmanuel Levinas attempts to offer one. It has the same Jewish roots as Paul's writings; and Levinas is also quoted as saying: 'All philosophy is in Shakespeare.' At the heart of his thought is the idea of an irreducible pluralism in being, whose primary form is the 'face to face'. There is no synthesizing of faces, no inclusion of their otherness in an overarching concept of sameness, a general notion of 'being'. The essence of the relationship is that it is ethical: the face of the other represents an appeal, even a command, which lays a primary responsibility on me. Levinas criticizes ontology for often attempting to conceive the unity of being as some sort of totality of which it is possible to have, at least in principle, an overview. The other whom I meet has an exteriority, an alterity, that resists all fusion, all comprehension, all inclusion in sameness.

Levinas connects language and reason as well as ethics with the plural reality of the face to face. The face is an ethical presence, appealing and appealed to, accompanying its presence with speech. Transcendence is to be understood from here, breaking through any idolatry of the face understood as just a visible form:

If the transcendent cuts across sensibility, if it is openness preeminently, if its vision is the vision of the very openness of being, it cuts across the vision of forms and can be stated neither in terms of contemplation nor in terms of practice. It is the face; its revelation is speech. The relation with the Other alone introduces a dimension of transcendence, and leads to a relation totally different from experience in the sensible sense of the term, relative and egoist.[15]

The theological conclusion of Levinas is: 'Monotheism signifies this human kinship, this idea of a human race that refers back to the approach of the Other in the face, in a dimension of height, in responsibility for oneself and for the Other.'[16] God therefore represents, negatively, a critique of any ontology that unifies being by ignoring the ultimate pluralism of the face to face, and, positively, the priority of ethics over ontology. This allows both the question of tragedy (how could a twentieth-century East European Jew fail to be gripped by that question?) and the difficult resolution; and, through and beyond that, the glory of the face.

I suggest that there is here a metaphysics which meets the demand MacKinnon makes, at the end of his chapter on 'The Transcendence of the Tragic' in his Gifford Lectures, for an ontological pluralism which is not atheist and which, by holding to the significance of the tragic, is protected against 'that sort of synthesis which seeks to obliterate by the vision of an all-embracing order the sharper discontinuity of human existence'.[17] But Levinas traces the discontinuity, the pluralism, not only to the sharpness of the tragic but to the face, which can express joy as well as agony. And in the face of Christ I see a manifestation of the Christian eschatological hope: for a non-tragic outcome of history which yet does full justice to the tragic.

Finally, I want to end with a question. As Kenneth Surin has written, MacKinnon's 'preference is for an interrogative, as opposed to an affirmative, mode of theological discourse'.[18] The question is from John Donne's sermon on the verse 'Jesus wept'. In it the themes of this essay converge – tragedy, atonement, eschatology, the face and the possibility of being 'sorrowful, yet always rejoicing'. And this genuinely open question comes from the sorrowful side, in deepest gratitude to Donald MacKinnon whose thought and, dare I say it, whose face have shown the intensity and yet sensitivity of the interrogation that the tragic must be allowed to conduct in theology and philosophy:

When God shall come to the last Act in the glorifying of Man, when he promises, *to wipe all teares from his eyes*, what shall God have to doe with that eye that never wept?[19]

Notes

1 'Philosophy and Christology', *Borderlands of Theology and Other Essays* (London, 1968), p. 81.
2 *Explorations in Theology 5* (London, 1979), pp. 70–89.
3 *Ibid.*, p. 84.
4 *Ibid.*, p. 89.
5 *Ibid.*, p. 74.
6 N. A. Dahl, *Studies in Paul* (Minneapolis, 1977), p. 31.
7 'The Future of Man', *Explorations*, p. 9.
8 For a fuller treatment of this and other aspects of 2 Corinthians discussed in this essay see Frances M. Young and David F. Ford, *Meaning and Truth in 2 Corinthians* (London, 1987).
9 'Philosophy and Christology', *Borderlands*, p. 80.
10 In 'Religion and Tragedy', *Religion and Literature* (London, 1971), pp. 13–118.
11 *Ibid.*, p. 104.
12 *Ibid.*, p. 88.
13 'Philosophy and Christology', *Borderlands*, p. 81.
14 'Religion and Tragedy', p. 34.
15 *Totality and Infinity: An Essay on Exteriority* (Pittsburgh, 1969), p. 193.
16 *Ibid.*, p. 214.
17 *The Problem of Metaphysics* (Cambridge, 1974), p. 135.
18 'Christology, Tragedy and Ideology', *Theology*, 89 (July 1986), p. 285.
19 Quoted in 'Religion and Tragedy', p. 78.

8 MacKinnon and the problem of evil

BRIAN HEBBLETHWAITE

Anyone who has heard Donald MacKinnon lecture on the problem of evil, or who has read him on this subject in articles and in the Gifford Lectures, will doubtless retain a number of very powerful impressions. For on this of all the topics in the philosophy of religion with which he has been engaged throughout his teaching and writing career, the characteristic qualities of MacKinnon's thought and work have been most evident. The refusal to accept any general argument or world view that avoided confrontation with the concrete and particular, the moral indignation with purported solutions, however venerable, that smacked of superficiality or evasion, the relentless wrestling with the utterly intractable cases of both wickedness and suffering which seem at the same time to challenge and yet to demand faith in the transcendent, provided for the patient listener or reader numerous instances of both illumination and frustration that come to mind again and again as one grapples with the issues of theodicy. Many a time have I been disposed to tear up what I had written about the problem of evil, on asking myself what MacKinnon's reaction would be to the book or the essay at hand.

I have selected three recurring themes in MacKinnon's writing and lecturing on the problem of evil for discussion in this essay. The first is his intense hostility to the analysis of evil as *steresis* or *privatio boni*. The second is his insistence that there is no theoretical solution to the problem of evil. The third – related to the second – is his insistence on the ineradicability of the tragic from Christianity. Tragedy is treated at greater length elsewhere in this volume, but its centrality in MacKinnon's treatment of the problem of evil makes it inevitable that I too shall have to consider it here. I shall not take space to document these three themes from MacKinnon's writings. My interest is in the themes themselves, and I assume that no one familiar with MacKinnon's work will quarrel with my selection of these as being the dominant motifs.

What MacKinnon has said and written on these topics has made me think long and hard and I am grateful for being made to face up to the kind of specific and intractable evils, both natural and moral, that have led MacKinnon to adopt the stance he has done on the *privatio boni* theory, on the insolubility of the problem of evil and on the place of tragedy in Christianity. But on each of these issues I intend to argue that MacKinnon simply cannot be right. I shall claim that, properly understood, the *privatio boni* analysis is a *necessary* element in Christian metaphysics, that the problem of evil *must* in the end find a theoretical solution, and that tragedy *cannot* be an ultimate category in a Christian view of the world. The mark of a great teacher is his ability to evoke respectful disagreement.

As is well known, the analysis of evil as privation was taken over from the Platonists by St Augustine as a way, indeed *the* way, to achieve intellectual, moral and spiritual liberation from captivity to Manichean dualism. I stress moral and spiritual as well as intellectual liberation since it is important to realize – and here I am sure MacKinnon would agree – that intellectual solutions to metaphysical problems have deep and pervasive moral and spiritual implications. Seriously to believe in dualism – an ultimate dualism between equally ultimate principles behind both good and evil, or even an ultimate dualism in the sphere of finite created substance – would have great, to my mind catastrophic, consequences for morality and spirituality as well as for intellectual comprehension of the nature of things. But it is indeed as the only way of ruling out an ultimate dualism from theistic and creationist metaphysics that the *privatio boni* theory functions and, as I shall argue, has a necessary place in Christian theodicy. But I shall also argue that that is its only function. It does nothing at all to diminish the problem of evil: that is, it does not in any way contribute to an answer to the question why God permits evil and suffering – any evil and suffering, so much evil and suffering, or evil and suffering of such horrific kinds – in his world. I shall argue that these questions remain just as pressing, just as perplexing, and just as demanding of an answer, when we accept the *privatio boni* analysis and thus rule out any ultimate dualism.

Before proceeding in this way, I want to stay with the question of dualism and to try to spell out the way in which the *privatio boni* analysis enables us to rule it out. What is at stake here is the ontological status of evil in the world. Evil is not a substance in its own right. This is to accept the dominant strands in Christian tradition which have equated *ens* and *bonum* in their range. Any and every substantial entity (whether finite or infinite), as such, is good. Christian metaphysics not only affirms here the goodness of God, but also takes up the Genesis affirmation that God saw what he had made and behold, it was very good. This means that matter is good, spirit is good, natural kinds are good, and the creation as a whole is good. Evil states of affairs, on this analysis, occur when created entities or systems, good in themselves, come into conflict and frustrate or deprive each other of their inbuilt or intended functions or fruitions. Alternatively, evil states occur when complex systems, such as persons, as such, parts of God's good creation, turn aside from God's intention or get perverted in their wills and bring about further clashes and deprivations both in themselves and in and between other complex systems in the world. These clashes, deprivations and perversions can be and are of the most horrific and appalling kind, but they do not, in themselves, belong in the category of substance. Good and evil are not, ontologically speaking, on a par.

MacKinnon has often drawn attention to the ferocity with which the Church, at various points in its history, as notably in the Albigensian Crusade, suppressed outbreaks of dualism in the West. The ferocity of the suppression was a sign, according to MacKinnon, that the Church's nerve was being touched on the raw. The threat of the dualists to the Church was only too real, since they might in fact be right, the subconscious fear that they might be evoking the ferocity of the suppression. I do not deny that the Albigensian Crusade, like all murderous Crusades, exemplifies the problem of evil right in the heart of the Church itself. But I think the Albigensians touched the Church on the raw, not because they were right, but because they were so plausibly wrong on so basic a tenet of the Christian faith as the goodness of God and his creation.

Always remembering that the anti-dualist, ontological analysis of evil as privation or perversion leaves the problem of evil just as horrific and unsolved as it was before, let us now examine some concrete examples of suffering and evil to see how this analysis applies. The most telling objections which MacKinnon brought against the *privatio boni* theory were always drawn from specific instances which seemed resistant to categorization as cases of privation. As an example of *Übel*, natural evil or suffering, I will take the case of the volcanic eruption in Colombia which engulfed the town of Armero. And as an example of *das Böse*, moral evil or wickedness, I will take the Holocaust, which looms so large in both Christian and Jewish consciousness as we try to understand a divine creation which permits an Auschwitz.

Many people feel that the latter, an extreme case of human wickedness, is less easy to categorize as *privatio* or *steresis* than the former, a peculiarly horrific natural disaster. For a volcanic eruption only creates a situation of natural evil when it destroys living beings, especially of course if it overwhelms a whole town, killing tens of thousands. We may still ask why it was allowed to happen there and then, or why it was not prevented, given the catastrophic consequences that were bound to occur if it happened there and then. Or we may ask why our physical environment has to be so generally precarious that such things can happen. But in itself a volcanic eruption is no more evil than a thermonuclear reaction in the heart of the sun. It is simply one among innumerable interactions of material substances, all part of God's good creation. A natural disaster, even one so utterly horrific as the Colombian volcano, consists in the deprivation of life and fruition caused by the accidental clashes of separately functioning systems within an overall system that is good. The loss of life and the suffering entailed for the victims and for their families and friends (and for all in any way involved) are negative phenomena – privations – solely in the sense that those lives and those relationships were frustrated and deprived of their natural and intended fruition and perfection.

I do not of course deny that deprivations constituting natural evil have positively evil consequences – but not, I suggest, in the category of substance. Deprived of my foot by a landmine, I experience excruciating pain. Certainly, the pain is not just lack of pleasure or of mental equilibrium. It is a positively evil mental state resulting from the deprivation of bodily wholeness through an accidental (or not so accidental) clash of independent systems. The pain mechanisms and their functions in bodily existence are in themselves good, but in situations of deprivation, they entail the positively evil mental states of excruciating pain. The *privatio boni* theory of evil does not require purely negative descriptions of such phenomena as pain.

Even those who are prepared to go along with the *privatio boni* theory where natural evil is concerned are often unable or reluctant to apply it in the case of moral evil. John Cowburn, for example, in his book, *Shadows in the Dark*,[1] insists that moral evil cannot be understood as mere lack of perfection. 'Deliberate murderous violence is not mere lack of gentleness', he writes; 'gross selfishness is more than a lack of consideration for others'. 'In general,' he concludes, 'a vice is not the mere absence of the corresponding virtue, but a driving force; it is not merely non-constructive, but positively destructive; it is not the non-assertion of some value or the non-willing of some good, but "active positive negation"' (he is quoting Emil Brunner there) 'and the willing of evil.' All these remarks are unquestionably true, and, if the *privatio boni* analysis of the ontological status of evil entailed that moral evil is mere absence of moral good, then it would indeed be quite untenable. I presume that MacKinnon's insistence that the evil of Auschwitz and of an Eichmann cannot be accounted for in terms of deprivation reflects just such a supposition. But I am not persuaded that this is the way to apply the *privatio boni* theory to moral evil. The monstrous and, in a sense, positive fact of a malicious and perverted human will is still not, in itself, a substance. It is the perversion of something inherently and in God's intention good, namely a human being. A will intended for perfection is perverted into imperfection of a most appalling and horrific kind, and the consequences in terms of attitudes, character and the suffering caused, are very far from describable solely in negative terms. But that is not the point of the *privatio boni* theory (any more than it was in the case of excruciating pain). The effects are positive and real enough, but they are effects of the radical imperfection or perversion of something in essence good and intended for perfection.

The case of moral evil, especially of monstrous evil such as Auschwitz, is indeed more complex and more deeply disturbing than that of pain, even excruciating pain. It is true, as MacKinnon says, that evil is often parasitic upon goodness, evil feeding upon good in a way it might not have done had that good not been there. I shall have more to say about this when I turn to the theme of tragedy. For the present I simply note the sense in which, while evil may be parasitic upon good, good is never parasitic upon evil. When we say good sometimes comes out of evil, we mean something different from what we mean when we speak of evil coming out of good. Evil may pervert or distort or even feed on good. Good, however, may transcend and overcome evil. This asymmetry between good and evil reflects the ontological status of the latter as *privatio boni*.

All the same, we are no nearer to solving the problem of evil by our rejection of dualism on the basis of the *privatio boni* theory. For nothing has been said so far about why the world is structured in such a way as to produce so many clashes, accidents and disasters which themselves produce so much suffering and pain. Nothing has been said about why God's personal creatures are allowed to become so perverse and destructive in their dealings with each other and themselves. The theodicy questions are just as pressing and just as difficult as they were before. Moreover the danger of glib, unrealistic or morally perverse answers to these questions is very great. MacKinnon's refusal to let us off the hook where the enormity and destructiveness of human suffering and of radical evil are concerned has been a constant and necessary challenge. But was he right to press the challenge to the point of asserting that there is no solution to the problem of evil for the Christian? I think not. For it seems to me that a foundational belief – a basic belief, in Plantinga's sense – in the goodness of God commits us to the necessity, if not of finding a solution, then of believing that there is a solution to the problem of evil. I find some support for this view in observing what tends to happen when one draws the consequences from insistence that the problem of evil is insoluble. Stewart Sutherland, in his book, *God, Jesus and Belief*,[2] regards the insolubility of the problem of evil as axiomatic. Where that is basic, something else has to give – in Sutherland's case, the goodness of God in any moral or personal sense – and we find ourselves encouraged to adopt an impersonal conception of deity. I cannot think that this is a path MacKinnon would wish to tread, but it is certainly a logically coherent view, given the insolubility of the problem of evil.

I cannot here expound and defend the theodicy which I myself find most plausible at present. I have tried to do so in a contribution to the forthcoming book which Geoffrey Wainwright is editing to commemorate the centenary of *Lux Mundi*. This theodicy is a combination of the free-will defence, itself defended against the compatibilist views of J. L. Mackie, and an examination of the necessary general conditions for the formation of any finite persons at all over against and in relation to the infinite Creator God. But I am encouraged to attempt and to pursue a solution to the problem of evil along these lines, not only by seeing what has happened in Sutherland's case, when the project is abandoned as impossible from the start, but also by observing Karl Rahner's thoroughly theological but extremely implausible attempt to ground the incomprehensibility of suffering in the incomprehensibility of God. I am referring to his article, 'Why Does God Allow Us to Suffer?'[3]

Rahner begins with an unintelligible distinction between allowing and permitting. He agrees that the question, 'Why does God allow us to suffer?', is the right way to put the theodicy problem; but he claims that this way of putting it does not involve the traditional distinction between permitting and causing. Granted that the notion of the permissive will of God is a problematic one, where the primary cause of all there is is in question (this was a point often stressed by MacKinnon too), nevertheless the actual nature of creation – the dignity of causality, as Aquinas put it, being imparted to creatures – surely requires us to employ this notion of God's permissive will. There is simply no way in which a Christian theist can affirm that God did what Hitler did. But he allowed or permitted it: the terms seem interchangeable.

Rahner proceeds to survey what he calls 'attempts at a theistic answer'. He touches on four of them. The first is the view that suffering is a natural side effect in an evolving world. Rahner admits that there is some force in this view, though he oddly begins one paragraph by saying that 'it is certainly not to be regarded as superficial or stupid' and ends the same paragraph by saying, 'in the last resort this answer is in fact unsatisfactory and superficial'. I prefer the beginning of the paragraph to the end, since, properly developed in connection with reflection on the purpose of an evolving physical world in the economy of creation, this view of suffering as inevitably bound up with the necessary conditions of the formation of finite persons has much to recommend it. It is the chief feature of John Hick's so-called Irenaean theodicy,[4] which, as I shall argue below, must not be construed moralistically as pointing simply to the necessary conditions of the formation of character, but rather as pointing, at a much more basic level, to the necessary conditions of the formation of finite persons as such.

Among other things, the law-governed, yet open and evolving, physical world is the necessary condition of the formation of finite, *free*, beings. And the second attempt at a theistic answer which Rahner mentions is the view that suffering is an effect of creaturely, sinful, freedom. Thus we come to the free-will defence. This certainly cannot answer all our problems concerning evil and suffering. Indeed in the context of the Christian tradition the free-will defence has its own peculiar difficulties in relation to the sovereignty and providence of God. But it is bound to play a role in any plausible theodicy.

The third attempt at a theistic answer, in Rahner's words, 'suggests that God allows us to suffer in order to test us and bring us to maturity'. Of all attempted theodicies, this falls most easily into the morally indefensible and outrageous. Whatever partial truth it may sometimes have, it cannot possibly explain or justify the extent and extremity of human suffering which often warps or destroys rather than ennobles. I recall the scorn which MacKinnon poured on this view, with its implied picture of the universe as a kind of moral obstacle race or, as he rose to the theme, a kind of 'cosmic Gordonstoun'. It was suspicion of this attempt at a theistic answer that made me want to distance myself from any over-moralistic interpretation of Hick's Irenaean theodicy.

Rahner's fourth attempt at an answer is the view that suffering points to another, eternal, life. I remain convinced that no theodicy can hope to succeed which derides or ignores the eschatological dimension.[5] But the hope of a future perfected consummation to the whole creative process in no way explains why God allows us to suffer. It may, one hopes, reconcile us to the cost in suffering of that creative process, if that cost can, on other grounds, be shown to be necessary. But the theodicy – the answer to the problem of evil – must consist in those other grounds. Rahner himself realizes that an eternal life without death, pain or tears cannot answer his basic question. But, since he is convinced that no one has succeeded in showing the *necessity* of our susceptibility to suffering and evil, and that therefore the creation of an eternal life without such things is theoretically quite possible, he can only conclude with an assertion of the incomprehensibility of suffering.

It is at this point that Rahner makes a characteristically theological move. Granting that there may be *some* truth in the above-mentioned attempts at a theistic answer, but insisting on their ultimate failure as a theodicy, Rahner tries to turn the tables on the critic by drawing on the long Christian tradition of belief in divine incomprehensibility. Rahner claims that the incomprehensible mystery of God positively requires the incomprehensibility of suffering if we are to love God absolutely selflessly and affirm him as the impenetrable mystery that he is. The incomprehensibility of suffering is part of the incomprehensibility of God. Rahner goes so far as to say that 'within our existence, which can be realised only historically in freedom, suffering is unavoidable insofar as its absence would mean that God would not be taken seriously as the incomprehensible mystery with which we have to cope here and now, but would remain an abstract theorem giving us no further trouble in the concreteness of our life'.[6] I detect here some echoes of the kind of thing MacKinnon said when he urged that the irreducibility of the tragic made one discontented with any sort of naturalism and opened up the dimension of the transcendent as the only alternative to trivialization. I shall have more to say about tragedy in a moment, but I very much wonder whether MacKinnon would want to go as far as Rahner in asserting that the incomprehensibility of God *requires* the incomprehensibility of suffering. I can make little moral sense of this paradoxical assertion. Divine incomprehensibility is indeed a venerable and ineradicable element in the tradition of Christian theism. Of course God is greater than anything we can think or say. We do not and cannot intuit the divine essence, and anything we finite creatures could fully comprehend would not be God. But the conviction of the divine mystery does not license any and every paradoxical assertion. Christian belief in the perfect goodness of God and Christian belief that God is love does not involve equivocal uses of the words 'goodness' and 'love', as MacKinnon would himself insist. On the contrary it is precisely conviction of the divine goodness and love that makes us search for a solution to the problem of evil. It is not excess of rationalism or lack of a religious spirit that makes the theodicy question such a pressing question in the mind of the believer. The quest for a theodicy, rather, is part and parcel of a genuinely spiritual desire for moral and religious credibility in basic Christianity. I have to confess that Rahner's position strikes me as not only rationally but religiously untenable. On the *premise* of the insolubility of the problem of evil, Sutherland's path is much the more plausible move to make. On the premise of the goodness and the love of God, however, there simply must be a solution to the question, 'Why does God allow us to suffer?'

It might also be pointed out that, on Rahner's view, the angels, if such there be, or the blessed in heaven, in an environment free from suffering, would presumably not be able to take God seriously, since there would be no incomprehensible suffering to underline God's mystery. I do not think much of a theology that has those implications.

I turn to the question of tragedy and its ineradicability from Christianity. Of course it all depends on what we mean by tragedy. If by tragedy we mean the kind of disaster and chaos that can defeat human goodness or greatness through a combination of fault and circumstance out of all proportion to any desert, then certainly Christianity must face up to the reality of the tragic. It is indeed part of the problem of evil that situations such as those portrayed in *Hamlet*, *King Lear*, *Macbeth* and *Othello* can and do take place. Christian theodicy must try to explain not only why God allows such things to happen, but why creation at the cost of such possibilities is nevertheless worth while. But those who have affirmed the ineradicability of tragedy from the Christian scheme of things have not only had in mind suffering and evil of such awesome magnitude as that portrayed in the tragedies of Shakespeare; they have also had in mind an even stronger sense of tragedy as including *ultimate*, eternal, failure and an *absolutely* unredeemable corruption of the good. That is why MacKinnon, with characteristic pertinacity, has focused our attention on the figure and fate of Judas.

Now it is very hard indeed to bring the ultimate Christian hope to bear upon situations of unspeakable tragedy without the appearance of trivialization, or indeed without blunting the practical imperatives of Christian faith. I can well understand what lies behind the following quotation from an article by Nicholas Lash:[7]

all theodicies – in the sense of theoretical attempts to demonstrate the compatibility of 'tragic disorder' with the goodness of God – are suspect as rationalisations of other people's meaningless suffering. Armed with a satisfactory theodicy, the need to contribute, in practice, to the redemptive liberation of human beings is sometimes less sharply felt. Christian hope remains a form of the tragic vision in the measure that it refuses to foreclose the question of the future by postulating in the imagination, some resolution to past and present tragedy, that in fact has not been resolved.

There are deep ambiguities in that passage, however. Lash makes his point in the course of reflection on Julian of Norwich's famous words, 'All shall be well and all shall be well and all manner of thing shall be well.' Now, whatever the Lady Julian herself meant by this, the pressures inclining the Christian mind in the direction of apokatastasis or universalism are not foreclosings of the question of the future by some imaginative postulate. They are, again, moral and spiritual, as well as theoretical, deductions from experience of redemption and the love of God. They exemplify the hermeneutics of eschatological assertions, as outlined by none other than Karl Rahner. Rahner himself refused to rule out the possibility of apokatastasis. This is a more persuasive theological stance than his use of the motif of incomprehensibility.

Lash's reference to 'postulating in the imagination, some resolution to past and present tragedy, that in fact has not been resolved' does not begin to do justice to the considerations which led not only Karl Rahner but also Karl Barth in the direction of universalism. The fact that life's tragedies in fact *have not been* resolved has no bearing whatsoever on the characteristically Christian faith that, in the end, they *will* be resolved, in the sense that their victims *will* participate in the resurrection, transformation and consummation of all things. It is perfectly true, as Lash says later on, that we are only enabled and entitled to pray the Lady Julian's words at the heart of darkness represented by Gethsemane and Calvary. But the whole point of the Christian story is that, while God is indeed there in the darkness of the Cross and of every cross, that is not the end. According to Christian faith and hope, the heart of darkness is not and cannot be the last word. If we are serious about the Christian faith, we have to apply the logic of redemption not only to the Hamlets and Othellos of this world, and not only to the innumerable nameless victims of life's tragedies, but to Judas as well.

It is of course extremely difficult to speak with moral and spiritual realism of the ultimate redemption of Judas, or, to take another of MacKinnon's examples, of Eichmann. But equally it is extremely difficult for the Christian mind to concede that any situation or person is ultimately and finally unredeemable for all eternity. As Lash himself puts it by way of exegesis of the Lady Julian's words, 'nothing, no circumstance, not even those in which all sanity and dignity, sense, structure and relationship, are cracked by chaos, disfigured by darkness, could justify resignation and despair'.

Consequently, I have to ask precisely what was meant by MacKinnon when he asked us to consider whether Jesus himself was a tragic figure and to ponder the degree to which Christianity takes seriously the reality of divine failure. Tragedy was there in the story of Jesus, not only for Judas and for the others who hardened their hearts against him, seemingly becoming no more than rejected instruments in the story of redemption. Jesus himself, the incarnate Son of God, failed to win the reception of his own when he came to them. Moreover, without the Gospel story and the history of the Christian Church, anti-semitism might well not have become the centuries-long horror that it did, reaching its unthinkable climax of mass genocide in the Holocaust of our own century. The kind of theodicy I try to work out certainly involves asking why these things were allowed to be and why the world is such as to render them possible. But the question before us at the moment is whether these failures, tragedies and horrors are ultimate, irredeemable facts, and the people involved in them for ever unforgivable, unchangeable and unresurrectable. Only if this is so can tragedy be said to be an absolute and final fact of human experience. I submit that Christianity is a faith which necessarily contradicts that view – not by attempting to diminish the horror of the tragic, nor by trying to reduce it to appearance or subsume it into a monistic whole, but by preaching a Gospel of redemption whereby the world's sorrow will be turned into joy and the inevitable sufferings and travail of the present phase of God's creative purpose will give birth to a glory beyond compare. That must mean a glory in which both victims and perpetrators (the former made new and whole and the latter transformed and forgiven) participate. Such a consummation may or may not occur. But Christianity is committed to the faith that it will occur. It is in that sense that I cannot concede to MacKinnon the ineradicability of the tragic. Another way of making the same point would be to suggest that David Ford's insistence on the 'sorrowful, yet always rejoicing' quality of 2 Corinthians 6[8] has to be, and can only be, spelled out eschatologically, and that the eschatological fulfilment of redemption will be such as to deprive all tragedy of finality.

I am well aware how dangerous a doctrine universalism is. But it does not entail the morally dubious consequences often drawn from it any more than does a theoretical explanation of why God allows us to suffer in the first place. Theodicy does not necessarily rationalize other people's suffering. Genocide remains an absolutely wicked and appalling thing, even when one understands in some measure why such a thing is allowed to happen in God's world. The need to do everything possible to prevent genocide remains just as pressing on us all, even when one believes that such a crime against humanity is not ultimately unredeemable and that, in the end, all will be well.

Rowan Williams has referred[9] to the way in which Teilhard de Chardin gives the impression of using his cosmic evolutionary perspective to evade the enormity of suffering and evil. But what is wrong with Teilhard is not his theoretical explanation of why suffering and evil are permitted to occur but his using that explanation in such a way as to downplay the significance of the outrageous things that happen and are done. The charge of evasion can be pressed in more than one direction. I grant that if explanations – or eschatological hopes – are used in such a way as to avoid facing up to what has happened or to what must be done, then Christian theodicy and eschatology become morally intolerable. But equally if moral outrage or practical imperatives are allowed to banish or downgrade the quest for theoretical explanation or eschatological justification of the ways of God with the world, then another evasion takes place. We avoid drawing the consequences of the conviction that the problem of evil is insoluble and tragedy ultimate. We evade the logical necessity of following either Sutherland's path and affirming an impersonal theism or Cupitt's path of rejecting an objective God altogether.[10] (I have already said why I am not impressed by Rahner's resort to incomprehensibility.) For the same reason suspicion must be voiced at any attempt to set theoretical and practical theodicies in opposition.[11] There is a theoretical evasion as well as a moral and practical evasion. As pointed out already, intellectual solutions to metaphysical problems have deep and pervasive moral and spiritual implications. The same is true of the refusal to press the theoretical questions. We are left with an incoherent faith.

The problem of evil breaks down into three pressing questions: Rahner's question, 'Why does God allow us to suffer?', Dostoevsky's question, 'Is creation worth the cost in suffering and evil that it has entailed?', and the practical question, 'How is evil to be overcome?' I have said little or nothing about the last question except to insist that it is just as pressing whatever our answer to the first two questions and to agree that any philosophical or theological theory that diverts attention from the practical problem is indeed suspect. But I do not think that the quest for understanding and consistency of belief and hope necessarily diverts attention from practice. On the contrary I think that good theory can inspire good practice as well as help to prevent despair. A plausible theodicy, spelling out the necessities involved in the world being such as to make suffering and evil possible, likely or even inevitable, and a consistent eschatology, enabling us to affirm that in the end all will be well, do not have the function of reconciling us to the world's evils and tragedies – nothing could reconcile us to Auschwitz – but they do go some way toward rendering belief in the goodness of God and the worthwhileness of the creation possible, despite Auschwitz. After all, only a coherent belief in God and his creation can allow the religious resources of inspiration, redemption and reconciliation to make their contribution to the overcoming of evil.

If someone asks me, how can you go on trying to work out a theodicy that reconciles you to the fact of Auschwitz, I reply that I do no such thing. My theodicy in no way reconciles me to that outrageous and appalling fact of twentieth-century history. It ought not to have happened. Such things must be denounced, opposed, and prevented in every possible way. But if someone asks me, 'How can you go on trying to work out a theodicy that reconciles you to a creation which contains the possibility of an Auschwitz?', I have to ask in reply whether the implications of the question put to me have been sufficiently seriously pondered. Have the possible reasons why the world is structured as it is been sufficiently considered? Have the nature and the basis of the Christian hope for a perfected creation, in which life's victims will themselves participate in the end, been thought through? And how is it possible to go on speaking of the love of God, if we cannot in any way at all be reconciled to his creation being what it is in this, its formative phase?

Notes

1 John Cowburn, *Shadows in the Dark* (London, 1979), p. 61.

2 Stewart Sutherland, *God, Jesus and Belief* (Oxford, 1984).

3 Karl Rahner, *Theological Investigations*, E.T. (London, 1984), Vol. 19, ch. 15. My attention was drawn to this article by Gerard Loughlin.

4 See J. Hick, *Evil and the God of Love* (London, 1966).

5 See B. Hebblethwaite, *The Christian Hope* (Basingstoke, 1984).

6 Rahner, *Theological Investigations*, pp. 206f.

7 'All Shall Be Well: Christian and Marxist Hope', reprinted in *Theology on the Road to Emmaus* (London, 1986).

8 See his chapter in this book, p. 125 above.

9 In the discussion at the MacKinnon conference.

10 See D. Cupitt, *Only Human* (London, 1985), p. 210.

11 As in Kenneth Surin, *Theology and the Problem of Evil* (Oxford, 1986).

9 Pride and international relations

BARRIE PASKINS

I suppose that every effort at creative thought, at thinking beyond the limits of what one knows already, is a kind of secret dialogue. A number of presences in the mind, imagined listeners and respondents, shape the direction and energy of the effort. How they will respond conditions the effort before one begins. How they take it shapes the endeavour as it proceeds. And very often, mercifully, they bury it without trace before it reaches the outer world, what we call the real world. To say anything very definite about one or more of these inner voices is difficult because they are at once so intimate and so withheld. It is not like reporting on rules that one is conscious of following, because the secret listeners do not respond on the basis of any rules that one can formulate to oneself. That is one mark of their being so personal. They are living presences precisely because their reply, which may be no more than a cocked eyebrow, cannot be predicted but must be heeded. For me to talk sense about Donald MacKinnon is therefore singularly difficult: one of my inner voices answers to that name, and at the same time there is also such a person out there in the real world, well known to you all and to himself. Of which of these two should I speak, knowing that the inner one is shaped by my sense of what the 'real' one is like? I do not know how to handle such conundrums, so I will confine to a paragraph a stab at characterizing my inner Donald, and then go on to speak of questions in philosophy in ways that have been shaped by my inner listeners, including my Donald if not yours.

My Donald is inseparable from two great funds of stories: the stories that are constantly buzzing in his head, and to which he so readily turns the conversation, and the stories about him, with which his friends are never at a loss to delight one another. The stories Donald tells seem to me important for the way that they constantly enforce the creative tension between discursive and intuitive thought. There is a great temptation, perhaps a necessary one, for the philosopher to iron out all the concrete particularities of stories in the quest for an intelligible intellectual structure. I do not believe for a minute that all of Donald's stories have a single moral, but they do fuse into a swarm that represents the buzzing of the real world, that busy energy of plurality which is the touchstone of philosophical truth. As for the stories about Donald, of which I propose to relate none, I suggest that they are a constant reminder to us of a particular, surprising and inspiring sort of mind: deeply compassionate, kind, and just; relentless in pursuit of the structure of reality, and more especially of the place within things of the good; tossed and distracted by the irreducible plurality of things; delightfully human and in no way aloof in its steady contemplation of the issues which are ultimately important. The stories about him are necessary too, of course, for it is the man himself, rather than any abstract list of character traits, which makes him a welcome participant in the secret dialogue within.

Donald never taught me directly, so it was from others that I learnt both the tedious necessary skill of worrying an argument into rigorous form and the equally vital lesson that philosophy is fun. But while we 'moral scientists' laboured over 'analysis' at Sidgwick Avenue, Donald at the Divinity School seemed to me, as he still does, the closest that I have come across to an incarnation of the Platonic philosopher, the boundlessly inquisitive and intensely engaging mind which nevertheless stands committed to the sovereignty of good above all. I should like to try to show what I have made of the sense of the proper task of philosophy which I take Donald to embody by trying to bring into the open an issue which seems to me important but neglected in what one might term the moral philosophy of international politics.

The dominant preoccupation in modern English-language moral philosophy has been with rule-based systems of thought, whose inter-relationship is often envisaged via the labyrinthine interconnections and tensions between utilitarian and Kantian ways of envisaging the world. The 'debate about the bomb' is one of many disputes about morality and public affairs which have naturally followed this pattern, with a great many varieties of utilitarian and absolutist positions on offer, and numerous attempts to steer some sort of middle way between the two extremes. There is no doubt that this is a necessary debate, but many of us consider that it rests on dangerously over-simplified fundamentals. There is a widely, though by no means universally, shared feeling that a necessary part of any corrective will be to take much more seriously what might be called the Aristotelian tradition in ethics.

What is much less certain is *how* we take that tradition seriously, how we conceive of its relevance to our modern concerns. One need only look into the work of Elizabeth Anscombe and contrast it with Alasdair MacIntyre's *After Virtue* and Martha Nussbaum's *Fragility of Goodness* to see how very variously the Aristotelian heritage might be understood. The conception I want to explore here is different from any of these three. What it takes from Aristotle above all is, first, his sense of the need for an outline of the excellent life and, second, his belief that this should be constructed via a consideration of the virtues. When we reflect upon international politics, we readily think such things as that the behaviour of states, the positions adopted by statesmen, the postures demanded by public opinion, are very often immoderate, unjust and imprudent. The philosophical question is, 'How seriously should one take such a way of talking?' In Aristotle's own writings, the virtues are characteristic of individuals, and he approaches politics in another, much more rule-oriented, way when he focuses on the comparison of constitutions. Is it excessively anthropomorphic to direct virtue-talk at the vast, impersonal edifice of the state?

This is a large question, of course. In this chapter I propose to tackle one small part of it, by examining one of the virtues which plays a very important part in Christian thought, and can be suggestive of a view of states which consigns them all to the devil in short order. I shall argue that much Christian and non-Christian thought in this particular area is misconceived, and that the state merits a little more patience in this particular regard than many of us find it natural to suppose. The virtue I shall discuss is humility. The problem with the state is that states are known to be very proud, jealous of their reputation, dangerous when their honour is at stake. One natural line of thought is that this universal characteristic of states, their pride, damns them, so that we should approach them in this regard with the caution that we accord to a dangerous evil power rather than with any suspicion that there might be something in their pride to be respected, even cherished. Such thinking encourages the humble to envisage a radical separation between their concerns and the preoccupations of the state. It is radically subversive of the concept of Christian citizenship. The question I want to raise, and to go a little way towards answering, is whether such a contrast between pride and humility is sound. I shall argue that it is not. Most of this essay will be concerned with aspects of orderly life within the state because this is the sphere we know best, where we can judge best of the nature of pride and humility. Towards the end of the essay I shall attempt one possible way of drawing out implications concerning the state and international relations.

A convenient starting-point is a book that has in its title a phrase which I used above in characterizing my inner Donald: 'the sovereignty of good'. Iris Murdoch's essay and essay collection under this title[1] offers an admirably terse and well-written exposition of a very influential dichotomy: on the one hand, man's natural selfishness; on the other, an 'unselfing' attention to the reality that is beyond the self. She says that the psyche resembles a machine, its consciousness not normally a transparent glass through which it views the world, but a cloud of more or less fantastic reverie designed to protect the psyche from pain; even its loving is more often than not an assertion of self; and so forth (pp. 78–9). Against this she pits an 'unpossessive contemplation' which 'resists absorption into the selfish dream life of the consciousness' (pp. 85–6). Her memorable illustrations of this latter are the following: first, 'I am looking out of the window in an anxious state of mind, oblivious of my surroundings', when suddenly 'There is nothing now but kestrel' (p. 85); secondly, a woman has taken against her daughter-in-law, but decides to question her prejudice, and suddenly is outside herself, seeing the young woman in a quite different light.

Iris Murdoch is such a clear and imaginative writer that it is illuminating to consider what she could and could not say if she were to undertake the testing discipline of attempting to write a novel. Her moral philosophy tells us that it would be of a peculiarly simple kind. Much of it would be a portrayal of selves caught up in their own dream-worlds, but occasionally there would be breakings-through to vision, and some people would be working at the consolidation of this discipline of attention. That is all. What would be missing from such an imaginative representation of life? One thing that would be necessarily absent would be any definite direction to the strivings of the good people. The focus in her moral philosophy is so much upon the delusions of self, and upon vision as the counter-balance to these richly documented follies, that there would be no space for the vision to deliver a content. Tolstoy's Pierre or George Eliot's Dorothea inhabit a definite enough world of substantive values for their strivings to be related as something more than projections of selfish delusion. The snares of the self are judged from without in a kind of reference-frame for which the moral philosophy of Iris Murdoch makes no provision.

This is, of course, no isolated limitation, either culturally or in terms of tradition. Iris Murdoch is an eloquent spokesman of a generation which has very good reasons for finding extreme difficulty in investing any substantive vision of the good with imaginative energy. Satire of a peculiarly rootless kind is its natural form of imaginative expression. And as to tradition, she is surely the kind of preacher who invites a remark which Küng applied to Barth's theology. He said that Barth was so insistent upon the otherness of God as to appear to leave nothing in man to be saved. In exactly the same way, selflessness in Iris Murdoch's *Sovereignty of Good* is so ethereal that it is incapable of playing any part in a human life thick enough to be the subject of a novel.

One of the greatest exponents of this kind of moral discourse, the kind that systematically squeezes out of human life any definite conception of the good, however much it may protest the sovereignty of good over other concepts, is the terrible Pascal, contemporary of Hobbes and a most penetrating commentator on our own appalling century. I quote from the Penguin translation of the *Pensées* (Harmondsworth, Middlesex, 1966):

2   Shall I believe I am nothing? Shall I believe I am god?

4   *Letter to induce men to seek God.* Then make them look for him among the philosophers, sceptics and dogmatists, who will worry the man who seeks.

44   *Imagination.* It is the dominant faculty in man, master of error and falsehood, all the more deceptive for not being invariably so . . . Put the

world's greatest philosopher on a plank that is wider than need be: if there is a precipice below, although his reason may convince him that he is safe, his imagination will prevail ... Anyone who chose to follow reason alone would have proved himself a fool ... Man has been quite right to make these two powers [reason and imagination] into allies ... Magistrates have shown themselves well aware of this mystery ...

26 The power of kings is founded on the reason and folly of the people, but especially on their folly. The greatest and most important thing in the world is founded on weakness. This is a remarkably sure foundation, for nothing is surer than that the people will be weak.

14 True Christians are ... obedient to these follies; not that they respect follies, but rather the divine order which has subjected men to follies as a punishment.

At this point, Pascal cites an interpretation, which he attributes to Aquinas, of a passage from the Letter of James. James appears to be delivering a message so simple and direct as to admit of no question of interpretation:

My brethren, show no partiality as you hold the faith ... For if a man with gold rings and in fine clothing comes into your assembly, and a poor man in shabby clothing also comes in, and you pay attention to the one who wears fine clothing and say 'Have a seat here, please,' while you say to the poor man, 'Stand there,' or 'Sit at my feet,' have you not made distinctions among yourselves, and become judges with evil thoughts? Listen, my beloved brethren. Has not God chosen those who are poor in the world to be rich in faith and heirs of the kingdom which he has promised to those who love him? But you have dishonored the poor man. Is it not the rich who oppress you, is it not they who drag you into court? (2: 1–6, RSV)

A simple message, one would have thought. If there is any politics in it, that must surely lie in the ringing declaration that there shall be real and simple equality in dealings among the congregation. Pascal is far from agreeing. This of all passages is tortured, with help from Romans, into requiring the faithful to be obedient to these follies, presumably giving pride of place in that grand erection the church building to the wealthy and powerful, while taking care to interpret the obvious meaning of such deference as a submission to divine punishment which receives no sort of overt social articulation. It is not surprising that Pascal has found so many secular admirers in this century among an intelligentsia that has flirted so readily with the various forms of totalitarianism. The great interest of Pascal is that he makes overt the political implications of that void which is undeclared in Iris Murdoch.

One further point about Pascal may be essential to my theme. He is emphatic that kings, magistrates, doctors, etc., 'win respect' by sagacious manipulation of the imagination. But he makes one exception:

41   Soldiers are the only ones who do not disguise themselves in this way, because their role is really more essential; they establish themselves by force, the others by masquerade.

This exception is not accidental. To ground his authoritarian vision, to make it immune from the charge of being but one more form of folly, Pascal has only two options. The option he does *not* take is that of declaring the powers that be to be directly ordained of God, so that submission to them is an article of faith. He is not, in other words, a fideist. The people are to be kept in line by a judicious mixture of reason and imagination, without appeal to the faith. This is one of the reasons why Pascal is so interesting to us. We want to see his rational deduction of political submission, as we would not be interested in any exercise of conjuring submission out of faith. Pascal has only one option left, which is to tell us that there is something out there in the world which he has understood and which requires submission. What is this something? It is force. Pascal, like Hobbes at this point, delivers a substantive argument, over and above the exposure of folly, through the claim to understand something that is real out there and thoroughly distinct from folly: force. If force is there to be understood, the clear-eyed may come to understand that you do not argue with it. Even Job, at the shatteringly disappointing end of the story, does not say to God, 'Cop out! Give me an answer!' He knuckles under, and is blest for his realism.

Pascal is wrong about soldiers. They are no more dealers in pure force than any other role-players. Even the most terrible of wars does not end with the total physical destruction of the losing side: rather, there comes a time when one side consents to admit defeat. How this decisive *psychological* move is secured is as much a blend of reason and imagination as any other of the operations that Pascal documents. And this is good news, if only of a negative kind, for the opponents of authoritarian realism. For it means that Pascal's system is left very much in the air, ill-equipped to deduce its political implications from any reality that has been securely separated from the miasma of folly which Pascal sees as the normal human lot.

But I do not want to dwell on this negative point, important though it is. Pascal matters to us above all as a challenge to establish what positive good we can affirm in the face of his penetrating negations. I shall suggest that a good way of exploring the question is by considering how to relate humility and humiliation.

This problem is acute in Iris Murdoch's *Sovereignty of Good*. She attaches great importance to the virtue of humility. In a way, it is *the* virtue from her point of view, in that humility is what we learn when reality breaks in upon the fantasizing self, and humility is the characteristic virtue of the attentive person on whom her account of goodness is focused. What she does not reflect upon is that there must be limits to humility without which there is inescapable confusion between this virtue and the affliction of humiliation. This is lost from view in *The Sovereignty of Good* because of its exclusive preoccupation with the pulling down of pride and illusion.

Sadly, there is much in Christian tradition which is bound to be unhelpful on this topic. The great tradition which sees martyrdom as the normal destiny of the faithful witness has within its logical structure an inbuilt resistance to the drawing of any contrast between humility and humiliation. So long as faith holds, bringing with it the humility of the faithful before the true God, nothing that the world calls humiliation can touch us. So-called humiliations are to be understood triumphally, as so many proofs of faith and divine loving-kindness. To the extent that Christianity concentrates its ethical thought on *the good death*, the faithful martyr, to that extent it obliterates the line between humility and humiliation by making the former into part of faith and the latter into a purely external circumstance through which faith is shown.

How are we to overcome the one-sidedness implicit in martyrology? Here is an outline of what I think needs to be said. First, several perspectives on human life are complementary, for all their apparent incompatibility. We cannot do without the long-range shot, in which God appears infinitely large and man infinitely small, but this is not the only legitimate or essential perspective. We also need a vision sufficiently close up for the real differences between good and evil in man, living flesh and blood, to be visible. As Collingwood said in *New Leviathan*, appropriately enough written at the time of Britain's supreme trial by war, we need to be able to think seriously in terms of Micah 6:8.

> He has showed you, O man, what is good;
> and what does the Lord require of you
> but to do justice, and to love kindness,
> *and to walk humbly with your God?*

'To walk humbly with' suggests a different perspective from that of abasement before the Almighty.

Second, therefore, where do we get this more intimate perspective? John Passmore, in *The Perfectibility of Man*,[2] draws a helpful contrast between two forms of pride. Aristocratic pride, pride in status and the status of the self, is in his humanistic view as vicious as Christian tradition has held it to be. But, he says, there is also the pride of the workman, his pride in what he is doing, and this is not vice, but a necessary virtue. The good workman will not be diverted from the standards of his craft, for he knows what is good and what is mere skimping or botching, what would be a betrayal of his calling. Nor will he hear of his craft being slandered, for it is a vulnerable thing in the world, a thing which liars and despisers can damage, a thing requiring to be cherished and nourished and stood up for. We probably need to add that the good workman will necessarily resist concealment of the pleasure that he naturally feels in doing what he knows to be good work, lest the killjoys misrepresent the possible place of work in the firmament of value. He will not conceal that his participation in this good makes him, too, a part of the good, that he, the workman, also merits part of the praise. He should certainly not be embarrassed, let alone censorious, when good judges of the work praise *him*. This is proper pride, and I think Passmore is exactly right when he insists that it is *the* line of defence against all that is shoddy and shameful in human activity. It is *the* measure of the skimped and the careless, and as observable in the proper pride of a parent as in that of a carpenter.

Proper pride offers a promising criterion for distinguishing between humility and humiliation. To humiliate a person is to deprive him of all capacity for proper pride, to take from him the inner or outer resources for participating in the right way in any of those innumerable activities in which it is right to take proper pride. This may take the form of dehumanizing hunger, or equally of a psychological slight so damaging that the person cannot look with proper pride on what he is doing, even when it is objectively appropriate.

Perhaps we should go further and recognize that humility and proper pride are *the same virtue by different names*. Certainly, proper pride is bound to bring humility with it, since it involves a clear recognition of all that is owed to others, to good materials, to favourable objective conditions, etc. And on the other hand, once we zoom in from the long-shot of the infinite God before whom the faithful martyrs are abased, proof against all humiliations, we see people engaged in an activity in which they can take proper pride, the cherishing of a certain fellowship and congregation and tradition, and as vulnerable to self-doubt or to the charge of unwarranted certainty as the practitioners of innumerable other activities. It is the inwardness of their activity which tells them when to say 'I can no other' and to endure the good death. It is from that which gives them a certain proper pride that they derive their reason for acknowledging their absolute dependence. Only the witness so unself-conscious about contingency that he sees himself as being *simply* alone with God would have a ground in his own patterns of thought for resisting the argument that humility and proper pride amount to the same thing.

It is worth hearing Pascal on one aspect of what I have just been saying:

35 *Heel of a shoe.* 'How well-made that is! What a skilful workman! What a brave soldier!' That is where our inclinations come from, and our choice of careers.

Here speaks the long-shot-man, for whom the workman's skill and the soldier's calling are dust and folly. Aquinas held that honour for virtue is the greatest external good at human disposal.[3] Pascal would undoubtedly stress the word 'external', intending it to mean 'manipulative': honour for so-called skill, etc., is the greatest manipulative good at the disposal of those with the sense to blend imagination and reason into effective government. Aquinas probably meant something rather different: something to the effect that the greatest outward visible sign at the disposal of human beings is to join in the proper pride of those who are doing the innumerable things which are good; something in the spirit of James's straight-forward involvement with the activity of the congregation.

Let me call one more witness about the relation between humility and proper pride before moving on to my final task, that of relating all this to thought about the nuclear age. One Christian writer who brought very great sensitivity and perception to the issues of humiliation and honour for good work was Simone Weil. 'What a skilful workman!' sneers Pascal, with all the aristocratic pride of pre-revolutionary France. In a series of reflections written in the 1930s, known as her First Notebook, she writes:

What shows that *work* – if it is not of an inhuman kind – is meant for us is its joy, a joy which even our exhaustion does not lessen . . .   (p. 8)

By work, man creates the universe around him. Remember the way you looked at the fields after a day's harvesting . . . How differently from a person going for a walk, for whom the fields are only a scenic background.
(p. 18)

The workers are reluctant to confess to this joy – because they have the impression that it might lead to a reduction of wages!   (p. 8)

In effect, Simone Weil proposes a critique of social organization whose cutting edge has yet to be tested. She asks in effect, how must society be organized so that work shall be the joyous thing that we know it to be when it is separated from social distortions? How must society be organized around the proper pride and humility of the workman?

Argument of this kind has extensive ramifications in our thinking about society within secure state boundaries, but I want to suggest that it also has a bearing on how we should think about international relations. I began by noting that most philosophical and theological input into 'the debate about the bomb' (a good example of what moral philosophy has achieved in this sphere) is concentrated on two main areas. One well-trodden field is the justice of nuclear deterrence: can there be a just use of nuclear weapons in war? Can deterrence be justified even if nuclear war cannot? The other well-covered area concerns what is rational: is deterrence playable? How do various forms of deterrence look in the context of game theory? These are both important, but concentration on them alone is unduly one-sided, for deterrence is but an instrument of foreign policy, and the underlying question is how we are to think about this. Support for the bomb derives from the (naive or sophisticated) conviction that weapons of mass destruction are necessary in the jungle of international politics: a decent state or alliance, it is felt, cannot do without them. To speak to such beliefs, and to the fears and ambitions that attend upon them, we have to consider the question of how to envisage a good state, and the background thought from the Aristotelian tradition which I am proposing that we try to take seriously is that this question of the good state, this question of what is excellent, should be approached via our under-standing of the virtues and vices.

The superpowers procure more or better weapons to practise containment, or to counter encirclement. What are we to say about the basis of such ideas as those of containment and encirclement? Clearly, no one sort of thing will suffice. We must have apposite views on the nature of international organization, the psychology of threat-perception, the particular characteristics of particular coun-tries, and much else. Among all this, one thought seems especially important for ethics: almost all of us incline to use the language of vice and virtue to characterize the conduct of the great powers. We speak of leaders and policies and public opinion as being intemper-ate, for example. Is such language appropriate? This question lands us in the same sort of area in which we have been operating throughout my argument. Starting from Iris Murdoch's eminently contemporary vision of the world, a vision largely prompted by the experience of war and other international phenomena, we got into an argument about the nature of a particular virtue. It is not difficult to see that just such arguments are necessary if we are to know what to make of discourse about the vices and virtues of international political behaviour. How directly does a consideration of humility and humiliation bear on the international question?

We saw earlier that Pascal directs contempt at something which Simone Weil cherishes, the work of the craftsman. Pascal's con-tempt is part of his one-perspective vision of human life, magnify-ing God to the point where humdrum human excellence vanishes. Something very like Pascal's attitude is a very typical attitude to the state: contempt, disillusionment, cynicism, scepticism at one level combined with a sense at another level of this despised thing being of enormous importance. Among many illustrations of this complex of attitudes, one of the commonest and perhaps most interesting is the loathing of taxes and cynicism about their being well-spent which is so very often combined with a roseate glow over the idea of 'the ultimate sacrifice' of dying for one's country. To cut a long argument short, people are very happy to die for their country (anticipating a good death, akin to the sublime good deaths of the martyrs), but would find it ridiculous to think of living for one's country. It is actually priggish, something worse than a vice, to be appalled at people's reluctance to pay their taxes. They want their country to be great and strong, and in a sense it would be wrong to say that they are unwilling to pay for it, so long as the price is in blood. What they do not want is for the state to be one of the things that they cherish in their everyday lives.

Doubtless there are many things of many kinds to be said about such attitudes, but I shall single out one. It is dismayingly obvious that we are far indeed from taking pride in the everyday workings of the state. The everyday machinery of government and politics is not something that is understood and cherished as a good workman understands and cherishes what he is doing. The state is indeed a false abstraction, is indeed nothing but the readiness with which we pay our taxes, but this clear understanding does not suit us. We prefer the state as it actually is to be described as something alien, just as in Simone Weil's commentary the alienated worker would resist any imputation of joy in his activity.

I suggest that this has profound implications for international relations. The desire for containment and the fear of encirclement are in practice inseparable from the ambitious desire for expansion. The aggressive–defensive urge of nation-states is, many of us certainly want to say, intemperate, imprudent and unjust. In other words, it is vicious. But is such virtue-talk seriously applicable to states? Part of the reason for thinking that it is lies here, in the power of this form of discourse to highlight the very odd attitudes upon which so much ordinary thinking about the state appears to rest. The modern great power is not understood in the somewhat minimalist, order-keeping terms that Hobbes and Pascal (on one reading) propose. It is charged with being the arena where ordinary flesh and blood can gain a good death. It is required to be an old-fashioned kind of hero, and woe betide a President Carter who fails to understand this. Yet this embodiment of our longing for grandeur is something we do not want to pay for, something whose everyday workings we despise. Here, surely, there is a *locus* for plain speaking about the virtues.

What might be said? It would be salutary to ask how a state would have to behave for it to make sense for us to cherish it, to pay for it gladly. We would need to be sure of something good in it, something good which we were doing by participating in it, some good in which we were sharing by this participation. If our nation-state were, in its national life, ministering to the real needs of others, so that the worth of our state was visible to others, and as naturally acknowledged by them as the good work of the craftsman is naturally acknowledged, then it would not be natural to hide our light under a bushel, to talk any language rather than that of craftsman-like pride in our nation. Perhaps there is something to be learnt from the admittedly equivocal experience of nineteenth-century British imperialism. The best of the imperialists thought that they were doing something in which a man could take pride. We know too much about the limitations of their merits, and the current plague of nostalgia for empire makes one reluctant to discuss such matters openly. But the thought we need to ponder is, perhaps, that a sense of pride purged of the aristocratic (racist) element which is all too present in our history, and directed to ends less dubious, more obviously conducive to the common good than those of the British in India, may conceivably be within the reach of flesh and blood, and ought to be one kind of norm from which we work towards sustained discourse about the virtues and vices of the state.

It is an open question whether the nation-state can do things which are for the common good, and as such can be a proper object of praise and pride. But suppose a nation were to find a way to live which could command the praise of the just and benevolent. Such a nation would be a proper object of pride for its citizens. They would look to it for part of their own self-esteem, as the Victorians somewhat too optimistically looked to their nation, and as we cannot look to our country now. If one cannot view one's country in that way, then it is far from clear how one should regard it. For the pride of the craftsman is the bastion against the slipshod and the meretricious. If we cannot view our nation in such terms, we have no intelligible basis for resisting the frankly manipulative views of the state which were pioneered by Hobbes and Pascal. It is therefore of great systematic difficulty for us to accuse our own leaders or electorates of intemperance, fantasy, paranoia, etc. Such accusations presuppose some principle of moderation, but the state-enterprise as we live it is devoid of any such principle. There is, therefore, in the international arena as in the sphere of social organization within the state's boundaries, scope for a radical criticism of existing practices guided by the question that I have attributed to Simone Weil: how must the state be organized to be a proper object of pride among its citizens?

I began by directing attention to the apparent radical contrast between the Christian virtue of humility and the characteristic pride of states. I have argued that this contrast is unreal. We need to envisage ourselves in several different perspectives. The long-shot which magnifies the glory of God has to be complemented by a closer view, in which it is arguable that humility and proper pride are one and the same virtue. This thought prompts radical questions about both the domestic politics and the external bearing of states. In effect I have argued that, rather than consign the pride of the nations to damnation, we attempt to draw the same distinctions in instances of it that we discern in fields of experience that we know well. If sound, the argument is but a small part of a large Aristotelian enterprise. Let me conclude by saying where I think the next step should lead. Aristotle held that the best way for us to approach moral truth was to consult as fully as possible the moral intuitions of both the wise and the many. The intuitions that I have been consulting in this paper are towards the perfectionist end of a spectrum. Towards the other end of that spectrum lie the dark convictions that states lie under a cruel necessity from which we individual mortals are shielded. I have not addressed these here. The next step, if the argument thus far is sound, is perhaps to inquire whether national pride can seriously be regarded as susceptible of the idealist interpretation proposed here.

Notes

1 Iris Murdoch, *The Sovereignty of Good* (London, 1970).
2 John Passmore, *The Perfectibility of Man* (London, 1970), esp. pp. 287–90.
3 See James Childress, 'Honor', in *A New Dictionary of Christian Ethics* (London, 1986), p. 275, citing *ST* II–III. 129.1.

10 'Between purgation and illumination': a critique of the theology of right

JOHN MILBANK

This chapter re-examines the post-Kantian character of modern theology. Its aim is to indicate how pervasive are its transcendentalist presuppositions and to suggest that these be eradicated. At the same time it argues that the possibility of theology 'at the end of epistemology' has to be construed at once as a historicism and as a 'metaphysics'.

In the first part of the paper I shall examine the way in which Kant is considered to have put a critical block in front of the 'way of eminence' and of what one might call the 'discourse of participated perfections' as discovered, especially, in Thomas Aquinas. Having shown that the basis of critique is here itself dogmatically metaphysical, and in a disguised fashion, political, I shall then proceed in the second section to suggest that theology proceeding in the wake of transcendentalism is partially reducible to a liberal rights ideology. This verdict will be applied both to theologies seeking for themselves epistemological foundations, and to theologies which assume that ethics has some extra-theological and well-grounded autonomy. In the final section I shall ask whether the recent revival of a neo-Aristotelian 'ethics of virtue' and a specifically theological exposition of 'the good' as prior to 'the right' points a way towards the retrieval of the 'discourse of participated perfections'. But the answer given will insist that there can be no relapse towards pre-modernity; rather, any retrieval must assume a post-modern, metacritical guise.

161

I

In his book *God As the Mystery of the World* Eberhard Jüngel seeks to escape not only from Cartesian foundationalism, but also from Kantian transcendentalism. The latter is for him the very consummation of a metaphysical tradition which is culpable, not because it illegitimately extrapolates from the limited to the absolute, but because of its rigorous agnosticism with regard to the content of that absolute. The achievement of metaphysics is 'to refer ourselves to an unknown without which we could not continue to exist', and

the theological critique to be directed against this metaphysical tradition focuses on the fact that in its obtrusiveness the unknownness of God has become an unbearably sinister riddle. For it is intolerable to live in the awareness of a condition which comes into view only in order to disappear again into unknownness. It is difficult enough for a person, with his earthly conditionedness to have an unknown father, as a procreator, but not a father.[1]

For Jüngel the *via negativa* in its classic form is a characteristic achievement of metaphysics, and its bad infinitude and projection of emptiness is the subtlest and most insidious form of idolatry.

However, one may well call into question Jüngel's effective conflation of the traditional *via negativa* with transcendentalism. The immediate context for his censure is a discussion of the treatment of analogy in Kant and Aquinas. In Kant's remarks on analogy in the *Prolegomena*, Jüngel discovers a culmination of the use of analogy in a strictly agnostic fashion. It is legitimate, according to Kant, to talk of God as cause of the world if we confine ourselves to true, original analogy (derived from the figure of analogy in rhetoric), namely, analogy of proper proportionality which involves comparison of two similar ratios, rather than two single things, or two things in relation to a third common element.[2] Pure reason demands that we regard the world 'as if' in a relationship of dependence on a highest cause, as a clock depends upon an artisan. This allows us, however, no room to speculate about that cause as it is in itself, and if we are forced to conceive this cause by reference to the schematizations involved in concepts of our experience, then this should involve us only in a 'symbolic anthropomorphism' which, as Kant says, 'only concerns language and not the object'. Hence for Kant, any apparent positive content in analogy only concerns certain necessities of our finitude with respect to the use of language, and analogy can certainly tell us nothing more about God than that all the conditions of the world that we know must be in a relation of total dependence upon him.

By making Kant's treatment of analogy pivotal, Jüngel associates an agnostic treatment of 'naming God' with proper proportionality. He tries to argue that, even in Aquinas, proportionality is more basic than attribution (the comparison of two things, or of two things in relation to a third element; although in theology, God as one pole of the comparison is also the medium of comparison), because, when Aquinas attributes, for example, 'goodness' to God 'in a more eminent sense', this merely means that an unknown goodness belongs to God in proportion to his unknown being, just as we possess goodness in due proportion to our being. Yet this conclusion certainly conflicts with at least the appearance of Aquinas's mature texts, which talk preponderantly about attribution, and it fails to reckon with the way in which, for Aquinas, any predication of goodness or being to finite things already refers to a dynamic ontological tension in which they are constantly drawn forwards towards the divine perfection. This ceases to be true only with Duns Scotus, who makes perfection language belong to a pre-theological metaphysical discourse concerned with a 'common being' indifferent to finite and infinite. One can almost say, with hindsight, that this metaphysics has a 'proto-transcendentalist' character.[3]

Still more significantly, however, Jüngel fails to reflect that while, from one point of view, proper proportionality is 'more agnostic' than attribution, from another point of view it is less so, because the common ratio can be univocally specified. In Kant's usage, analogy of proper proportionality tends to posit a specifiable, fixed, precisely known sort of relation of God to the creation; God is only related to creation as efficient cause – he 'constructs' the world outside himself as an artisan manufactures a clock.

This observation can open the way to our grasp of a hidden contradiction in many recent treatments of analogy. In so far as they characteristically try to combine a preference for analogy of attribution seen as 'more agnostic' with a post-critical confinement of analogy to 'our use of language' detached from questions of participation, they then fail to be aware of the alliance of the latter perspective with proper proportionality.[4] What emerges to view is that there are really two possible agnosticisms – the metaphysics of Kant, which is totally agnostic as concerns God-in-himself, but in a way dogmatic as concerns his relationship to finite beings, and the metaphysics of Aquinas, which is less agnostic concerning God-in-himself, but also more agnostic concerning the conditions of our relationship to God. It is only Aquinas's agnosticism which really exemplifies the principle that there is no *ratio* between finite and infinite.

Let me try to substantiate this, first of all with respect to Kant. Recent Kantian scholarship has tended to stress that, while Kant is giving a critical, agnostic version of the Leibnizian–Wolffian metaphysics, none the less he remains within the basic terms of this metaphysics which posits a noumenal substrate to appearances, a world of monads without composition in themselves and without external relations, on which spatial–temporal relationships are yet themselves founded.[5] Metaphysics has, in this world, a specific and 'scientific' object, and while for Kant this sphere of pure reason becomes very restricted of access, it is still, all the same, attainable. That we possess theoretical 'ideas' which we use regulatively with respect to the concepts of the understanding, and that we are able to exercise a practical reason with respect to the self-grounding logic of the rational will itself, means that we are truly able to stand at the *boundary* of reason and understanding, of noumena and phenomena. Unlike a limit, says Kant, which involves merely an asymptotic progress towards an unreachable goal, and is an aspect of pure phenomenality, a boundary has something positive to it – to grasp it one must in some way stand outside it.[6] Nevertheless, this standing outside is for Kant very minimal: one knows absolutely that there is an outside, but not the content of 'things in themselves' in this realm beyond the boundary. Kant's *entire* philosophy is in a sense an aesthetic of the classical sublime in which one is brought up against the margin of organized, formal, 'beautiful' experience, and at this margin becomes overwhelmed by the intimation of the materially formless, and infinitely total. In the *Critique of Judgement* Kant tells us that the sublime in the imagination is the indeterminate form of pure reason, and also that the sublime, unlike the beautiful, more enters into itself when we pass from imagination to the theoretical.[7] Here vague intimation becomes a known relation to other noumena, and fears of the overwhelming and pleas for grace are transformed into awesome respect for the moral law within us.

The minimality of content with respect to the sublime reasonings concerning the noumena can easily cause us to overlook the fact that for Kant the supposition of transcendental relation to unknown things-in-themselves is all important. For it is upon this formality of relationship alone that he constructs the centrepiece of his phil-osophy, a natural moral law derived sheerly from the self-establishing of the rational will. Furthermore, the differences between Kant's attitude to finite things-in-themselves, to other transcendental egos, and to the quasi-intelligences which underlie physical substances on the one hand, and to God the supreme thing-in-itself, the Monad of monads, on the other hand, are not as marked as is sometimes supposed. If one surveys the entire course of Kant's post-critical writings, including the *Opus Postumum*, then it would seem that in relation to both God and things-in-themselves there is an element of an 'as if' attitude, a positing for regulative purposes, which none the less does not belie an ultimate require-ment for belief in a realm of inner, noumenal relationships as the ultimate reason for the necessity of this 'as if' attitude, for our naturally given, metaphysically speculative disposition.[8]

Given the above kind of analysis, it is easy to show that Kant's strictures on attribution, on a metaphysics of eminence, are them-selves grounded in a metaphysics that may well seem to us more sheerly dogmatic than much of the metaphysics of the Middle Ages. It is not at all the case that Kant offers us an innocent, descriptive account of our finitude, the permanent limits of our human being. One can see this in two ways: first of all, Kant's confining of categories like cause and substance to the world of our experience is mainly impelled by the 'scientific' establishment of a metaphysical world, as strictly distinguishable from the phenomenal world in terms of the realities of freedom and a pure reason able to proceed from possibility to actuality. Only then, because one stands meta-physically above phenomena, is one able to determine dogmatically the 'range' of concepts like cause and substance.

In the second place, it can be pointed out that the Kantian demand that such categories should not be applied outside the range of their possible schematization is not the simple equivalent of a Thomist reminder of our *modus significandi*, but instead assumes, in 'empiricistic' fashion, that there is a mass of information, a 'sensible manifold' recognizable as separate from its categorization, and that it is this that the categories of the understanding must 'apply' to. One can call into question this dualism of organizing scheme and empirical content by suggesting that it is entirely unwarranted to suppose a mass of information somehow coming 'into' our 'mind' from 'outside' – once one abandons this picture of a 'mind' as a mirror or a receptacle, there is in fact no reason to posit such 'unorganized' material at all.[9] But without this atomistic material base, it no longer appears that categories like cause and substance have a necessarily restricted orientation towards finite, material things, in accordance with what can only be (as clearly emerges in the *Critique of Judgement*) a divinely pre-established harmony.[10] They simply belong to our linguistic being-in-the-world, and the question, 'Can they be extrapolated?' just belongs with the question, 'Is there a "beyond", a transcendent, at all?'

It follows from this that Kant's refusal of any extrapolation from phenomenally instantiated categories and content depends wholly upon his 'metaphysics of the sublime', according to which one can step up to a boundary where one 'sees' that phenomenal categories no longer apply, and where one grasps, with necessity, that there are things-in-themselves, even if one can give no content to them.

This agnosticism does not simply register a margin outside our empirical and practical knowing; on the contrary, it is the very *mode of being* of our practical and political existence. While physical science is not able to deal with things-in-themselves, the laws of the state – we are told in the *Metaphysics of Morals* – *must* treat things as things-in-themselves in so far as they are not here regarded as a chain of causal appearances but rather are correlated with human freedom, so as to become 'private property'.[11] In the world of human relationships, both 'personal' and political, it is the very vacuity of things and the very lack of specific content in genuine freedom which is made to organize rational behaviour. Hence 'agnostic' emptiness of content with regard to things-in-themselves is so far from being irrelevant to human empirical practice that it actually *defines* genuine, normative human practice. Rational, moral behaviour is universalizable behaviour which treats every rational being as equivalent in his formal freedom, and every object as equivalent in its ability to be possessed and its standardized exchangeability. To say that God can be conceived as being in a relation to the whole world which is similar to the relations of freedom between things *within* that world, and to postulate this God as the ultimate harmonizer of the laws of nature with the law of freedom, is to say that God is *fully* known as the guarantor of the noumenal relations of rational law and so fully known as law-giver. That this is really to know quite a lot about God is indicated by the *Opus Postumum*, where it is suggested that God as rational will remains unknown in his ultimate ground even to himself.[12] In the metaphysics of the sublime the absolutely equal and formally fixed relationship in which we all, as liberal subjects, stand to the unknown absolute, serves to confirm the world (the enlightened, bourgeois world) as it is.

Thus this metaphysics, including *especially* its agnosticism, is reducible to the ultimately political promotion of abstract, negative right as the foundation of human society, as opposed to any positive conception of a common 'good' as a collective goal. It is important to stress – because this is obscured in certain 'benign' readings – that this formalism is affirmed most of all at the metaphysical level. Although it is true that Kant is religiously concerned with more than the pragmatic workings of mutual respect for negative freedom in liberal society, the truly moral will, asymptotically approaching the 'holiness' of the divine will which is moral by nature, simply has a genuine, and not merely self-interested, respect for this freedom.[13] This 'genuineness' is construable in terms of moral *virtue* only in so far as human beings are engaged in a struggle with an originally perverse will which subordinates our noumenal to our phenomenal nature. Otherwise, as regards the *telos* of holiness, the moral will is genuine merely by according with the formal–practical rules governing the relations of purely noumenal beings, and following from the necessities of their being by nature free. This is why, in Kant's version of 'justification by faith', the moral will, abstracting entirely from its real, phenomenal 'character', can be wholly converted all at once as regards 'principle', and 'cast of mind', although only gradually can this grasp of principle be translated into a constant disposition to subordinate phenomenal interest in our own happiness to noumenal disinterestedness. Hence it is not the case that for Kant human virtue strives to instantiate an unknown plenitude of good belonging to the *telos*. Rather, what is essential to the eschatological goal, namely the formal principle, is already known, and this knowledge takes precedence over any actual virtuous formation. If one is not misled by the very particular manner of Kant's separation of practical from theoretical reasoning, then one will clearly see that Kant in fact perpetuates the post-Suarez severing of natural law from *Aristotelian* practical reasoning by continuing to ground moral imperatives on theoretically known conditions of rational nature. The ideological supremacy of 'right' over 'good' is correlated, after Suarez, with the notion that one can 'read off' from the given world the permanently divine-willed formal conditions of true human behaviour. 'Agnosticism' in Kant is the reverse face of a great formalist confidence – even as regards metaphysics.

Let us turn in the second place to Aquinas in order to demonstrate that *his* agnostic reserve obeys an entirely different economy, one which is ultimately in harmony with the supremacy of 'good' over 'right'.

It is easy to suppose that when Aquinas says that one can know nothing of God save that he is, what he is not, and his relationship to creatures, he is coming close to the critical position of Kant. In a number of ways recent writers have sought to make this connection, but it is possible that in the wake of a growing anti-Kantianism this move may have outlived its hermeneutic usefulness. To take an important example: David Burrell, in his brilliant book, *Aquinas: God and Action*, endeavours to exploit the notion of *modus significandi* in such a way as to make it appear that Aquinas employed specu-lative grammar to indicate the range of possible meanings available to us in our finitude, and by this operation to show, indirectly, what terms cannot apply beyond our finitude, and what terms might enable us to 'go on talking' with respect to the unknown, though without providing us with any real knowledge.[14] This involves the assumption that Aquinas thought in terms of straddling the bound-ary of the sublime in a way different from, but not wholly dissimilar to, that of Kant. It is wholly relevant to say here that such an aesthetic was not culturally available to Aquinas. It is also relevant to ask whether associating Aquinas with 'speculative grammar' of this precise type is not slightly anachronistic in terms of the chronology of mediaeval thought; as I indicated with respect to perfection terms, it is rather Scotus who later uses grammar in a 'quasifoundationalist' way to delimit the scope of certain meanings prior to their employment in theology (although Burrell alludes specifically to twelfth-century grammar, some elements in his treatment of *modus* seem more consonant with the reflections of the post-1270 *modistae*).[15]

Burrell does not recognize that there is a tension between his notion of a 'grammatical' approach to the unknown beyond the known, and the very different idea that throughout his writings Aquinas is spelling out the specific 'grammar' of creation *ex nihilo* in which the 'unknown' and the 'known' are specified together according to a particular religious assumption about ultimate reality – an assumption that Aquinas may have seen as universally available according to rightly-directed reason, but which, it is hermeneutically important to stress, is actually rooted in the Biblical tradition. Burrell's own exposition in fact veers between these two different notions – grammar as giving the transcendental possibility of a negative specification of the unknown, and grammar as explication of the culturally-specific meaning-presuppositions involved in the logic of creation *ex nihilo*. (In the latter case the term 'grammar' is a heuristically useful term quite apart from arguments about the mediaeval discipline. Where grammar refers in this way to culturally specific assumptions, then linguistic analysis is saved from being a new mutation of transcendentalism.)

It is only when one sticks to the latter notion that one can really make sense of Aquinas's 'discourse of participated perfections'. As Burrell says, the key principle here must be that being is not a 'mere fact'; rather, being, even when it concerns our own doings and makings, is sheer 'givenness'. On the other hand, it has to be said that Aquinas is not at all interested in the later Leibnizian question of why there is 'being in general', or in the related quest for sufficient reason, and neither is he concerned with the Kantian principle that being is not a predicate.[16] Rather, his 'real distinction' of *esse* from *essentia* is concerned firstly to establish a new supremacy of act over form and thereby to deny that reason and intelligibility have any priority over activity, and secondly to associate the concrete and particular subsistence of things with a constant and unpredicatable 'addition to' given essence and species (*ST*, 1 Q.1 a.4). From a usual modern perspective, Aquinas's terminology appears strangely muddled, because the *essentia/esse* contrast mixes comparison of the possible with the actual and that of the categorically general with the contingently particular. Yet this 'muddle' is wholly germane to the 'grammar of creation' because it both secures a new connection between substance and particularity and allows that the actual always 'supersedes' a foregoing determination of possibility. In this way ultimate *differentia*, extending especially to the differences of human persons, are made relevant to the teleological directedness of things. One might say, by making essence to be in 'active potency' to being for every finite creature Aquinas effectively 'eschatologizes' the notion of teleology throughout every level of reality, a move which can then be understood as a preparation for the theology of grace. That which is aimed for, especially as regards human beings, is always, also, that which is 'superadded' (*ST*, 1 Q.5 a.1 ad.3, a.4 ad.2). (I do not, of course, endorse this explication of the 'grammar of creation' as in any way final. Following Erich Przywara I should prefer a more dialectical account in which 'essence' no longer figures as the definitely identifiable principle of finite limitation but marks an active possibility sometimes transcending given actuality. This makes the dynamic non-identity of being and essence *itself* the mark of finitude.)[17]

There is nothing, in a sense, 'mysterious' about these 'superadditions'. They involve, simply, further acts of intellectual synthesis, further strengthening in virtue, further insight into the truth that virtue, as, especially, charity, is not merely perfection in us but a constant spilling over into the strengthening of others after the pattern of the divine creative perfection itself (*ST*, 1 Q.5 a.3 ad.2). But this is not at all to say – following interpreters like Rahner and Metz – that Aquinas builds on an anthropological foundation. On the contrary, there is for Aquinas no grounding of the good in a given, self-transcending rational nature. Instead, to define humanity as located in the increasing imitation of divine goodness, and of divine being, is to have a wholly theological anthropology; it is to say that human beings are only properly known within our imitation of God. To start to specify what is humanly common to us is already to enter into theological discourse, and at the same time, according to our *modus significandi*, to keep our attention upon the very particular sorts of goods that are actually realized by human beings in specific kinds of social existence. There is no appeal, as with Kant, to an abstract non-phenomenal source of validation, but by the same token there is no appeal to God as the transcendent guarantee of a world construable as good and finitely existent within its own terms.

For Aquinas the possibility of analogy is grounded in this reality of participation in being and goodness. Analogy is not, for him, primarily a linguistic doctrine, even if (as I shall insist later) it must become so for us – though not in a manner which persists in the transcendentalist illusion that a 'semantic' account of analogy can be given before an ontological account of participation. Signs, for Aquinas, reflect ideas, which (more or less perfectly in different instances) reflect existing realities (*ST*, 1 Q.13 a.1). It is things themselves which declare to us their relationship to God. Restriction of theology to knowledge of this relationship means for Aquinas something quite different from that indicated by apparently quite similar statements in Kant, because Aquinas thinks of divine causality in terms neither of sufficient reason nor of efficient causality alone, but rather in terms of a complex unity of formal–final–efficient causality which suggests that as all being is from God, then everything in some sense pre-exists within the fullness of the divine simplicity (*ST*, 1 Q.13 a.3, a.5, Q.12 a.11, Q.6 a.4) (or within the divine *Ars* that is the second person of the Trinity). Hence, to know God as cause is not just to know him as cause of the good, but also to propose him as the perfection of goodness, and in a certain sense as the exact, perfect reality of one's *own*, human being (*ST*, 1 Q.6 a.1 ad.2). The degree to which this is not a purely empty attribution is precisely the degree to which one thereby conceives, and personally enters into, the dynamic of created being. Aquinas sums it up in the *Summa Contra Gentiles*: 'God is called wise not only in so far as he produces wisdom, but also because, in so far as we are wise, we imitate to some extent by the power which makes us wise' (*SCG*, 1. 31, 2).

This version of analogy, and Aquinas's metaphysics as a whole, is only comprehensible in terms of the absence of any 'critical', transcendentalist claim to have surmounted finitude, to be able to catalogue its categorical conditions, delimit their relevance and pronounce upon the foundationally formal conditions of the realm beyond finitude. *Because* this is impossible, neither is it possible to know (and one will be likely to assume otherwise) that our knowledge of finitude is not inextricably bound up with partial, but substantive knowledge of infinitude. Yet this 'knowledge of the infinite' may go along with a much greater degree, as compared with Kant, of agnosticism about the conditions of our relation to God. It may be that only an allowance of this imperfect substantive knowledge permits a rigorous adherence to the rule that there is 'no proportion', no 'third measure of comparison', between finite and infinite. This is the case with Aquinas: to say that 'God is eminently good' is for him in effect to make a statement in which the *analogans-analogatum* 'good' can itself be explicated as an entire theory of that participation which makes all analogy possible. 'Good' offers us a semantic depth not because this word already happens to have this character within some sphere of ordinary secular language which Aquinas could never have conceived of, but because actual, given human being is involved in some indefinition in relation to God. Against Burrell one must say that to ascribe real degrees of perfection to being, indeed any use of evaluative perfection-terms, *already* assumes a metaphysics of participation, such that grammar here grounds itself in theology, not theology in grammar. Thus to have some knowledge of virtue, of perfection, is imperfectly to know one's humanity, which is only absolutely comprehended in the divine inclusion – as *esse ipsum* – of all *differentia*. To say 'good' for Aquinas, is not to allow oneself any semantic resting-place; instead religious–moral self-dissatisfaction here colours the very conditions of possible meaningfulness. And this indefinition extends to both the content of virtue and the indissociable 'eternal law' of the formal–final terms of our relationship to God.

   To sum up this section: knowledge of God for Aquinas is change within the circumstances of a certain formal, 'beautiful' constancy of teleological development; knowledge of God for Kant is confirmation of this world as it is, or else a sublime aspiration which is a contentless bad infinitude, unrelated to actual social behaviour.

II

From the foregoing analyses it would seem possible to suggest that the Kantian agnosticism is dominated by a liberal priority of right, while the Thomist agnosticism is grounded in a notion of common and always particular good, conceived both as fact and as value, but imperfectly known and subject to an always revisable practical judgement. One can then perhaps argue that the choice between these two agnosticisms is not really a speculative matter at all, but a matter of different ethics, different politics, different ecclesiologies. However, by posing the matter in this way I do not mean to suggest that the position of Aquinas is retrievable without revision.

In the second part of this essay I shall switch to this level of practical consideration. First of all I want to consider the presence of liberal deontology in modern theology. The most extreme form of this occurs in the guise of attempts to provide theology with 'foundations', or to determine *a priori* the precise, scientific subject-matter of theology in terms of a general positioning of all scientific knowledge, just as Kant sought to determine the subject-matter of metaphysics. The most striking and exemplary instance of this occurs in Helmut Peukert's *Science, Action and Fundamental Theology*.[18] More, perhaps, than any previous theologian, Peukert seeks to build his whole theology from the base of Kantian practical reason. Following Jürgen Habermas and Karl-Otto Apel, he argues that philosophy of science has now led us to see that theoretical knowledge and political authority have precisely the same ground of legitimation – namely the unlimited extension of free communication pursued without coercion or domination. He attempts to show that there is an *aporia* in the restricting of this ideal merely to communication among the living. Resurrection of the dead, of the victims of past injustice, as a new equivalent of the Kantian eschatological harmonizing of nature and freedom, thus becomes the site of genuinely rationally-authorized theological consideration. However, this doctrine of 'anamnestic solidarity' really bursts the bounds of the theory of normative communication with which Peukert begins, and reveals that, far from being a uniquely foundational starting-point, the doctrine of resurrection belongs within the whole wider context of Christian life and teaching. This is because normative communication is only concerned with adjudicating relations of mutually compatible freedom between subjects present in a single space. As it has no concern with the interruptive *difference* of subjects and the way in which real communities find their direction and their identity in the narrative relating of these differences, it cannot really have any interest in resurrection; where one thinks only in terms of abstract subjective will, then death altogether removes the person, and any problem of justice due to her.

There is also the danger, within this kind of approach, of treating the *natural* limitation of death as a sort of transcendental limitation, and then deploying death, after the manner of Heidegger, as a categorical organizer of the content of our historical lives such that the 'fundamental' problem of our lives is our own death, or (for Peukert) the death of the other. This will not do as a foundation for ('authentic') knowledge, because the social possibility of knowledge is partly constituted by our collective survival of death, our writing on tombstones. And we always write specific names, which are precisely the *personae* which we ourselves inherit. In fact only identities *unlimited* by death define our humanity, if one remembers that we do not first of all exist as isolated individuals.

Peukert is important because he gives an extreme example of an attempt to proceed from a liberal deontology, legitimating a secular, pluralist politics, and then to conjoin to this base a Christian theology which is precisely a 'theology of right', or, one might say, of the liberal cemetery, the anonymous tombs. But much more interesting than the case of theologies which seek foundations is the consideration of how a broadly 'neo-orthodox' theology which refuses foundations may sometimes seek to relate itself to the Kantian heritage. It is here that a reflection on the thought of Donald MacKinnon can prove highly instructive.

MacKinnon's thought straddles the boundary of the sublime, but it does so with more perplexity and more intensity than almost anyone else's. The perplexity is shown in the hesitation MacKinnon exhibits about moving forwards from 'purgation', from a strictly 'descriptive', and not speculative, metaphysics, conceived in broadly Kantian terms, towards 'illumination', or some sort of positive affirmation of transcendence. 'The Problem of Metaphysics' delineates for MacKinnon a certain groping towards a version of an analogy of attribution, and an attempt to build theology in its entirety upon a kenotic and tragic Christology. However, my analysis of Kant would suggest that to conceive of purgation entirely as a *prelude* to illumination, or of 'description' as a task innocent of speculation, may forestall illumination altogether, or else radically determine its instance. Thus it might be possible to argue that MacKinnon does not altogether escape the 'theology of right'.

Let us consider first MacKinnon's thoughts on representations of the absolute. He tends to suggest cautiously that a deontological ethics requires qualification in so far as our conduct may be radically guided by attention to particular facts or particular persons regarded as embodying particular sets of values. Likewise he suggests that metaphysics may have to become constitutive rather than merely regulative to the degree that our naturally-given metaphysical disposition cannot help assigning to this or that representation a better clue to ultimate reality than what is found elsewhere. If at moments MacKinnon seems to endorse a certain positivity of revelation in relation to Christology, at other times he more interestingly associates Christology itself with the possibility of metaphysics. And this is an association I would want to uphold.

Nevertheless, the metaphysics cautiously brought forward itself seems to carry a certain freight of positivity, which can be doubly related to MacKinnon's 'Butlerian' inheritance. In the first place only this specifically Anglican background helps to clarify how MacKinnon understands a critical metaphysics as sitting quite naturally with a belief in revelation. Both in Butler and in Mansel there is an absence of the Kantian rationalist notion of access to a non-phenomenal realm of 'pure reason', and this means that, correspondingly, the grounding of natural law becomes more vague – appeal is made to universal 'dictates of conscience', as well as (in Butler) to considerations of benevolent utility. Yet it is even more the case for Mansel, following Butler, than for Kant (as he makes clear) that natural law is derived from the total set of the given conditions of finitude (as Mansel puts it, it is these and not transcendent speculations which are *regulative*) rather than from the pull towards transcendence.[19] Given the positivity, and at the same time the derivational vagueness, of the principles of natural law in this tradition, it becomes easy to understand revelation as a *supplementary* legal system of essentially practical injunctions regarding both morality and worship (hence 'the analogy of religion to the course and constitution of nature' as a new version of a theology conceived as 'ecclesiastical polity' and within the terms of post-Suarez natural law). The new 'facts' and ordinances belonging to revelation give us no more knowledge than does natural law about the content of the infinite. Mansel is consequently anti-mystical and clearly stresses that the positive critical determination of the 'limits of religion' and positive finite knowledge of revelation is *opposed* to any *via negativa*.[20]

MacKinnon, by contrast, wrongly supposes that the Kantian–Butlerian critical path and the *via negativa* naturally belong together. And yet one can discern in his theology also a contradiction between the two. Following Scott Holland, MacKinnon effects a sort of Christological reworking of the Butlerian analogy, such that the essential content of revelation tends to be reduced to a more intense affirmation of the essential 'natural' limits of human existence, as providing sufficient guidance for our lives.[21] We shall return to this shortly.

The second 'Butlerian' element, making for positivity, concerns MacKinnon's 'realist pluralism'. The tendency of this doctrine is to insist that things can be adequately known and distinguished as they are in themselves without believing that their full determination awaits upon the infinity of relations they may have to everything else. Yet it is perhaps possible to hold the latter, essentially Hegelian, view within an open perspective of infinity, rather than Hegel's own perspective of quasi-finite totality. This should adequately avoid any absolute determinism, because here there can be no 'whole' distinct from the network of relationships, which are always relations of particular, distinguishable things. Certainly, to maintain this distinguishability, one needs to say that entities may be relatively discrete, relatively indifferent to certain relations in which they may fall. And yet even such indifference, such 'resistance' can help negatively to determine what they are and what they become. The antinomy between simpleness and compositeness which Kant located 'at the margins' of the normal processes of the understanding, in fact runs dialectically throughout our reasonings about the composition of the world. Hence while MacKinnon is right to insist on the category of 'substance' as a barrier against any metaphysics of pure 'process' which is necessarily 'totalizing', 'substance' needs to be reconstrued as a linguistic marker for certain patterns of narrative consistency in which, none the less, we can never identify any 'underlying' constant element.

But by sticking with a non-dialectical, Aristotelian notion of substance, and with some sort of logical atomism, however qualified, MacKinnon pays insufficient attention to the kind of antinomies that can open up here. As things are, in fact, entirely constituted through networks of changing relationships, the more one seeks to isolate them in their determinate finitude, the more their concreteness altogether escapes us, and their sheer particularity becomes paradoxically their *only* remaining property: a particularity about which we can say nothing, with the result that for all practical purposes one particular becomes the same as all other particulars. We are back to the Kantian things-in-themselves which turn out to be the economic and political equivalences of liberal, post-enlightenment society.

MacKinnon's ideas about the representation of transcendence are affected by this kind of antinomy. Thus, while he is concerned with the unique relevance, for ethics, of isolated figures like Socrates, he does not consider how their virtue is located in a particular social practice, a particular *paideia* designed to be formative of character. The same tendency in Christology can lead towards a Christo-monism, in which not enough attention is given to Jesus's specific social practice, its rooting in a tradition and its ecclesial viability. Attempting to establish Jesus's uniqueness in isolation from his social practice and social relations naturally focuses upon Jesus's invisibility, his aloneness at Gethsemane and his inner perplexity. Foregrounding perplexity as the mark of the specific is another manifestation of the transmutation of concrete content into absence of content.

A similar thing is true of MacKinnon's analysis of parables. Very significantly he attests affinity for the romantic notion of the symbolic which contrasts the parabolic with the allegoric (whereas traditionally both are 'chains of metaphor').[22] This notion suggests that the parabolic–symbolic conveys us out of language towards some underlying transcendent essence, rather than that the category 'symbolic' is intended to register a non-arbitrary dimension of essential 'resemblance' within the play of signs itself (even if this can never be abstractly isolated from 'conventionality'). Within the latter conception – which denies that one can reach the sublime 'edge' of language – it can be seen that the associations of a story, which control its interpretation, are never free from the socially-historic instantiated network of connotations which might be said to constitute the 'allegorical' (unlike the Greek tradition, which aims for mimesis, and seeks to contain allegory as a 'device' – so tending to mechanical 'equivalence' – the biblical and post-biblical tradition actively promotes the allegorical condition of narrative, so fore-grounding its preemptive, 'prophetic', as well as its recapitulatory, character). The formality and conventionality of the signifying substitutions at work here tend to put limits upon the 'realistic' construal of parabolic characters – for example of the woman seeking after the coin as 'obsessional', or the father of the prodigal as approaching Lear's blindness towards filial loyalty.[23] MacKinnon can contrive such readings because he takes the parables as woven out of a 'real life' unmediated by emplotment and carrying all the freight of a 'given' human ambiguity which can then become the symbolic vehicle of a gesture towards transcendence. There is half a suggestion in MacKinnon that the element in the parables which indicates the absolute is the pointing up of some finitely irresolvable hesitation. In a series of brilliantly 'deconstructive' readings (but, given the 'realist' fallacy, it is as if deconstruction were being done by A. C. Bradley) MacKinnon appears constantly to suggest that their implications, their bias, might just as well be 'the other way round'. And yet, perhaps, he does not *quite* do this. This 'not quite' I shall return to.

After this consideration of 'representation of the transcendent', let us pass, in the second place, to MacKinnon's understanding of the tragic. Here very similar considerations apply. It can be suggested that besides MacKinnon's intense existential concern with tragedy, there may also be a disguised formalist reason for his concentration on this mode of narrative. In his reflections upon transcendence he is much more preoccupied with the Platonic notion of presence than with the Aristotelian version of *telos*, and therefore concentrates on tragic indecision which occasions a kind of *exit* from the narrative instead of remaining in the plot and seeking for resolutions. One's suspicion here is that it is not that MacKinnon simply *discovers* history to be tragic, but that he also *emplots* history within a privileged tragic framework.

Thus MacKinnon appears to convert the categorical imperative itself into something very like the view that it is *only* in tragic perplexity that we know we are free, and at the same time are brought up against the very margins of the humanly responsible world.[24] When we do not any longer know how to act, then we discover ourselves as transcendent subjects standing 'above' our usual narratively instantiated characters. But this has to be read as an extremely subtle version of the aesthetics of the sublime, of the liberal discourse of modernity.

To substantiate this: in *A Study in Ethical Theory* MacKinnon pursues an elusive 'Butlerian' balancing of the claims of deontology as against the claims of utilitarianism. The latter he associates with public duty, with refusal of the kind of 'personal' sentimentality often associated with the doers of good works, and also with the concept of *raison d'état*. It is important here to note that this tension, especially when utilitarianism is spelled out in the manner indicated, need not necessarily project one outside the scope of comprehension of deontology. In Kant himself the embodiment of (noumenal) natural right in (phenomenal) legal right involved the intrusion of a certain hypothetical imperative which permitted, in public affairs, an element of merely prudential calculation. Nevertheless the tension becomes for MacKinnon, as not for Kant, the site of tragic conflict. And one should stress that this frequently is *the* site of tragic conflict in MacKinnon. There consequently opens up a suspicion that when he insists on the 'tragic' as virtually a surd element in human affairs, there is unconsciously smuggled into this view an ahistorical assumption about the permanence of the conflict between a public sphere of objective, and strictly equivalent justice, and a private sphere of forgiving cancellation of fault. Yet this is surely a failure to historicize which may mean both a 'taking for granted' the liberal state, and also a failure to reflect that *Antigone* and the Gospels have the place in our culture which they do because they record the extraordinary *institution* of an entirely unprecedented degree of scruple, belonging to a new sort of social imagination.

MacKinnon, of course, is totally right to take seriously the way in which good intentions can have tragic consequences, and the way in which one virtue can in itself inhibit other excellencies. There can be no flippant resolution of this sort of question; none the less it is legitimate to ask whether the ultimate Christian perspective may not be one of tragi-comic irony rather than unappeased tragedy – that is to say *in retrospect* it may become possible to determine our failure to attain the Aristotelian mean, or else we may be able to trace these sorts of conflicts, and these sorts of 'perverse upshots' of apparently desirable courses of action, to a lack of integration in our society, or the lack of a sufficiently encompassing social imagination. To say this is also to say that every evil is traceable to some lack, or perhaps rather to some sort of symbolic distortion, some imperfect vision. This sort of Augustinian analysis can accommodate the Baroque 'play of mourning' (*trauerspiel*), whose allegoric deciphering of the action in terms of our voluntary fallen submission to sin and death yet must of itself always signify the resurrection hope (drama exemplified in Calderon and the Shakespeare of the 'romances' rather than Racine), if not pure classical tragedy.[25] At the same time it seems also in keeping with a process of constant social self-revision, of historicizing critique.

By contrast one must be suspicious of any suggestion that evil is a surd and tragic element. This seems to suggest that we are irretrievably locked into essentially private, genuine, yet fatally partial intimations of the good, which will never receive any adequate communicative mediation. Our only true community is then in abstract repentance and formal forgiveness (which MacKinnon significantly implies at times is 'fact-defying', compared to legal justice) that can scarcely receive social embodiment. The tragic gap between the political state bound to justice and the finally non-mediable wills of individuals then becomes the ontological abyss, which is nevertheless a sublime opening beyond our perplexity. Evil, in this conception, seems akin to Kant's 'radical evil' – almost a necessary background for the *söllen*, the moral will towards the absolute. Moreover, the absolute for MacKinnon, as for Butler, Mansel, and Scott Holland, is encountered as a confirmation of the conditions of our perplexity. God himself dies in the space opened up by the tragic abyss, and the meaning of the resurrection tends to be limited to a corroboration of the fact that God is the God who is with us in our suffering – the unlimited God who yet enters fully into our (tragic) limits, without mitigating them. One needs, perhaps, in this context, to be reminded of Rousseau's reflections on the way in which sympathy can turn into a kind of displacing or usurping of the experience of the person sympathized with. Without some notion of evil as ontologically predatory it becomes indeed impossible to grasp that while God may truly have suffered evil, he can yet, in some important sense have 'left evil behind'. For if evil is not a surd element outside the world-text which human beings write, then within this narrative it can be constantly re-enacted, re-presented, shown up as mere subjectivity, and so contained.

Indeed, unless the contingency of evil is privative, such that those caught in its toils can always go on hoping for total liberation, one can say that kenotic theology itself (and MacKinnon's thought is self-questioning enough to be alert to this danger) may become a new mode of consolation or theodicy. For here one tries to 'deal' with evil conceptually by relocating it within the context of providence as kenotic suffering, while yet leaving evil as a 'limit' element of the known world. This remains subtly within the eighteenth-century theological paradigm of design/theodicy, whereas *traditional* teleology suggests a narrative restriction and redemption of an evil construed as subjective and contingent. Only this latter view avoids pretending that evil is not really evil: *because* evil is evil it is, in its innermost experienced subjectivity, not rightly 'to be known' – rather, in this aspect, to be 'forgotten about'.[26]

There are, then, genuine grounds for suspicion of the Scott Holland/Forsyth/MacKinnon (metaphysically Butlerian–Kantian) tendency to restrict kenosis to the making known of limits and of evil. MacKinnon rightly follows his predecessors in eschewing any notion of a temporary 'putting off' of omnipotence – it is rather that we must re-understand omnipotence as creative love, and therefore as not conceptually opposed to the idea of the 'limit' represented by the assenting (so possibly not-assenting) will of created persons. Yet it may be that these (in certain respects not sufficiently Hegelian) thinkers stress only one side of the *communicatio idiomatum*, the God–humanward direction. If we are 'redeemed', and if this is more than 'legal' conformity to ahistorical limits compensated for by a notional faith that God himself has also submitted to these limits, then 'omnipotence' must be inscribed within the form of Christ's life and the Christ-formed world (but no one, and not Christ himself, is the simple 'possessor' or manipulator of this form). In MacKinnon's more recent writings there is a profound search for a way to hold together an 'ethical' attention to Christ's actual life and teachings with an 'objective' doctrine of the Atonement. But this can only be achieved if the mode of the inescapable 'failure' in Christ's mission can yet be ecclesiologically integrated into an account of a historical practice which uniquely provides resources even in and through 'defeat'.

My suspicion, then, is that there is a hiatus in MacKinnon's work. The secular groundwork in ethics is all designed, following Kant, to safeguard the absolute disinterestedness of ethics, and the purity of ethical freedom, by stressing agnosticism with regard to transcendence as a counterpart to an existential refusal of any materialist necessitarianism. It is an insistence on the inescapable significance of a 'modern' biography like that of George Eliot (yet does not the positive content of virtue here now appear to derive from the religious resources of the past?). The problem with this is that, by severing ethics from theoretical knowledge, and failing to observe that terms like 'good' and 'right' are no less caught up in imaginary cultural constructs than the term 'God' (such that the separation of ethical from religious language is itself just another 'convention'), MacKinnon really endorses an empty, abstract notion of the individual subject, from which it is impossible to derive any concrete notion of desirable human goals. This remains true even though MacKinnon reworks the transcendental subject in terms of categories of performative linguistic action, giving to Butler's 'deliverances of conscience' a slightly existential note in which certain forms of discourse carry the burden of upholding the possibility of freedom. Yet what is still seen as metaphysically significant is just this possibility, a freedom which can go counter to any perceived subjective 'interest'. Where notions of the 'good' are divorced from visions of 'happiness', of what is ultimately desirable, then only negative precepts of 'right' can finally remain in place.

This 'quasi-Kantianism' with regard to the moral subject shows up in MacKinnon's comparison of ethical decision to a creative act – it is, as regards its formal freedom, 'without grounds'.[27] In this respect he is actually *less* realist than the Hegelian tradition which sought to remind us how all our values and any possibility of freedom follows from *sein*, from an always already-realized (in some real degree) goodness. On the other hand he tends to prescind from the real site of an 'absolute' human creativity, namely the erection of entire cultural formations which represent new 'types', in no essential way imitative of anything naturally given. Thus while MacKinnon acknowledges the importance of Hegel's attention to the historical, he thinks of historical situatedness in semi-Kantian terms as a further categorical restriction on knowledge and behaviour, and not as the positive fact of the culturally constructed character of theoretical and ethical categories. Hence culture is seen too much as the given, too little as the imagined, and 'surd' elements of evil are supposedly brought to view.

The 'agnosticism' of the secular groundwork finally rehearses the thoroughly ideological conditions of secular liberal autonomy. The practical 'contentlessness', which is essential here, is the disguised theoretical source of the insistence on a contentless infinite which goes with an exclusion of constitutive metaphysics. When MacKinnon passes to theology, and the quest, after all, for such a metaphysics, including an analogy of attribution, then an attempt is made to pass beyond epistemological and deontological closure. Yet here arises the hiatus, which can only be overcome in positivist, Butlerian terms. For the Kantian backdrop, however much it may be seen as the setting for 'something else', always dominates the entire later performance.

III

In the previous section, I hope that I have shown how modern theology, both 'liberal' and 'neo-orthodox', can have a tendency to be overwhelmed by the ideological character of transcendentalism and deontology and consequently to present something really at variance with the traditional *via negativa* and *via eminentia*.[28] In the final section I want to pose tentative questions about the retrieval of a 'discourse of participated perfections', and at the same time to show where I think MacKinnon's thought still retains an inescapable value.

Discontent with both consequentialist and deontological ethics among Christian and non-Christian thinkers has led recently to a revived Aristotelianism, which is characterized by the view that to act ethically is to act out of a certain steady habit of virtue and to aim for a certain sort of perfection of character.[29] In this conception, aiming for a *telos* is understood as a practice in which the goal sought is internal to the nature of the activity (and hence quite different from an external 'consequence' and yet more 'factual' in character than a deontological law or principle). A society in which such an ethics is instantiated is a society taking seriously *paideia*, or the idea that its purpose is the formation of its members through the assigning to them of certain worthwhile roles. Ethics here depends upon a collective notion of the particular goods, or even the ultimate Good, to be aimed at.

Certain problems, however, arise for all these theorists, that are to do with relativism and 'ultimate grounding'. These no longer concern the descriptive rather than prescriptive character of the word 'good' – once fact/value dualism is abandoned in a 'holistic' theory of language this is seen not to be a problem at all. However, if one admits that this description is always socially mediated, and also allows that societies have the capacity for increasing insight into the nature of the good, then how does one discriminate between these mediations, and how is the immanent capacity for revision possible?

In the wake of MacIntyre's *After Virtue*, recent writers favouring a *sittlich* conception of ethics, like Jeffrey Stout and Sabina Lovibond, have been preoccupied with these problems. However, secular writers (as these are) have an obvious interest in qualifying the scepticism concerning uninflected 'reason' evinced by the French 'post-modernists'. Consequently they tend to present historicism as a sustainable secular option, an adequate context for the development of the virtues. But theology is bound to ask whether this is any more convincing than the ahistorical Kantian attempt to secure a sphere of secular neutrality.

Thus Stout plausibly contends that scepticism is the upshot of a disappointed quest for foundations, such that once one realizes that practical and theoretical truth are not in need of 'founding', scepticism also dissolves; one is, in Richard Bernstein's phrase, 'beyond objectivism and relativism'.[30] In essence, this conclusion is perfectly valid, because once foundationalism is abandoned truth ceases to be a set of 'principles' that we can manipulate; instead we have to conceive of truth as working itself out through our reasonings, of a participation in something which we intimate, but never fully grasp. Although this is implicitly the case for all our human discourses, this does not normally lead to a sceptical paralysis.

However, this will not solve the problem for theoretical scepticism of drastically divergent intimations, and of radical change within particular traditions of reason. At times Stout seems content just to say, quite validly, that relativism is not a real *practical* problem because people are constantly convinced by all sorts of 'good reasons', which lead to conversions. A diachronic, historicist approach will soon reveal that humans do not conceptually occupy tidily discrete and mutually exclusive 'world views'. Yet to cope with *theoretical* scepticism Stout has to go further to imply that, at given points of time, certain sets of reasons or certain intellectual programmes present themselves irresistibly to those reacting 'rationally'. This, however (as Feyerabend has shown in relation to

Lakatos), must still suggest that some 'evidence' disentanglable from the theory-laden terms of the programme is objectively decisive in causing a change of mind. Davidson, Stout and others are quite wrong to suggest that relativism is basically an upshot of scheme–content dualism; on the contrary, it is precisely because thinkers like Feyerabend and Foucault have rejected this dualism that they can contend that there is no accessible 'content' which can ever adjudicate between clearly incommensurable theories.[31] Likewise, when we are engaged in 'radical interpretation', or a situation where we must simultaneously ascribe beliefs to, and find equivalents for the words of, alien others, then the indissociability of their beliefs from the system of their language must mean that where this language demands that a radical (and even contradictory) 'difference' be made in our language in the process of translation, then there is no way for us to avoid the ascription of alien beliefs. This seems a more basic implication of 'radical interpretation' than what Stout stresses – namely the possibility that any apparently radical alien meaning may always be an effect of false belief ascription, demanding a revision in our finding of linguistic equivalents. The point is that when, as happens, we cannot carry out such revision, we are left with no further, 'extra-linguistic' recourse.[32] It is true that in any such encounter there is always a large area of negotiable meaning, and true that we can scarcely ever say that an apparently radical incommensurability may not be transformed by a new synthetic development; yet this should not obscure the fact that this does not make such syntheses self-evidently 'superior', or that most intellectual revolutions are not straightforward syntheses, but usually contain elements of seemingly 'arbitrary' theoretical change.

It is highly significant that with the same instrument Stout seeks to show that scepticism is beside the point, and that secular reason is now non-foundationally secured in a way that also makes theological reason permanently marginal and out-dated. This instrument is the 'new probability', deriving from the logic of Port-Royal, which, according to Stout, following Ian Hacking, introduced the notion of 'internal evidence', or the inherent probability of a thing, as distinct from an older meaning of probability, which was confined to 'opinion of trusted authorities'.[33] Stout considers that this new scientific standard both made Cartesian foundationalism redundant because now 'well-attested belief' could become synonymous with 'true knowledge', and meant that any not merely fideist theology must strive to make its beliefs 'well-attested' after a probabilistic fashion, as, for example, in Butler's *Analogy*. Hume then finally showed that theology could not meet this standard: so Hume, not Kant, becomes the pivotal figure in Stout's intellectual history of modernity.

However, this argument can be easily broken down. First of all, Hacking is not quite right about the 'old probability'; appeal to authorities was complexly conjoined with 'probable' arguments from analogy, jurisprudential considerations about testimony and theories of the imprecise knowledge obtainable for the sense of *phronesis* in ethical reasoning. Secondly, the 'new probability' was a strictly formal affair, linked to the discovery of the calculus, and belief in its ontological value had to be strictly correlated with either an empiricistic confidence in sensory evidence or a Stoic–rationalist confidence in ordered chains of rational representation (as in Leibniz) as giving in themselves an adequate ontology. A collapse of these confidences, as Stout advocates, is not compatible with the view that the new theory of probable evidence can shield us from scepticism, and be our basic guide. The 'new probability' will not provide us with the necessary and necessarily conventional *standards* of what is likely, outside a given set of formal rules, nor of what counts as factual, or a good explanation, or catastrophically 'anomalous'. (Stout's claim that a decisive difference, beyond simple concentration on prediction and control, between scientific and pre-scientific thought is a 'refusal to accept the anomalous' is highly tendentious, and involves him in projecting back into the Middle Ages a 'paradoxical' appearance for theological beliefs which clearly did not appear as so sharply paradoxical within the mediaeval rational construal of things. The mediaevals did not need sheer recourse to 'authority' to help them out here.) And probabilism of the recognizably modern sort in fact proved perfectly compatible with a 'calculus' of theological authorities in so-called 'positive theology', and the attempt to argue with this formal instrument alone in fact *encouraged* a more sheerly positivistic view of 'authority'. Hence one can conclude in the third place that theological probabilism did not represent the only remaining way to avoid fideism, but rather was simply an aspect of theology's bondage to empiricism/rationalism. And Stout's over-estimation of what probabilism can achieve suggests that empiricism/rationalism is still at work in any secular attempt to be at ease with historicism.

More convincing is an effort like that of Lovibond, working in a Wittgensteinian mode, to account for the 'semantic deepening' of our increased insight into the good in terms of a gradual unmasking of ideological subterfuges.[34] This supposes that without such subterfuges good reveals itself unreflectively as a given feature of our 'undistorted' interaction with nature, including other human beings. But this ignores the kind of exposure made by thinkers like Baudrillard and Castoriadis of such theories (including aspects of Marxism) as new variants of natural law, because they arbitrarily associate cultural construction more with ideological distortion than with approved, non-ideological values.[35] In these sorts of theories it is implied that 'real' human needs are just 'given', whereas, in fact, all needs are constructed through complex signifying processes which direct and promote desire. It is in this area of concrete cultural values that one can see the continued *inevitability* of metaphysics, and the continuing significance of Hegel's argument that the enlightenment claim to 'end' constitutive metaphysics is itself the result of ideological moves to guarantee the self-sufficiency of a hopelessly pluralist liberal 'civil society' – a move initially conjoined to the promoting of a private relation to an empty deity.[36] This insight of Hegel's is perfectly separable from the form of his own metaphysics as a rationalist determinism, a form in fact traceable to his failure fully to *emancipate* himself from the Kantian–Fichtean stress on history as the rational coming-to-be of freedom.

The foregoing considerations may lead us to conclude that Stout too easily concludes that there is a third way 'after historicism' between some sort of scepticism on the one hand, and a metaphysical and teleological history on the other, even if this be disconnected from Hegel's continuing foundationalism. Without desperate devices like Stout's probabilism, or Lovibond's naturalism, it becomes apparent that the science of the order of our changing reasons and actions is but a branch of aesthetics, a matter of the formation of 'taste'. There is no way out of this aesthetic historicism, and it cannot be epistemologically founded. But an ultimate metaphysical grounding is a different matter; a tradition does not simply maintain itself within a cosy humanistic hermeneutic circle (this can be the last, remote permutation of transcendentalism) because the normative sense of 'where it is going' is indissociable from, is in fact the same thing as, conjecture about how things ultimately *are* such as to render this tradition valuable and truthful. As the artist is always painting also his aesthetic, so our acts and constructions can only be really moved and shaped by a kind of 'metaphysical faith'.

For this reason, to say that our moral virtues get legitimated within a 'narrative framework' cannot itself be a solution to the post-transcendentalist problem of legitimation, if this be taken to mean that narrative is for us a substitute for a natural human *telos* which is now, after historicism, no longer available. (I am not convinced that the fate of teleological biology is relevant here.) Nevertheless the narrative mediation of goal, virtue and character, stressed by MacIntyre and Hauerwas but necessarily invisible to Aristotle and Aquinas, is now inescapable. It marks our historicist sense that we are the authors of the human text, and at the same time the names marked within that text. It is this sense that can itself be regarded as the irreversible 'turn to the subject', a turn which thinkers like Descartes and Kant attempted to hijack in order to neutralize its sceptical implications. The same historicism is able to carry out a 'metacritique' of Kant, but at the same time it places us at a distance from Aquinas's 'discourse of participated perfections'. This can only again be possible if we take account of that other Christian Aristotelian, Hegel, and his reflections on history, ideology and metaphysics as referred to above.

This approach is preferable to a more purely 'Barthian' one which thinks of the Christian moral narrative too schematically as presenting to us plots and goals provided by revelation, reflecting a revealed 'story of God'. But Stanley Hauerwas has progressively moved away from any such suggestion towards an emphasis that the Christian narrative is, first and foremost, the lived narrative of the Church.[37] A development of this perspective would allow one to say that the site of theology is at one with a specifically Christian metaphysics (a 'metaphysics of faith', one might say). Talk of 'metaphysics' here serves to register the idea that the process of 'revelation' is essentially at one with a particular rational quest for God. Also that through the encounter with Greek culture this tradition has passed definitely into a more reflective mode; but as Hegel realized, there is no limit to the possibility of the transformation of specifically Greek metaphysics – i.e. 'philosophy' – through its subsumption into Christian tradition: we can say, into theology. In this conception the *sensus eminentior* is given not just through the dynamic of individual *praxis*, but through the whole practical *and* 'poetical' activity of constructing the narrative, projecting forwards the divine horizon, and living out this plot – always supposing that it has been formed in a finally exemplary way by Jesus Christ. Ecclesiological mediation might then finally allow the *analogia entis* and the *analogia Christi* to come together.

But in this reconception of analogy one has to say that the imitation of the divine power spoken of by Aquinas (an imitation which in the elusive yet concrete centre of the Christ-*figura* and in the eschatological prospect of the spirit is actually an identity with) must also include the creation of language itself, because language does not stand for ideas, as Aquinas thought, but constitutes ideas and 'expresses' things in their disclosure of truth for us. In this case language itself in its expressive relation to beings belongs to the *analogatum*. Language is also 'like God', and our linguistic expression mirrors the divine creative act which is immanently contained in the *Ars Patris* that is the Logos. 'Analogy of being' becomes 'analogy of creation' because our imitative power is a participation in the divine originative–expressive capacity (this also accords with a more dialectical conception of the *esse/essentia* difference). Teleological constraint is here mediated through our sense of the 'rightness' of our emergent linguistic product.[38]

Language, however, is always particular and traditioned. Those suspicious of the strictly ecclesiological character of this new 'discourse of participated perfections' might very well want to ask about how one conceives of the relation of the ecclesial tradition to secular society and secular reason. The minimum, but very significant, 'concession' that can be made here is that the principle of non-obfuscation of historicity and non-obfuscation of our cultural constitution through language can operate in a way as a 'control' upon our ecclesiology, with the proviso that no secular historicism (not even Marxism) can provide positive content to the *sensus eminentior* – to suppose otherwise would be to lapse back into the formalist foundationalism of the natural law tradition which characterizes modernity. Also it should be stressed that this valuation of history and language is actively promoted by Christian faith; for another tradition these conditions might appear restricting, or something that we need to obscure or forget (but this does make them, in some absolute sense, 'irrational'). This control then provides a new sort of minimal 'natural law'.

However, there might arise another and more serious doubt. Hauerwas is absolutely right to proclaim that to be a Christian must mean to live in the Church, to be formed by the Church. But how far is this *possible* – the tendency of a *sittlich* ethic may be to insist that we can really only be fundamentally formed by the political community, as being the real community of power and interest. The shadows of F. H. Bradley and T. H. Green are not so easily banished. And in this light one can read far more sympathetically MacKinnon's retreat into deontology after the Second World War; somehow it seems to reflect the Church's minimal and very ambiguous social presence. One can also read more sympathetically MacKinnon's account of our tragic sundering between deontology and consequentialism. This could be taken as reflecting a reality *not* dominated by genuine *sittlich* 'practices', by the virtues, but one in which true 'internal goals' were scarcely available. It could be that in such a society there is a tragic sundering of virtue into integrity of motive on the one hand and measurement of consequence on the other. This more 'sympathetic' reading, then, entails an understanding of MacKinnon's ethical writings as implicitly recording, in a finely-attuned manner, the objective fragmentation of social processes making 'virtue' possible.

To show more clearly what I mean, let me refer to Hauerwas's more recent endorsement of pacifism. Hauerwas exhibits great originality in showing that the theme of peace has a more natural home in a *sittlich* ethics than in deontology because deontology only considers peace as a contractual limitation of preceding or possible conflict (just as for Kant 'duty' can only be resistance to contrary inclinations), and not as a fundamental way of being with other persons. One may also want to agree with Hauerwas that it is not that nation-states just *happen* to find themselves tragically involved in wars – it is rather that the whole 'narrative plot' of the nation-state presupposes war as the dimension outside law between states and as the ultimate threat which finally conserves the nation's identity and nurtures certain preferred 'heroic' virtues.[39] Given this dark and Clausewitzian, yet irresistible, analysis, it is difficult to disagree with Hauerwas that (at least usually) for Christians to fight is to assign to the nation-state greater ultimacy than the ecclesial community.

Nevertheless, one might ask in relation to a situation like that in South Africa, whether it is not the case that the Church there is simply robbed of certain possibilities of realizing certain practices that should define its nature (and in a less apparent, but no less acute way, this is true of the Church everywhere). Here exercising peaceableness *may be* precisely not exercising other Christian virtues such as justice, or even comfort and support of others. In this sort of situation does one not have to say that our action is in a way alienated from itself, such that we cannot evade tragic choices, none of which seems perfectly to instantiate integrated 'practices'? In this kind of perspective MacKinnon may be quite right to insist that one cannot legislate in advance the criteria for correct choices even in the case of Jesus's decision to go up to Jerusalem and not to become a messianic leader. To say that a particular mode of action – here 'non-coercion' – should be persisted in whatever the circumstances must tend to lapse back into deontological schematism, because an ethics of virtue can never escape the problematic of 'moral luck' which reveals that all possibilities of good require a particular social context for their viability. Hauerwas wishes to stress that we need the imagination to realize that a peaceful response always has capacities to transform an apparently fixed, tragic situation; *Christian* virtues of charity and forgiveness are directed towards transforming the very conditions of moral luck themselves. This is important, and yet one wants to reply that given the stress on *habitus* in the Aristotelian tradition, there must be cases where one practically knows that a sudden change of heart on the part of the violent and unjust is virtually impossible.[40] One can, however, hold out for a tragic refusal of the pacifist position without denying that it is likely that any implication in violence is likely to prove futile in the long run.

And when we consider the *via crucis* it is true, as I intimated in relation to the parables, that the bias for MacKinnon can never quite go 'either way'. This 'not quite' can then rejoin Hauerwas's insistence that the way of peace, the way of exemplary persuasion and forgiveness, is always the more final way, not on account of a sublime imperative, but because it belongs to a more desirable way of life that we should strive to realize – a way of life no more and no less 'imaginary' than existing social practices which always write violence into their scripts.

What we seem to need, however, is some account of the *sensus eminentior* which takes into account the partial (never complete) alienation of the very possibility of virtuous action. Perhaps in our modern plight, as Walter Benjamin implies, it is the *narrator* of alienated action, of disjointed and so inoperative virtues who is initially the 'just man', the 'just woman'.[41] Only redemptive re-narration or 'recapitulation', may open up a new space for future practice. The tragic abyss that is *represented* rather than mutely indicated is *contained* in its historical occasion and final non-necessity; the obscurity of its opening is yet bounded and enabled by the concrete instance of a 'ruin' (which is always an emblem of Golgotha). And in this redemptive movement we have not to do with the empty sublime of the classical, but with the baroque sublime, the represented rupture and 'suspension' of our reaching towards transcendence; the angels fall half out of the ceiling, because the boundary which they cross is just as much an illusion in so far as we seem to fix and comprehend it, as their seeming to appear three-dimensionally in the space below. An historicist theology knows that the *whole* thing – 'God', 'heavens', and the economy of their relation to *our* finitude (the counterfactual of angelology by imagining 'another finitude' reminds us that we have no transcendental knowledge of finitude 'as such') – is the product of our representation, and it is this whole picture which must, if anything, be an imperfect registration of final reality.

If art as redemption is modernity's own antidote to modernity, then *poesis* as a central aspect of Christian redemption – redemptive re-narrating and so 'explaining' of human history under the sign of the Cross – may be the key to a retrieval of the *sensus eminentior* and to a post-modern theology.[42]

Notes

1 Eberhard Jüngel, *God as the Mystery of the World*, trans. D. L. Guder (Edinburgh, 1983), p. 277.
2 Immanuel Kant, *Prolegomena to Any Future Metaphysics that Will Be Able to Present Itself as a Science*, trans. P. G. Lucas (Manchester, 1962), pp. 121–8.

3 Duns Scotus, *Philosophical Writings*, trans. A. Wolter (London, 1963), pp. 2, 5, 9–12, 24.

4 See Thomas Aquinas, *Summa Theologiae*, Vol. 3, ed. Herbert McCabe O.P. (London, 1964), McCabe's Appendix 4, 'Analogy'.

5 See J. N. Findlay, *Kant and the Transcendental Object* (Oxford, 1981), and C. M. Turbayne, 'Kant's Relation to Berkeley', in Lewis W. Beck, ed., *Kant Studies Today* (La Salle, Illinois, 1969).

6 *Prolegomena*, pp. 119–20. It should be noted here that, while Hegel views the 'boundary' still more positively than Kant, because the antinomies are not, for him, static, but can be dialectically deployed, he none the less also refuses the *sensus eminentior* because he sees this as illegitimate extrapolation of concepts of the understanding. But this refusal would collapse if one questioned the dualism of reason and understanding, which for Hegel remains a serious, *ontological* dualism such that there is a realm of 'mere' externality, mere 'fortuitousness'. This for Hegel is the restricted, but legitimate, sphere of the operation of a capitalist economy in 'civil society'. So in Hegel also, refusal of eminence turns out to be connected with liberal politics. See Charles Taylor, *Hegel* (Cambridge, 1975), p. 292 (though Taylor's evaluation here differs from mine).

7 Immanuel Kant, *The Critique of Judgement*, trans. J. C. Meredith (Oxford, 1978), pp. 96–128.

8 *Kant and the Transcendental Object*, p. 274.

9 See Richard Rorty, *Philosophy and the Mirror of Nature* (Oxford, 1980).

10 *Critique of Judgement*, pp. 90–1.

11 Immanuel Kant, *The Philosophy of Law*, trans. W. Hastie (Edinburgh, 1887), p. 67.

12 *Kant and the Transcendental Object*, p. 275.

13 Immanuel Kant, *Religion within the Bounds of Reason Alone*, trans. T. H. Greene and H. H. Hudson (New York, 1960), pp. 27–38, 40–51, 60.

14 David Burrell, *Aquinas: God and Action* (London, 1979), esp. pp. 4–12, 55–68.

15 *Philosophical Writings*, pp. 9–12, 15. In the latter place Scotus denies that we know God only as what he is not, because 'every denial is intelligible only in terms of some affirmation'. However, this is not an affirmation of the *via eminentia*, but rather an assertion that one can find a 'simple concept' of God's essence/being (this turns out to be infinity–unity). Already in Scotus 'foundationalist' moves in relation to meaning and 'transcendentalist' moves in relation to metaphysics go along with a drawing from the traditional mystical 'paths'. For the point about speculative grammar I am indebted to Dr Graham White of Clare Hall, Cambridge: see Jan Pinborg, *Logik und Semantik im Mittelalter* (Stuttgart, 1982) and the article 'Speculative Grammar' in *The Cambridge*

History of Later Mediaeval Philosophy (Cambridge, 1982), pp. 254–71. The use by Aquinas of the term *modus significandi* at e.g. *ST*, I Q.13 a.3 is perhaps different from that of the *modistae* and more in line with Gilbert de la Porrée's Aristotelian 'psychologizing' of philosophic grammar. Aquinas wishes to draw attention to the ontological conditions of our knowledge as governing our *intentional* access to the *res*, in this case God. But the *modistae* were interested in dealing with sense in abstraction from reference and for them the *res significata* was primarily a 'general meaning' (of an essentially nominal character) which attaches to a particular *lexeme*. This *lexeme* is then reflected according to various *modi*, including usual parts of speech, which are basic categories of meaning. Although both the general meaning and the *modi* have ontological equivalents, this philosophic grammar tends to a Platonic contrast of focal nominal sense with contingent inflection, such that the *res/modus* contrast is really to do with what is most primary in the realm of meaning, regarded as 'mirroring' the realm of substance. In Thomas this contrast is genuinely to do with our limited and unverifiable access to substance; he is trying to explicate how an intention can direct itself to its object, although its *modus* is not strictly homologous with the object. Although Burrell emphasizes the connection of *res/modus* with intention (like Gilbert and Aquinas) he makes it sound as if (as for the *modistae*) the ontological and epistemological constraints embodied in the *modi* categorically determine the possibilities of sense and meaning, whereas for Aquinas's 'pre-critical' perspective sense derives mainly from the object of reference, to which the intention has imperfect, indirect access. The contrast is not between sense and reference, but between a mode of being and comprehension of the knower not fully commensurate with the mode of being and sense of the thing known, which none the less, in the case of God, indeterminately constitutes the existence of, and meaning available to, the knowing subject. See Burrell, p. 62, where he questionably compares the *res/modus* distinction to that between *Bedeutung* and *Sinn*.

16 *Aquinas: God and Action*, pp. 42–55.

17 Erich Przywara, *Polarity*, trans. A. C. Bouquet (Oxford, 1935), pp. 117–49.

18 Helmut Peukert, *Science, Action and Fundamental Theology* (Cambridge, Mass., 1986).

19 H. L. Mansel, *The Limits of Religious Thought* (London, 1859), pp. 252–3.

20 *Ibid.*, p. 83. See also pp. 311–12 for Mansel's response to Maurice. *Both* these thinkers are working within the 'English positivist' tradition of a 'discoverable divine government', and both favour 'literal' and not mystical or allegorical interpretation – quite unlike the Lowth-

Coleridge tradition by which Newman, at his best, is influenced. Maurice misreads Mansel as giving a liberal doctrine of divine *historical* accommodation, whereas Mansel teaches a once-for-all accommodation, and Maurice insists that the revealed 'system' more 'Platonically' reflects God as he is in himself. Neither thinker provides in these respects a good example for today, but at least Maurice, unlike Mansel, conjoins to the tradition of 'revealed government' a reflection on the social character of knowledge – here reflecting the path that leads in France from theology to sociology (Bonald to Comte).

21 See Henry Scott Holland, *On Behalf of Belief* (London, 1892), pp. 187–238.

22 On allegory see especially Walter Benjamin, *The Origin of German Tragic Drama*, trans. J. Osborne (London, 1977), pp. 159ff.

23 D. M. MacKinnon, *The Problem of Metaphysics* (Cambridge, 1974) pp. 84–93.

24 *Ibid.*, p. 145.

25 See Benjamin, *The Origin*, p. 129: 'Fate is the entelechy of events within the field of guilt' (this describes the Augustinianism of baroque drama). Compare MacKinnon, *Borderlands of Theology* (London, 1986), pp. 100–1: tragedians are true 'to the facts', 'an irresistible element in the scheme of things that brings even the most steadfast moral fidelity to nought'.

26 It is possible to have a genuine Christian reworking of Nietzschean 'forgetting', as an antidote to the secular, 'scientific' delusion that curiosity is always justified, self-apparent and innocent in its motivation. See Friedrich Nietzsche, 'On the Uses and Disadvantages of History for Life', in *Untimely Meditations*, trans. R. J. Hollingdale (Cambridge, 1983), pp. 57–125.

27 D. M. MacKinnon, *A Study in Ethical Theory* (London, 1957), p. 97.

28 These two ways are not 'stages', but presuppose each other.

29 For example, Alastair MacIntyre, *After Virtue* (London, 1981), Stanley Hauerwas, *Character and the Christian Life* (San Antonio, 1985), Michael Sandel, *Liberalism and the Limits of Justice* (Cambridge, 1983).

30 Richard Bernstein, *Beyond Objectivism and Relativism* (London, 1984).

31 Paul Feyerabend, *Against Method* (London, 1975), pp. 181ff.

32 Donald Davidson, 'On the Very Idea of a Conceptual Scheme', in *Inquiries into Truth and Interpretation* (Oxford, 1984), pp. 183–99.

33 Ian Hacking, *The Emergence of Probability* (Cambridge, 1975), Jeffrey Stout, *The Flight from Authority* (Notre Dame, 1981), esp. pp. 95–179.

34 Sabina Lovibond, *Realism and Imagination in Ethics* (Oxford, 1983).

35 See Jean Baudrillard, *Pour une Critique de l'économie politique du signe* (Paris, 1972) and *The Mirror of Production*, trans. M. Poster (St Louis, 1975), Cornelius Castoriadis, *L'Institution Imaginaire de la société* (Paris, 1975), esp. pp. 457–98. Castoriadis argues that even in a socialist society, just distribution would be a matter of convention in which different

things and activities would be accorded roughly equal value depending on their considered worth, without this necessitating the capitalist 'imaginary institution' of abstract equivalence. Likewise, Baudrillard shows that a 'pure use value' thought of naturalistically outside linguistic exchange is a myth.

36 See Gillian Rose, *Hegel Contra Sociology* (London, 1981). This essay is much indebted to Rose's arguments.

37 Stanley Hauerwas, 'The Church as God's New Language', in Garrett Green, ed., *Scriptural Authority and Narrative Tradition* (Philadelphia, 1987), pp. 179–98.

38 It is in fact with Thomas Aquinas, in relation to both the Trinity and the *verbum mentis*, that a certain conflation of the *forma exemplaris* with the *imago expressa* begins, so transforming the notion of an exemplary idea such that the idea now only *is* in its constant 'being imaged'. Taken further by Eckhart and Nicholas of Cusa this development dynamizes our participation in the divine ideas and finally makes our creativity the reflection of the divine rationality. Yet at the same time, teleology remains fully in place, because our 'art' is always a 'conjecture' concerning the completion of the divine 'art'. It is not far-fetched to see here one major and original version of the 'turn to the subject', which later – in thinkers like Vico, Hamann and Herder – becomes an 'alternative version' of this turn, in opposition to the obscuring ambiguity of its 'Augustinian' and foundationalist versions in Descartes and Kant. See, for example, on Eckhart, Umberto Eco, *Art and Beauty in the Middle Ages*, trans. H. Bredin (Yale, 1986), p. 113.

39 Stanley Hauerwas, *Against the Nations* (Minneapolis, 1985), pp. 132–98.

40 Stanley Hauerwas, *The Peaceable Kingdom* (London, 1983), pp. 135–51. There may also be a slight tendency, at this stage of Hauerwas's work, to turn the narrative into a *schema* by stressing to an extreme, though necessarily corrective, degree the idea that given virtue pre-empts the 'moment of decision' (this is confusing in relation to my point in the text, because it means that Hauerwas himself has tended to put all the emphasis on *habitus*). A balanced narrativist re-working of Aristotelianism would have to find a place for the idea that our decisions informed by *phronesis* constantly give slight new inflections to the narrative and develop the form of our virtues.

41 Walter Benjamin, 'The Story-Teller', in *One-Way Street* (London, 1977), and *The Origin*.

42 'Post-Modern theology', in my usage, goes further than 'neo-orthodoxy', because it does not, like the latter, tend to leave unquestioned the 'godless' and autonomous self-enclosure of secular modernity, which then for this theology forms a 'background' for the unprecedented workings of faith. In this last section, I am indebted in several ways to past discussions with Kenneth Surin.

11 On being 'placed' by John Milbank: a response

STANLEY HAUERWAS

I have always thought that one of the most interesting questions in philosophical psychology is whether another can understand us better than we understand ourselves. In principle I have wanted to argue the positive side of that case not only because it often empirically seems to be the case but because questions of the truthfulness of narrative construals hang on that issue. MacIntyre makes this point quite nicely in the 'Postscript' to the second edition of *After Virtue* by noting:

> If some particular moral scheme has successfully transcended the limitations of its predecessors and in so doing provided the best means available for understanding those predecessors to date *and* has then confronted successive challenges from a number of rival points of view, but in each case has been able to modify itself in the ways required to incorporate the strengths of those points of view while avoiding their weaknesses and limitations and has provided the best explanations so far of those weaknesses and limitations, then we have the best possible reason to have confidence that future challenges will also be met successfully, that the principles which define the core of a moral scheme are enduring principles. (p. 270)

It is therefore with some concern that I respond to Milbank's extraordinary and wide-ranging paper. I feel at once embarrassed to be associated with a thinker so substantive and profound as MacKinnon but complimented that Milbank is able to put us in conversation. I feel like the young student who is told that what he just said is extremely interesting and important and is not even sure what it is he said. What I understand Milbank to have done is offer a historical narrative that helps some of us better understand the role

197

we are currently playing. In this response all I wish to do is express a few reservations about the story in which Milbank has cast me without denying that he may well understand me better than I understand myself.

Before responding more directly to Milbank's narrative, however, a comment needs to be made about Milbank's style. I once had a professor who divided the world of thinkers into 'splitters' and 'lumpers'. 'Splitters' are those who like to divide problems into ever smaller units for analysis and arguments. In contrast 'lumpers' range wide across the intellectual landscape making connections and generalizations that leave the rest of us a bit breathless. While this taxonomy is not exhaustive, and most of us do a little of both, it is illuminating for an essay like Milbank's. For clearly we have an extraordinary exercise in 'lumping' as we begin with the difference between Aquinas and Kant's negative theology, some extremely apt observations and criticisms of Kant's metaphysics, an interesting defence of Aquinas's doctrine of analogy as grounded in his metaphysics of participation (rightly *contra* Rahner and Metz), why Kant's metaphysics necessitates the priority of right in morals and politics, how MacKinnon tries but fails to have it both ways as he smuggles into this theology an ahistorical assumption about the necessity of conflict, setting the stage for us to understand the challenge facing those who work from a consistent historicist starting point, why both Stout's and Lovibond's secular attempts to avoid relativism fail, why some narrative mediation of goal, virtue, and character is unavoidable, involving a strong claim for the *locus* of theology being the Church (which may allow for the metaphysical joining of the *analogia entis* and *analogia Christi*), helping us appreciate why MacKinnon's 'retreat into deontology' makes sense in the light of the Church's ambiguous social presence, all of which leads to why we must be open to the use of violence in South Africa. An extraordinary story, and I have left out many of the sub-plots. Indeed I will be interested if Milbank thinks I have even picked out the main plot.

I call this way of going about things a matter of style, though of course it is more than that. Style cannot be separated from substance, and Milbank's wide-ranging story testifies not only to his extraordinary erudition but also to his considerable synthetic power, as well as the extremely provocative constructive position he is developing. While I cannot pretend to match Milbank's learning and skill, I want to try to raise some doubts about Milbank's account if for no other reason than that it may help us to better understand his position.

As much as I stand in awe of Milbank's *tour de force*, I am also unsure whether I think the story can be told so coherently, or to put it another way, while I am sure a story must be told I am not sure if I share Milbank's sense of what purpose such telling has – which, of course, only indicates a difference in what story or stories is or are told and who is doing the telling. My concern, therefore, is broader than the many objections that can be made about Milbank's judgements about particular thinkers – for example, MacKinnon's objection that Kant is correctly understood as a deontologist. While I do not know enough to decide on many of Milbank's wonderfully suggestive insights and judgements – for example, that MacKinnon may associate Christology itself with the possibility of metaphysics – generally I find his individual suggestions quite insightful. Nor do I mean to raise questions about how the various sub-plots of the story are inter-related even though I do have considerable questions about how the metaphysical analysis in the first section is to be related to or informs the last section's discussion of contemporary social and theological themes. Rather, my difference with Milbank has to do with his presumption that in order for Christian theology to work it must supply the kind of history he has provided.

Put differently, Milbank's story almost seems to make our current situation more coherent and hopeful than I take it to be. Milbank suggests that MacKinnon does not simply discover history to be tragic, but he also emplots history within a privileged tragic framework. Whether that is true of MacKinnon I cannot say, but I suspect that Milbank has come close to doing something very similar in the way he tells the story, particularly in the last section. For in spite of his very suggestive but cryptic suggestion of how the Cross may provide a way for a redemptive re-narrating of our history, it is quite unclear to me where Milbank gets his confidence that we have the power to narrate one single history that combines the story of both the Church and world. That I work in a more restrictive manner at least partly reflects my theological conviction that the story that the Church tells about herself and her relation with the world may not provide the kind of story that the world will recognize as its own – in short, we do not live at a time in which there can be one story; there must be at least two.

Of course, this is not just a point about 'this time' but rather a point about all time since the resurrection of Jesus. Nor do I think this 'dualism' means there is no relation between the two histories or that the histories are ontologically irreconcilable. There are two histories for one reason only – some worship God and lead their lives accordingly and others do not. While it is our hope these histories will ultimately be one, such a hope can only be grounded eschatologically in God's promised consummation of history.

In order to try to make this issue more exact I want to respond to a few of Milbank's extremely interesting suggestions toward the end of his paper. He asks how the ecclesiological character of his reconstruction of the 'discourse of participated perfections' might determine the relation between ecclesial tradition and secular society and reason. He suggests that at a minimum a very significant concession can be made by acknowledging the principle of non-obfuscation of historicity and that our cultural constitution 'through language can operate in a way as a "control" upon our ecclesiology with the proviso that no secular historicism (not even Marxism) can provide positive content to the *sensus eminentior* – to suppose otherwise would be to lapse back into the formalist foundationalism of the natural law tradition which characterizes modernity'. I am not sure I understand what is being said here. But if Milbank means that the Church must live in this time, as I think it should have had to have lived in the past, without the comfort of being able to construct the story of the world so that our faith in God's providence must be exactly that, i.e. faith, then I am in fundamental agreement with him. Yet I am not sure if Milbank is content with that, as he seems to want to write a history that will give him a way of knowing how and where God is guiding history – thus one history.

Thus Milbank wonders if it is possible to sustain a non-violent ethic as a *sittlich* ethic, since he seems to accept Hegel's contention that such an ethic can finally only be formed by the political community – by which I understand him to mean the community that has the power to determine which story is to be told that is inclusive of all other stories. Given the lack of the Church's social power today, Milbank seems to reappropriate MacKinnon's 'retreat into deontology' as the only means the Church can have to fulfil its own internal commitment to maintain an ethic that unifies motives and consequences. This seems to be why he cannot accept my 'pacifism', even though he accepts my account of the status of the nation-state, for to rule out violence on principle might be to lapse back into an ahistorical account.

Though I am sympathetic to the profound concerns that lead Milbank to this view, I remain unconvinced that the Christian commitment to non-violence as an unqualified way of life must be open to question when new circumstances arise. That would be the case only if one believes that we live in one history; I do not believe that, nor do I believe it is easy to correlate the two histories in which we live. That we do live in two histories is the reason I continue – though, as Milbank notes, with a good deal of qualification – to think that there is no way around the 'Barthian' notion that God has plotted the story of the Church in a way that is decisive for our judgement of any subsequent story of the Church.

This is clearly not a revelational positivism, since like Milbank I think the *sensus eminentior* is given through the 'whole practical and "poetical" activity of constructing the narrative, projecting forwards the divine horizon, and living out this plot – always supposing that it has been formed in a final exemplary way by Jesus Christ'. What I do not understand, however, is given his commitment to one history, what basis Milbank has for assuming the 'finality' of Jesus Christ. To see the rationality of that I think we cannot avoid recognizing that the Church cannot help but be part of a plot that the world cannot know as its own – and, of course, that is the true history of the world.

Index of Names

202

Index of Subjects